Educating
African American Males

Studies in the
Postmodern Theory of Education

Shirley R. Steinberg
General Editor

Vol. 383

The Counterpoints series is part of the Peter Lang Education list.
Every volume is peer reviewed and meets
the highest quality standards for content and production.

PETER LANG
New York • Washington, D.C./Baltimore • Bern
Frankfurt • Berlin • Brussels • Vienna • Oxford

Educating
African American Males

Contexts for Consideration,
Possibilities for Practice

M. Christopher Brown II,
T. Elon Dancy II,
James Earl Davis,
EDITORS

PETER LANG
New York • Washington, D.C./Baltimore • Bern
Frankfurt • Berlin • Brussels • Vienna • Oxford

Library of Congress Cataloging-in-Publication Data

Educating African American males: contexts for consideration, possibilities for practice /
edited by M. Christopher Brown II, T. Elon Dancy II, James Earl Davis.
pages cm. — (Counterpoints: studies in the postmodern theory of education; vol. 383)
Includes bibliographical references.
1. African American men—Education. 2. African American men—Education (Higher)
3. African American young men—Social conditions.
4. African American men—Social conditions. I. Brown, M. Christopher.
LC2731.E33   371.829'96073—dc23   2012032463
ISBN 978-1-4331-0852-5 (hardcover)
ISBN 978-1-4331-0853-2 (paperback)
ISBN 978-1-4539-0915-7 (e-book)
ISSN 1058-1634

Bibliographic information published by **Die Deutsche Nationalbibliothek**.
Die Deutsche Nationalbibliothek lists this publication in the "Deutsche
Nationalbibliografie"; detailed bibliographic data is available
on the Internet at http://dnb.d-nb.de/.

The paper in this book meets the guidelines for permanence and durability
of the Committee on Production Guidelines for Book Longevity
of the Council of Library Resources.

After a decade of birthing new sons and brothers,
we celebrate the emergent and future generations of engaged scholars
committed to moving onward and upward
toward the great lights of
manly deeds,
scholarship,
and love for all mankind.

— *mcb2, ted2, & jed*

Invictus

Out of the night that covers me,
Black as the Pit from pole to pole,
I thank whatever gods may be
For my unconquerable soul.

In the fell clutch of circumstance
I have not winced nor cried aloud.
Under the bludgeonings of chance
My head is bloody, but unbowed.

Beyond this place of wrath and tears
Looms but the Horror of the shade,
And yet the menace of the years
Finds, and shall find, me unafraid.

It matters not how strait the gate,
How charged with punishments the scroll.
I am the master of my fate:
I am the captain of my soul.

William Ernest Henley

Contents

Preface

It is now more than a decade since M. Christopher Brown II and James Earl Davis (2000) published their Peter Lang classic, *Black Sons to Mothers: Compliments, Critiques, and Challenges for Cultural Workers in Education*. In the years since publication, the issues defining and setting the context for understanding the relationship between Black males and education remain complex. Associated with each issue are multiple questions and problems facing Black boys/men and their families—both blood and fictive kin. Although there has been substantial discussion about the plight of Black boys in school, only modest attempts have been made to connect male lives to meaningful sources of influence and support, such as their mothers.

While the lives of Black males create much public interest (and fear) as evidenced by extensive national debate, media fixation, scholarly inquiry, and social interventions, little attention is paid to the roles and responsibilities of academic structures incident to the education of African American males. Indeed, families, friends, spouses, and lovers of Black boys/men, who at times benefit from and fall victim to relationships with Black males that are fraught with economic and emotional challenges, provide voice to both public and private concerns about educational contexts and practices. These precarious relations are facilitated by a combination of structural economic changes that have moved many jobs off shore, demographic shifts in household arrangements and compositions, and changes in male role expectations as fathers, sons, spouses, and significant others.

Black Sons to Mothers illustrated the ways in which questions (and others of similar language) about Black sons and their mothers were epistemologically biased. That volume pushed against assumptions that mothers are biological and only female. Rather, men too can mother and, yes, a mother can be nonbiological. Mothering is not just familial, but also a form of cultural work. That early work pressed everyone involved in the life of a learner (from the minister to the rap star to the school bus driver) to consider the ways in which they "mothered"—intentionally or unintentionally.

This new book, *Educating African American Males: Contexts for Consideration, Possibilities for Practice*, responds to and extends the conversations in *Black Sons to Mothers* in a similar vein—exploring meanings and connections of Black boys'/men's lives and offering literary, scholarly, and personal space to interrogate the seemingly elusive intersection of race and gender. Evoking a similar nostalgia as *Black Sons to Mothers*, *Educating African American Males* is offered in two voices: one where men speak to the education of African American males as cultural workers and another representing the transformation of African American males into the cultural space of educator.

Educating African American Males will continue the epigenetic discourse of *Black Sons to Mothers* by offering higher-ordered understandings of Black male pathologies, schooling, and cultural work. This understanding continues the tradition of its predecessor text by connecting the experiences and identities of Black boys/men to the cornerstone of cultural work—(un)learning. The confluence of social and political mandates, ideologies, and alleged pathologies is most profound in educational contexts.

The politics and social realities of race continue to complicate the gendered experiences of Black men. What has emerged from this genderless construction, however, is an archetype of masculinity that is viewed as deficient under the weight of racism, economic marginality, and cultural expectations. *Educating African American Males* joins *Black Sons to Mothers* in imploding archetypes of masculinity that too narrowly define and defend Black men's roles in cultural work.

The contributors for this volume are committed to exploration and analysis of the lives, both personal and professional, of Black men that engage the multiplicity of the Black male subject in relation to race and identity, as well as others similarly situated. With that goal, authors extend, push, and potentially contest thinking in *Black Sons to Mothers* through both traditional scholarship and personal narrative. We as editors, along with our contributors, are committed to *Educating African American Males*.

Acknowledgments

The editors and contributors of this volume wish to acknowledge Alpha Phi Alpha Fraternity, Incorporated—in which we all hold membership. In particular, we celebrate the initial years of the Alphas in the Academy Committee that was created by the 33rd General President in 2009. Alphas in the Academy was designed to "*to address issues of concern to our brotherhood related to collegiate life, higher education employment, and promoting increased postsecondary participation for African American males.*"

Alphas in the Academy Committee identified a number of worthy activities, deliverable outcomes, and work projects. The consensus around a published book project emerged as the "must do" and "premiere" activity for the Committee. In the year 2000, two brothers of Alpha Phi Alpha Fraternity, Incorporated—M. Christopher Brown II and James Earl Davis—published a highly celebrated book on African American males—*Black Sons to Mothers: Compliments, Critiques, and Challenges for Cultural Workers in Education*. The contention was that ten years after the publication of *Black Sons to Mothers* there was substantial opportunity to further address the plight of black boys in school in relation to meaningful sources of influence and support (i.e., Project Alpha, Go to High School-Go to College, Big Brothers-Big Sisters).

Alphas in the Academy Committee members resolved that one important contribution for Alphas in the Academy would be to extend and expand the work of that volume making it relevant for 2012 and beyond. *Educating African American Males: Contexts for Consideration, Possibilities for Practice* is the result of those efforts.

The committee members who served on Alphas in the Academy by region are:

Eastern Region
Bro. James Earl Davis, Ph.D. (Rho)
Dean, College of Education, Temple University

Bro. Arthur L. Fields, Ph.D. (Mu Lambda)
Senior Program Manager, District of Columbia Public Schools

Bro. John M. Lee, Ph.D. (Kappa Xi Lambda)
Research Scientist, The College Board

Bro. George L. Wimberly, Ph.D. (Omicron Eta Lambda)
Director of Professional Development, American Educational Research Association

Midwestern Region
Bro. Waldo E. Johnson, Ph.D. (Iota Delta Lambda)
Professor of Social Service Administration, University of Chicago

Bro. Vernon C. Polite, Ph.D. (Gamma Lambda/Omega) *deceased
Dean of the College of Education, Eastern Michigan University

Southern Region
Bro. M. Christopher Brown II, Ph.D. (Theta Sigma Lambda)
President, Alcorn State University *Committee Chair

Bro. Roland W. Mitchell, Ph.D. (Delta Phi Lambda)
Associate Professor of Higher Education, Louisiana State University

Southwestern Region
Bro. T. Elon Dancy II, Ph.D. (Beta Eta Lambda)
Assistant Professor of Higher Education, University of Oklahoma

Bro. Walter T. Tillman, Jr., M.Ed. (Theta Iota Lambda)
Executive Associate of Academic and Student Affairs, Southern University System

Western Region
Bro. Willie L. Neal, M.S.Ed. (Zeta Sigma Lambda)
School Administrator, Millennial Tech School

Chapter One

Sociohistorical Contexts of African American Male Education

An Analysis of Race, Class, and Gender

T. Elon Dancy II

America's history is a turbulent legacy of social exclusion in many ways. Not surprisingly, this bitter legacy has undergirded disparate trends among African Americans across national sub-institutions. More specifically, events of the past have uniquely troubled African American male lives. For instance, scholarship documents how histories and contemporary social contexts persistently trouble this group's experiences in education (Brown & Davis; 2000; Brown & Dancy, 2010; Davis & Polite; 1999; Lee, 1992). This chapter seizes a rare opportunity among educational texts to interrogate the unique lives of African American males at the intersection of history, society, and culture. Ultimately, this knowledge will be used to comment on the role of identities and identity intersections in African American male educational attainment and experiences.

I conducted a multidisciplinary review of the literature, drawing most heavily from history, African American studies, anthropology, cultural studies, women's and gender studies, sociology, and education. In a broad sense, the following question is at the center of this review: How has a changing sociocultural landscape in America impacted African American male identity constructions over time? More specifically, how have African American men evolved with respect to their manhood? *Manhood* is defined as responsibilities to self and others, existential philosophies and worldviews, and self-definitions and behaviors (Dancy, 2012; Hunter & Davis, 1992).

Chronological literature reviews are often selected in the presentation of history to aid the reader in interpreting changes over time, giving a series of examples of key developments, and ending with future directions (Anson & Schwegler, 2000). The organization of this review is chronological to keep identity changes in African American men with the social contexts that predispose them. This chapter highlights the raced, classed, and gendered experiences of African American males throughout six turbulent periods in history that largely defined and redefined African American male identity: pre-transplantation Africa, post-transplantation America, the Antebellum and Reconstruction eras, the New Negro Movement (the Harlem Renaissance), and the Civil Rights Era. This distinction between eras is made in an effort to demonstrate the different ways in which the evolving American context influenced African American men's constructions of self over time. The chapter ends with meditation on the role of education in positively or negatively influencing this process.

Pre-transplantation: Men in the African Diaspora

In *From Slavery to Freedom*, Franklin and Moss (1994) chronicled African male lives prior to transplantation, or, removal from Africa and replacement in America. The authors argue that the preexisting system of enslavement in many African countries shaped class distinctions among African men and families at the time of transplantation. Accordingly, African men were either dignified or degraded relative to the work in which they engaged to create a life for themselves and their families. For example, "good men" were those who could prove an ancestry of free men and were, therefore, entitled to positions of respect and recognition as members of nobility (Franklin & Moss, 1994, p. 18). African men who worked the soil were considered the most noble. Following in order were cattle raising, hunting, fishing, construction, navigation, commerce, gold mining, and the processing of commodities (i.e., soap, oil, and beer). Working-class men in Africa were those who could not prove a noble ancestry and subsequently were not entitled to socially revered positions. However, African men of lower socioeconomic status could still achieve power and wealth, which substituted for nobility of origin (Franklin & Moss, 1994).

African men largely felt responsible to their families, communities, and culture. In fact, the presence and power of community was and continues to be deeply embedded in the identities of African men (Ouzgane & Morrell, 2005). Familial and political leadership in Africa were both intertwined as well as the patriarchal, or, in other words, men were positioned at the center of this leadership. Families combined to form village states throughout most of Africa. Among these families were small kingdoms, which were the largest, most influential families (Franklin & Moss, 1994). In this government, African men were selected by designated families to serve as kings of their localities. Subsequently this form of government led to many village states and subsequently many Black male kings. Franklin and Moss (1994) observe that kings of larger empires were careful not to intrude in the sovereign rule of other African kings in similarly sized empires or smaller ones. In Africa, this sense of constraint respected the communal bond between kings, families, and village states, but among African men more deliberately.

The social organization of the family was a patriarchal one. African men decided that, while women did not necessarily legally belong to their husbands, women did belong to their families (Franklin & Moss, 1994). Meanwhile, husbands were free to have multiple wives, and, in fact, polygamy was valued among Black men. While constructions of polygamist families clearly supported patriarchal interests, there is some evidence to suggest that women exercised autonomy in families and rights to property (Hine & Jenkins, 2001). Still, positions of authority were largely reserved for and controlled by African men (Hine & Jenkins, 2001). Moreover, patriarchy was not only evident in men's relationships with women but also other men and boys.

A growing historical literature considers how gay and bisexual African men made meaning of their identities and constructed families (Evans-Pritchard, 1971; C. A. Johnson, 2001; Junod, 1962; Murray & Roscoe, 1998). Evans-Pritchard (1971) describes the ways that many young African men in the Zande engaged in marriages and other intimate relationships with other boys. For instance, he writes that "the boy fetched water for his husband, collected firewood and kindled his fire, bore his shield when traveling and also a small bag containing wava leaves" (p. 1430). Similarly, C. A. Johnson (2001) found a similar pattern of marriages among African men in the Berber culture of Siwi where "men and boys entered into alliances. . . with family approval and these alliances had many of the traits of formal marriages" (p. 136). Even more, C. A. Johnson (2001) added that many African communities were fundamentally bisexual. He argued, "Among both the Zande and Siwi, boy-wives were eventually married to women, their former husbands paying the bride price. The new husbands subsequently took boy-wives of their own" (p. 136). Across many African cultures, males who were diverse in their sexuality were not necessarily hindered in participating and holding class importance in African society (C. A. Johnson, 2001).

In *Boy-Wives and Female Husbands: Studies in African Homosexualities,* Murray and Roscoe (1998) document intimate relationships among men across African communities including Zanzibar, Angola, Simbabwe, Cameroon, and Hausa. In the text, the authors recount conflicts concerning gender roles between a French priest and a precolonial African society in the Congo kingdom. The French priest, Jean Baptiste Labat, objected to the feminine behavior of the shaman (governing priest) of the Giagues people of the Congo kingdom. The shaman, Ganga-Ya-Chibanda, often dressed in women's clothing and was frequently addressed as "grandmother" (Murray & Roscoe, 1998, p. 10). Labat's disgust for Ganga-Ya-Chibanda is an example of the early European condemnation of the diverse social constructions of African men. Additionally, this conflict is emblematic of the ways in which Europeans sought to change African behavior once Europeans decided it was reprehensible.

As the authors of *Boy-Wives* point out, the social constructions of sexuality in Africa differed from those they encountered after their enslavement in America. In America, same-sex relations were (and still are) conflated with masculinity (and femininity), mental health, and morality (Murray & Roscoe, 1998). In many countries of Africa, however, the social code around sexuality required that African men express same-sex desires, but did not allow these desires to overshadow or prevent procreation, which would compromise cultural strength (Murray & Roscoe, 1998). However, the cultural strength of African peoples would be compromised during capture and a new life of bondage in America.

Post-transplantation America: Negotiating Identity against Bondage

Once in America, Black men (and women) were subjected to patriarchy as defined by White men. hooks (2004a) defines the American patriarchal system as a political-social one in which White men inherently dominate; are superior to everything and everyone deemed weak, especially women; and are endowed with the right to dominate the weak and to maintain that dominance through various forms of psychological terrorism and violence. Thus, White men are interested in maintaining a "natural" position of dominating gendered and cultural others. As a result, patriarchy is the deliberate and systemic process used in inculcating Black men with such traits as weakness, docility, and ignorance to place them into inferior positions. After transplantation, men of the African diaspora were forced to develop new meanings of themselves and new behaviors consistent with what their oppressors desired.

The ways in which Whites treated the enslaved of the African diaspora represented a different form of patriarchy in America than existed in Africa (Hine & Jenkins, 2001). Perhaps the greatest atrocity is that men of the African diaspora did not own themselves. The institution of slavery denied enslaved men the natural right to construct their own identities. Enslaved male efforts to develop independent identities often conflicted with the intentions of Whites who systemically placed Black men in chattel positions and defined them as things or privately owned commodities (Marable, 2001). The result was often harsh and dehumanizing treatment which enslaved men experienced.

White enslavers denied certain characteristics (i.e., authority, familial responsibility, and property ownership) to African and African American men in cruel and sadistic ways (Mercer, 1994). Slave codes, for example, were used to control the enslaved (Du Bois, 1903/2005; Franklin & Moss, 1994). *Slave codes* were defined as the repressive body of laws which covered every aspect of the life of the enslaved and redefined these persons as property (Franklin & Moss, 1994). Laws protected the ownership of the enslaved inasmuch as they were property, and laws protected Whites against any dangers that might arise from the presence of large numbers of enslaved men.

Enslaved men and women had no standing in the courts: they could not be a party to a lawsuit; they could not offer testimony, except against another enslaved or free man of the African diaspora (Franklin & Moss, 1994). Enslaved persons could make no contracts or own property, though, in some states, the enslaved were permitted certain types of personal property. The enslaved could not strike a White person in self-defense; but the killing of enslaved women and men, however malicious the act, was rarely regarded as murder (Franklin & Moss, 1994). The rape of an enslaved woman was regarded as a crime only because it involved trespassing. Also, many of the enslaved were not permitted to leave plantations without the written permission of their masters (Franklin & Moss, 1994). Enslaved persons who behaved or acted in any way incongruent to slave code policies were considered affronting to White male interests and were severely punished (Akbar, 1991). Whipping, branding, imprisonment, and hanging were commonly used penalties to ensure adherence to slave codes as well as to condition enslaved men and women to perceive themselves as psychologically, intellectually, spiritually, and emotionally inferior. In many cases, Whites cut off the body parts of the enslaved as punishment (Franklin & Moss, 1994).

The creation of caste systems is another example of the patriarchal relationships between Whites and enslaved of the African diaspora. Whites resocialized enslaved men and women by dividing them into two general groups when they arrived on Southern plantations—laborers and house slaves. The laborers worked in the fields harvesting rice or tobacco, cutting sugarcane, picking cotton, or building roads and structures. Additionally, enslaved men who were laborers bore the tasks of smelting iron, digging wells, or laying bricks. In fact, many enslaved persons built the very plantations and buildings around which they worked (Graham, 1999). Conversely, enslaved men in the master's house usually served as butlers and were perceived within the enslaved community as favored in their master's household (Graham, 1999). The terms *house niggers* and *field niggers* emerged in this caste system as labels. The enslaved in the house gained better treatment and had access to better working conditions, better clothing, minimal education, and intimacy with the master's family (Graham, 1999). Whites and "house niggers" came to consider "field niggers" (who were often darker skinned and worked outside the home) to be less civilized and intellectually inferior (Graham, 1999). These early caste systems worked to create resentment between and among men of the enslaved community (hooks, 2004b). White slave owners advanced a greater rift in the enslaved community by placing lighter-skinned servants in the house. Lighter-skinned servants were primarily the children of White slave owners and enslaved women who engaged in (often nonconsensual) sexual relations.

The skin-color caste system was an advancing force behind new sexual politics between Whites and the enslaved of the African diaspora. One way White men exercised their patriarchal masculinity was through sexual brutality. Enslaved women were used by White men for sexual gratification and to demonstrate their power (Marable, 2001). Across American plantations, enslaved wives, daughters, and betrothed women were sexually ravaged, causing emotional distress to them and those who loved them (Franklin & Moss, 1994; Marable, 2001). Scholars argue that many men of the African diaspora were psychologically affected as a result of these often violent and aberrant relationships (DuBois, 1903/2005; Graham, 1999; Marable, 2001). DuBois (1903) in his text *The Souls of Black Folk* poignantly argues:

> Nor was the Negro man's burden all poverty and ignorance. The red stain of bastardy, which two centuries of systematic legal defilement of Negro women had stamped upon his race, meant, not only the loss of ancient African chastity, but also the hereditary weight of a mass of corruption from white adulterers, threatening almost the obliteration of the [African American] home. (p. 19)

Du Bois's (1903/2005) work asserts that the sexual degradation of enslaved women denigrated many enslaved men in immense psychological and emotional proportions and threatened to destroy African American families. Du Bois also suggests that a key problem in the construction of African American manhood is that many African American men suffered from an inability to protect African American women from the sexual transgressions and aggressions of White men. However, enslaved women were not the only sexually victimized of the African diaspora.

Wallace (2002) suggests that many White men also sexually victimized enslaved men when he writes that "the sodomitic threat was as real during slavery as the heterosexual rape of women" (p. 88). Wallace (2002) illustrates an example of this threat in Harriet Jacobs's (1861) *Incidents in the Life of a Slave Girl*. In Jacobs's biographical account, Luke (a slave) was savagely raped and forced to endure sexual treatment by White men in excess (Wallace, 2002). The master is described as performing degrading acts of masturbation and sodomy on Luke. Wallace (2002) chillingly recalls in the text, "[I]n the end, the young master takes to his bed a mere degraded wreck of manhood" (p. 89). Wallace's work describes the sexual decadence exercised by many White men that greatly imposed on the masculine identities of men of the African diaspora. Other work supports the existence of sexual degradation of African diaspora men by White men as well

(Montejo, 1968). Additional scholarship asserts that many sexually humiliating acts performed by White men on African American men are masked in the writings of Frederick Douglass and others (Clifton, 2001; Wallace, 2002). Sex, however, was not the only patriarchal tool used to maintain the subordinance of people of the African diaspora.

Whites also sought to psychologically terrorize the enslaved by attempting to change the ways the enslaved saw and thought about themselves. Research identifies two patriarchal images of enslaved men of the African diaspora that emerged during this period—the beast and the Sambo (Gossett, 1965; Hoch, 1979; Jones, 2005; Mercer, 1994). The two images bifurcate men of the African diaspora as either violently resistant (beast) or docile (Sambo). In *Race, Sex, and Suspicion: The Myth of the Black Male*, Jones (2005) describes how the distinctions of these images reflected the White men's psyche. The beast represented the savage, or the hyperaggressive and hypersexualized man of the African diaspora. As Patricia Hill Collins (2005) writes, these types of enslaved men were seen as "big, strong, stupid, and naturally violent" (p. 56).

Beliefs about African and African American men's physical stature informed White attitudes and responses. According to Dyson (2001), enslaved men of the African diaspora were believed to have big sexual desires and even bigger sexual organs to realize their lust. Dyson (2001) further adds that White men created the myth that enslaved men were obsessed with White women to attempt to relieve the guilt of White men for raping enslaved women. After slavery, White men continued to beat, burn, hang, and often castrate African American men in response to perceived sexual envy and threat (Dyson, 2001). Additionally, Dyson (2001) notes that Whites made enslaved men and women aware that Whites perceived them as ugly, disgusting, and sordid. To further illustrate this notion, Dyson (2001) writes that "black bodies were spoken of in the same breath, as say horses and cows" (p. 312). Also, Thomas Jefferson illustrates Dyson's argument about the perceived hypersexual nature of enslaved men:

> They seem to require less sleep. A slave after hard labour through the day will be induced by the slightest amusements to sit up till midnight or later, though knowing he must be out with the first dawn of the morning. . . They are more ardent after their female? But love seems with them to be more an eager desire, than a tender delicate mixture of sentiment and sensation. Their griefs are transient. . . In general, their existence appears to participate more of sensation than reflection. . . Their love is ardent, but it kindles the senses only, not the imagination. (Quoted in Perkins, 2000, p. 15)

Enslaved men were viewed as hyperaggressive as well. For instance, Jones (2005) argues that the beast reflects the White enslaver's psychological fear that he would be murdered by his enslaved community. Jones quotes a description offered by Blassingame (1972) in describing African American male revolt leader Nat Turner as a beast:

> Nat was the rebel who rivaled the Sambo in the universality and continuity of his literary image. Revengeful, bloodthirsty, cunning, treacherous, and savage, Nat was the incorrigible runaway, the poisoner of white men, the ravager of white women who defied all the rules of plantation society. Subdued and punished only when overcome by superior numbers or firepower, Nat retaliated when attacked by whites, led guerrilla activities or maroons against isolated plantations, killed overseers and planters, or burned plantation buildings when he was abused. . . Nat's customary obedience often hid his true feelings, self-concept, unquenchable thirst for freedom, hatred of whites, discontent, and manhood, until he violently demonstrated these traits. (Quoted in Jones, 2005, p. 19)

In contrast, Jones (2005) writes that the Sambo represented the White enslaver's desire for power. The Sambo is described in the literature as buffoonish, docile, and loyal (Blassingame, 1972; Franklin & Moss, 1994; Jones, 2005). Jones (2005) asserts that the Sambo was "always dull, always immature, always a child; he never became a man" (p. 27). White belief in this bizarre manhood of enslaved men hence satisfied the subconscious need of slave-owning Whites to remain in command. However, enslaved men thought about their manhood differently. In this period, "true" manhood was represented by the attainment of freedom. Thus, stupidity and intimidation were largely behaviors enslaved men used to honor (and often disguise) a manhood desire to be free. Accordingly, these behaviors would significantly change in the Antebellum and Reconstruction eras.

Antebellum and Reconstruction Eras: Fighting Wars, (Re)Constructing Families

Research offers the term *resistant masculinity* to describe rebellious acts of Black men in fighting for freedom (Estes, 2005; Hine & Jenkins, 2001). Acts of resistant masculinity persisted throughout slavery in the form of revolts. More specifically, enslaved men and women showed signs of dissatisfaction, plotted rebellion against their masters, and committed acts of sabotage, arson, theft, and murder. African American men and women worked in harmony to resist enslavement and maintain inner strength and integrity. For example, enslaved men and women participated in conscious, voluntary day-to-day protest including the destruction of agricultural implements, burning crops, stealing Whites' personal food and property, and deliberate delays during fieldwork (Marable, 2001). Even civil rights leader Frederick Douglass describes in his autobiography his own exercise of resistant masculinity that culminated in a two-hour brawl:

[The fight with the slave overseer] rekindled in my breast the smoldering embers of liberty. It brought up my Baltimore dreams and revived a sense of my own manhood. I was a changed being after that fight. I was nothing before—I was a man now. (Quoted in hooks, 2004b, p. 3)

Revolts, fights, and other acts of resistance on plantations were not the only contexts for resistant masculinity. Eventually, African American men gained the opportunity to exercise resistance through military service.

Military Service

One way enslaved men resisted oppression was through military service, particularly in the Civil War. Prior wars for American territorial expansion (i.e., the Revolutionary War and the War of 1812) attracted the involvement of few enslaved men or held little symbolic importance for them because it did not mean liberation for enslaved men (Hine & Jenkins, 2001). This distinction is not made to negate the efforts of enslaved or free men of the African diaspora who fought in these wars. In fact, the Revolutionary War presented one of the first opportunities for enslaved men to understand how military service could serve as a conduit to win freedom (Hine & Jenkins, 2001). Thus, the Revolutionary War became a fight for freedom even though the enslaved men who participated were largely fighting for the independence and economic gains of White Americans. Some enslaved men in the South escaped and would often join enemies of America to attain freedom. Southern White men feared and resisted enlisting and arming enslaved Black men. In response, the enslaved often fought for enemies of America or escaped (Hine & Jenkins, 2001).

However, Hine and Jenkins (2001) also note an interesting pattern that fueled enslaved men's resistant masculinity after the Revolutionary War—the growing racism and practice of exclusion. The authors write, "[W]henever the country was at peace, and the need for combat soldiers was at a low level, the military excluded black men" (Hine & Jenkins, 2001, p. 40). Black men served in all divisions of the army during expansion wars including the Continental Army, the state militias, units made of U.S. allies, and the navy (Hine & Jenkins, 2001). However, African American men were excluded from newly formed military forces after the end of these wars because Whites widely believed that enslaved men would use military participation as a catalyst for attaining freedom. The Civil War, however, provided African American men with an opportunity to intensely fight against racial exclusion, rather than for White America's expansion of resources and other ideals that did not include people of the African diaspora. Thus, "the meaning of black manhood in America became inseparable from freedom and equality" (Hine & Jenkins, 2005, p. 46). Though free African American men also fought in the Civil

War, African American soldiers in the Civil War were largely African American men who had been enslaved (Hine & Jenkins, 2001).

Military service influenced the identity constructions of Black men both similarly and differently from White men (Cullen, 2001). Namely, duty and responsibility were clear dimensions of manhood for both African American and White men. Both also conflated masculinity with fighting, but manhood meanings (i.e., protection of human freedoms, rights, and ways of life) differed as African American men felt a sense of entitlement to experience what many Whites denied (Cullen, 2001). Accordingly, African American men fought in the Civil War to attain a sense of pride in themselves. Accordingly, Cullen (2001) writes that many African American men expressed masculinity in terms of protecting their families. He points to the narrative of Civil War army veteran Thomas Long, who wrote,

> Suppose you had kept your freedom witout enlisting in dis army; your chillen might have grown up free and been well cultivated as to be equal to any business, but it would always have been flung in dere faces—"your fader never fought for he own freedom"—and what could dey answer? Neber can say that to dis African race any more. (Quoted in Cullen, 2001, p. 499)

Many African American men were willing to fight because they believed they would not be regarded as men in the eyes of their families and others until they proved their manhood by their willingness to go into battle and fight for their principles (Cullen, 2001).

Military service also provided African American men with a stronger civic voice. Many African American men expressed unwillingness to serve in the military unless they could serve on an equal basis with White men (Cullen, 2001). Even though this right was largely denied, many African American men who served in the military during the Civil War were yet affirmed as men by their military experiences. According to Cullen (2001), a former slave exclaimed, "This was the biggest thing that ever happened in my life. . . I feel like a man with a uniform on and a gun in my hand" (p. 496). Even one White soldier observed, "Put a United States uniform on his back and the chattel is a man. . . You can see it in his look. Between the toiling slave and the soldier is nothing but a god could lift him over. He feels it, his looks show it (Cullen, 2001, p. 496)."

Cullen (2001) writes that African American men who served during the Civil War era killed two prominent racist conceptions of African Americans as children and animals "with one stone" (p. 496). In the years before the war, Southern Whites had thought about enslaved men and women as children or animals to make the institution of slavery appear "rhetorically defensible" (Cullen, 2001, p. 496). However, these enslaved men were neither as armed soldiers. Cullen's synthesis surmises that African American men's resistant masculinity during the war not only redefined how others saw and thought about African American men but also endowed enslaved men with a new power to prevent the abuse of themselves and those they loved. After African American men won their freedom in the Civil War, they returned to their families and sought to build a life of their own.

Reconstructing Life and Families

E. Franklin Frazier's (1939) cornerstone work, *The Negro Family in the United States*, was considered cutting-edge in its exploration of the African American family pre- and post-slavery. After the Civil War, African American men and women wandered "aimlessly about the country" in a "modified plantation system" (Frazier, 1939, p. 209). In other words, Southern Whites attempted to "re-enslave" African Americans in new ways to maintain labor needs in the South. In these days, new constructions of manhood emerged for African American men.

After slavery, African American leaders like Alexander Crummell, Frederick Douglass, and W. E. B. Du Bois emerged to endorse a different framework for the African American family, specifically for African American men—the patriarch. However, scholarly work argues that implicit in this framework was the idea that African American men would approach family life in similar ways to White men in their homes (hooks, 2004b). In fact, hooks (2004b) argues that enslaved African American men were socialized during slavery by Whites to believe that they should endeavor to become family patriarchs. Family patriarchs were those who were free and who provided for and protected women and children. hooks (2004b) refers to those men who exercised this power without force as benevolent patriarchs. Frazier (1939) supports this assertion, writing that many African American men were "exceedingly jealous of their newly acquired authority in family relations and insisted upon a recognition of their superiority over women" (p. 127). hooks (2004b) also observes that a large majority of African American men adopted the dominator model set by White masters. The *dominator model* refers to the force (sometimes violence) used to dominate African American women in similar ways that White men dominated White women (hooks, 2004b). hooks (2004b) argues that some newly freed African American men would even beat their wives following the example of White enslavers.

hooks (2004b) highlights, however, that many African American men did not engage in patriarchal manhood and masculinity. Rather, many African American men sought refuge among Native Americans whose cultures did not insist on violence and/or subjugation of women and children. hooks (2004b) observes that, in these cultures, marriages between Native women and African American men "created a context for different ways of being and living that were counter to the example of white Christian family life" (p. 4). Notwithstanding, many African American men who married African American women sought to subordinate women as a very important part of manhood construction.

Frazier (1939) identifies two factors that African American men used to so-lidify positions as leaders in the home. One factor was the way in which African American men were positioned in African American churches. Since the Afri-can American church was under the domination of African American men, the church's work tended to confirm men's interest and authority in the family (Fra-zier, 1939). A second factor involved the acquisition of property and homes. Fra-zier (1939) writes that, even before slavery's end, African American men became interested in developing superiority in the home. Before slavery, many ambitious African American men felt it was their duty to attempt to purchase their freedom and the freedom of their wives and children (Frazier, 1939). African American men, Frazier (1939) posits, used economic arrangements like these to place them in a position of authority. In some cases, women refused to become subject to the authority of their husbands (Frazier, 1939). A manhood trend was established. African American manhood, which was largely resistant during the Antebellum Era, had evolved to mimick White men's patriarchy after the formerly enslaved were freed.

The New Negro Movement:
Intersections of Class, Ritual, and Identity

During the New Negro Movement (early 1900s), African American men would strive to develop industry and attempt to protect their communities. Exercising re-sistance seemed to have its gains. Politically, African American men had gained the right to vote. However, women were denied this right until the twentieth century. Some African American men, though, had been elected to public office despite White backlash (Collins, 2005). As some African American men gained politically and financially, a class divide also emerged. *Class* is largely defined as the grouping of individuals according to economic and cultural criteria (Weber, 1958).

In *Manliness and Its Discontents: The Black Middle Class and the Transformation of Masculinity, 1900–1930,* Summers (2004) writes, "[H]egemonic discourses of manliness clearly shaped how [African American] men thought about themselves as men" during this period (p. 14). *Hegemony* is defined as experiences that sustain the power of particular groups while subordinating others to states of powerless-ness. Summers's (2004) analysis concerns the rise of two organizations that influ-enced classed constructions of African American male identity—the Prince Hall Freemasons and the Universal Negro Improvement Association (UNIA).

African American fraternal organizations are largely influenced by Freemasonry. Wallace (2002) traces the origins of the African American masonic movement in the United States back to March 6, 1775. Prince Hall, a free Afri-can American artisan and Revolutionary War veteran, entered an encampment at Bunker Hill in Massachusetts where he and fourteen other free African American men were initiated by an outfit of Irish Freemasons belonging to a British regiment. Hall and his fellow African American members petitioned for nine years to obtain a charter from the confederate-operated American Grand Lodge, with no success (Wallace, 2002). In 1784, Hall obtained a charter for Provisional African Lodge I from the Grand Lodge of England. African Lodges eventually became Grand Lodges and attracted African American men nationwide over the subsequent thirteen years (Summers, 2004). African American men were attracted to these organizations because they unified men under ideologically bourgeois constructs of manhood (i.e., wealth, social respectability, and political power) (Summers, 2004). During the New Negro Movement, Prince Hall Freemasonry would attract African American men who sought to redefine themselves as political, economic, and social leaders. Summers (2004) writes that between 1904 and 1955, membership in the order grew from 46,000 to more than 300,000, with most gains occurring prior to 1930.

Summers (2004) also argues that African American men's manhood in the New Negro Movement Era was largely influenced by gender, class, status, age, and their intersections. Specifically, African American men used class in defining themselves against African American women, other men, and boys (Summers, 2004). African American men became biased, in a collective sense, toward other African American men who had not been influenced by fraternalism and middle-class values. Freemasonry increasingly attracted the first emerging middle classes of lawyers, prosperous farmers, and independent tradesmen. Freemasons became ideologically bourgeois and sought to assert their masculine privilege and authority in African American communities in similar ways to White men in America. This "imaginary claim" to traditional manhood meanings subjected African American women to subordinate roles, since Freemasons appointed themselves as protectors of women and children (Summers, 2004, p. 27).

The membership of Freemasons grew in exclusive ways. Summers (2004) notes that the majority of accepted members into the masonry fell within middle-class economic lines. A masonic handbook obtained by Summers (2004) identifies the following membership guidelines: "[H]e [must be] free-born and [not] a bondsman, of good report, hale and sound, so as to be capable of earning a livelihood for himself and family, and to perform the work of a member of the Lodge, and he must have some visible means of gaining an honest livelihood" (p. 35). Few men with "questionable reputations" or in menial positions were proposed for admission to the lodge (Summers, 2004, p. 35). Women were excluded from joining the Freemasonry to maintain the masculine character of the organization (Summers, 2004). Freemasonry was not the only organization, however, that sought to improve the sociopolitical and economic conditions of African Americans during the New Negro Movement Era.

The Universal Negro Improvement Association (UNIA) also emerged in America during the New Negro Movement and was the largest secular organization for people of African descent in the world. The UNIA grew from a small group of Jamaican men and women who shared similar ideologies about self-reliance, anti-European colonialism, and racial purity (Summers, 2004). The international standing of the UNIA distinguished it from Prince Hall Freemasonry which was a national organization. Members of the UNIA were often referred to as Garveyites to recognize Marcus Garvey, who was the chief philosopher of the UNIA movement and its president-general. Garveyites believed that entrepreneurship was both a means to manhood development as well as racial advancement. The work done by UNIA chapters and their various auxiliaries resembled self-help organizations. The UNIA pushed for African Americans' economic empowerment through the creation of restaurants, clothing factories, stores, cooperative markets and financial institutions, and laundries, among other pursuits. Men who worked in these areas often held leadership and membership positions in the UNIA.

Garvey articulated a largely eclectic ideology of the "self-made" man to guide the UNIA. Like Freemasons, the UNIA first adhered to and then reshaped Eurocentric, middle-class standards of manhood. Unlike Freemasons, the UNIA pushed a more radical, "racially chauvinistic and nationalist agenda" (Summers, 2004, p. 69). Specifically, UNIA officials delivered rousing speeches and wrote scathing editorials in the *Negro World* that often referenced African American manhood as the subject, while the work of Freemasons was often subtle and understated. Summers (2004) presents several models of self-made manhood that informed the more radical ideology espoused by Garvey. These models combined to comprise the "producer outlook" of African American manhood which focused on achievement as defined by three important ideals: (1) gaining leadership in industry, (2) adopting bourgeois standards of respectability, and (3) implementing frontier ideologies posited by Theodore Roosevelt and American imperialists (Summers, 2004, p. 85). In addition, the notion of frontier manliness (demonstrated by Native American warriors and White homesteaders) represented the aggressive aspect of African American masculinity. Garvey advocated the "cult of strenuosity," developed by Theodore Roosevelt, to encourage African American men to strengthen their "physical muscles" as opposed to "spiritual muscles" (Summers, 2004, p. 80).

The self-made-man ideology was clearly embedded in the masculine discourses among Garveyites and Prince Hall Freemasons. For instance, both organizations used rituals to create in their members a heightened sense of manhood. Rituals are defined as actions and interactions performed symbolically (Summers, 2004). Freemasons and Garveyites also used rituals to define their organizations as exclusive. The rituals performed in both organizations served to bind the members together but also to divide African American men into disparate groups. Rituals formed a sense of cohesiveness among African American men who joined these organizations. Specifically, members who continued the artisanal, social, and political work of the organizations were perceived as reflecting an informed sense of self separate from nonmembers and women.

Middle-class ideals of domesticity and the public-private organization of gender roles played an important part in the manhood constructions for African American men in both movements (Summers, 2004). During the New Negro Movement Era, African American men would begin to use class in defining self and distinguish self from other African American men, women, and boys. Garveyites sought to politically and economically rally both African American men and women around an entrepreneurial agenda to effect change in Africa, while Freemasons aspired to unify like-minded, bourgeois men through secrecy to ascend to prominence in America. Both Garveyites and Prince Hall Freemasons shared fundamental ideas about what it meant to be a man in the early twentieth century (Summers, 2004). Members in both organizations subscribed to bourgeois ideals of manhood shaped by production and engagement in the marketplace and also sought to provide and protect African American women and children. In the years following the New Negro Movement, African American men and women would employ strong resistance to political inequality.

The Civil Rights Era:
Identity Crisis and the Emergence of a "Cool Pose"

Economically, the climate of America shifted at the dawn of the Civil Rights Era (Perkins, 2000). Specifically, Perkins (2000) identifies the economic sources that contributed to dramatic shifts in African American male identity: (1) the impacts of deindustrialization, job losses, and the globalization of the economy on African American working-class and underclass households, and (2) the exponential growth in the number of unmarried mothers after World War II. The number of unmarried mothers tripled between 1940 and 1957 (Perkins, 2000). The growth in numbers of unmarried mothers, in turn, led to an increase in welfare dependence for many African American families. As welfare dependency expanded, the age structure of African American households dramatically changed. In particular, birthrates among older, better-educated, middle-class African Americans declined, while birthrates among younger, less-educated, lower-socioeconomic African Americans rose and resulted in an increase in the number of births to unmarried African American women (Perkins, 2000). Scholars write that these economic trends were linked to the overt racial segregation in this period (Collins, 2005; Perkins, 2000). However, in this section, gender relations among African American men and between African American women and African American men are additionally considered as contributors to these trends.

Collins (2005) identifies "the political economy of racism," which, she argues, mandated the separation of African Americans and Whites on many levels of social interaction (p. 62). In her discussion, she maps how the political, legal, and social system affected African Americans differently relative to the region of America in which they lived. In the South, African Americans endured Jim Crow laws which legally separated African Americans and Whites. The term *Jim Crow laws* refers to the laws that upheld the "separate but equal" doctrine between African Americans and Whites. The "separate but equal" doctrine was the accepted, legalized separation upheld in a Supreme Court review of the *Plessy v. Ferguson* case (Collins, 2005). In this case, Homer Plessy, an African American man, took a seat in a passenger car designated for Whites, was ejected, and sued on the basis of discrimination. Whites achieved separation in the North through covert segregation, customs, and "traditions" (Collins, 2005). African Americans in the North were made to work the worst jobs, confined to the worst neighborhoods, and generally restricted or prevented from movement in White neighborhoods and other areas (Collins, 2005).

In this economic and political climate, African American men's constructions of self evolved. Two trends impacted new negotiations of African American male identities: (1) the political disenfranchisement of Jim Crow laws and failure of the general public to assist African Americans who were formerly enslaved, and (2) the patriarchal imagery of African American men as hypersexual and naturally violent (Collins, 2005). Across America, African American men were relegated to the dirtiest and lowest-paying jobs in America, that is, if African American men were hired at all. As a result, African American families were pushed to live in crowded, unhealthy, and unsanitary living conditions. Urban African American neighborhoods came to be known as "ghettos," or what Collins (2005) terms "a new form of prison," due to the egregious conditions African Americans were forced to endure (p. 69).

Scholars argue that movements led by African American women and gay, bisexual, and transgender African American men would contribute to feelings of Black male disempowerment (Collins, 2005; hooks, 2004b; Perkins, 2000). Collins (2005) observes that the urbanization of contexts allowed for a "freeing" of African American women who longed for life outside the imprisoning domestic life they lived in the South. African American women began to challenge patriarchal ideas about their own womanhood constructions. As a result, many African American women chose to be single in urban areas during the Civil Rights Era. At the same time, urbanization "freed" some closeted, gay African American men, as some openly gay African American men would begin to comment about diverse constructions of manhood in which same-sex intimacy was natural.

Many African American men found it difficult to challenge new constructions of African American womanhood and diverse constructions of African American manhood. According to Collins (2005), African American men either escaped the responsibility for their families (setting the stage for women-headed households) or formed new constructions of themselves as respectable African American men. However, this was ideologically difficult for African American men as their constructions mimicked the constructions of White men in a racially segregated and oppressive society (Collins, 2005).

African Americans refashioned a more "cool" manhood during this period, one that would free them from the obligations of marriage and fatherhood (hooks, 2004a). According to hooks (2004a), this new "freedom" for many African American men was envied by White men who wanted to redefine themselves as "cool." hooks (2004a) posits that African American men's new desire to be cool became the antithesis to family life and ultimately resulted in a trend in which African American men turned away from family responsibility in significant numbers. Interested in this trend, White researchers began to formulate scientific ideas that sought to uphold African American inferiority, justify separation, and to argue that African American men were being emasculated by African American women (Collins, 2005; Perkins, 2000).

Emergent theses largely informed the Moynihan Report (Moynihan, 1965; Marable, 2001; Perkins, 2000). The report, issued at the heel of the Civil Rights Act of 1964, argued that government must intervene in rebuilding the paternal role in African American families. The report, titled *The Negro Family: The Case for National Action*, argued that the African American man's role in the family had been weakened due to poor employment rates among African American men and the escalating prominence of African American women in African American homes. The Moynihan Report posited that government intervention was necessary to place African American men in economic positions that would enable them to become empowered in African American homes. The widespread belief in this report was that strong African American fathers would serve as value-added role models to African American youth. This, in turn, would socialize African American families, and particularly African American men, into American society. This led to a theory which asserted that African American men's employment would repair the African American family and begin to reverse the sociopolitical and socioeconomic damages of slavery.

This theory reinforced two patriarchal notions: (1) African American men needed to fight in wars on behalf of America (which had denied the interests and freedoms for African American families for years), and (2) African American men's sexist beliefs were legitimized and their efforts to subjugate African American women were supported (hooks, 2004a). The report is largely identified as sparking gender-conflict between African American men and African American women. Subsequently, these conflicts were precursors to other identity-tied resistance movements including the Black Power, Gay Liberation, and Women's movements. (hooks, 2004a; Marable, 2001; Perkins, 2000).

How History and Culture Matter: Meditations on Education and Society

In this chapter, African American male identity was explored throughout six eras of history: pre-transplantation Africa, post-transplantation America, the Antebellum and Reconstruction eras, the New Negro Movement Era, and the Civil Rights Era. Major themes in the development of African American male identity throughout history emerged. From deeply embedded connections to community to resistance to coolness, the ways in which African American male identities evolved have mirrored the evolutions of sociopolitical, cultural, and economic contexts. Subsequently, the turbulent sociocultural histories of African American boys and men hold valuable lessons for how they are served and underserved in education.

School and college educators are reminded that the identity-sorting devices used in society permeate educational contexts as well. Specifically, economic, cultural, racial, and social differences are still found to result in differential privilege in schools (Alexander, 2004; Brown, Dancy, & Norfles, 2006; Lareau, 2000). For instance, resources that contribute to educational success, such as supplies, books, computers, a place to study, and tutors, are available to children whose families have greater income and wealth. To maintain advantage, persons in positions of power use schooling to preserve vantage points of themselves and their progeny. Privileged parents continually investigate ways to pass on their advantages to their children, given America's history of systemic inequality (Alexander, 2004; Lareau, 2000). These contexts, to which the past is predisposed, leave many students, particularly African American males, behind.

Schools also perpetuate privilege among groups of students that cluster along racial lines. Schools and colleges are largely predisposed to White, middle-class values (Alexander, 2004; Diamond & Moore, 1995; Gay, 2000). Consequently, the values of middle-class students are congruent with school and college values. Thus middle-class students, more likely to be White or Asian, potentially respond to the requirements of schooling more easily than those who are not from middle-class families, excluding other differences that may be philosophically at odds with schools (Alexander, 2004). Concurrently, economic advantages confer benefits by supporting variation among individual students within schools. In other words, students from higher-SES families locate access to activities and opportunities less likely for students from lower-SES families. However, the goal of using school resources to enhance children's opportunities may be thwarted by differences among public schools (Alexander, 2004).

As in society, the social and cultural identities of African American males and those who serve them represent a growing degree of cultural mismatch across many schools and colleges in America (Delpit, 1995; Gay, 2000). The responsibilities for educators cluster in two broad areas. First, school and college educators must have a keen awareness and understanding of the historical and sociocultural contexts of their school and campus communities if their work is to be successful. They must familiarize themselves with histories of discrimination, systems of oppression, and contemporary manifestations of marginalization, which may contribute to mistrust, skepticism, and cynicism by communities and cultural groups that may have been excluded or devalued by an institution and its leaders. Where particular subgroups (i.e., African American males) are identified as "at-risk" populations, educators must familiarize themselves with critical information at identity intersections including race, gender, class, sexual orientation, and other identities. This information can be gained through historical research and artifacts including newspaper reports; governmental data; school, district, and university performance reports; and informal interviews that capture the experiential knowledge of people who have been marginalized, underserved, or silenced in a particular community.

Second, school and college educators must discern patterns of exclusion and segregation as perpetuated through administrative policies and practices. They must analyze policies and practices with the intent of identifying those that continue to grant privilege and a sense of entitlement to one group while only offering disadvantage and limited access and opportunity to others. For instance, African American males are more likely to be punished for their behavior vis-à-vis other student groups (Ferguson, 2000). However, African American males are found to engage more eclectic pathways to masculine identities that reflect cultural combinations of Black, White, and alternative standards that this chapter has outlined (Harris, 1995). Thus, recognizing the evolving sociocultural context of education is critical. Effectively identifying and resisting the cultural reproduction of educational inequities helps disrupt trends (i.e., hypercategorization as discipline problems, underrepresentation in college) that challenge African American males in the education pipeline. Inequality and inequity are reproduced when education leaders fail to address diversity issues concerning decision making, allocation of resources, and power distribution. Thus, education leaders must be unafraid to speak about what matters.

References

Akbar, N. (1991). *Visions for black men*. Tallahassee: Mind Productions and Associates.

Alexander, K. L. (2004). Public schools and the public good. In Ballantine, J. H. and Spade J. Z. (Eds.) *Schools and society: A sociological approach to education (2nd.ed)*. pp. 234–249. Belmont, CA: Thomson Wadsworth.

Anson, C. M., and Schwegler, R. A. (2000). *The Longman handbook for writers and readers* (2nd ed.). New York: Longman.

Blassingame, J. (1972). *The slave community: Plantation life in the antebellum South*. New York: Oxford University Press.

Brown, M. C. and Dancy, T. E. (2010). African American male collegians and the sword of Damocles: Understanding the postsecondary pendulum of progress and peril. In V. Polite & E. Zamani Gallaher (Eds.), *The State of the African American Male: A Courageous Conversation*, pp. 249–264. East Lansing: Michigan State University Press.

Brown, M. C., Dancy, T. E., and Norfles, N. (2006). A nation still at risk: No child left behind and the salvation of disadvantaged students. In F. Brown (Ed.), *No child left behind and other special programs in urban school districts*, pp. 341–364. Oxford: Elsevier.

Brown, M. C., & Davis, J. E. (2000). *Black sons to mothers: Compliments, critiques, and challenges for cultural workers in education*. New York: Peter Lang.

Clifton, C. (2001). Rereading voices from the past: Images of homo-eroticism in the slave narrative. In D. Constantine-Simms (Ed.), *The greatest taboo: Homosexuality in black communities*. Los Angeles: Alyson Books.

Collins, P. H. (2005). *Black sexual politics*. New York: Routledge.

Cullen, J. (2001). "I's a man now": Gender and African American men. In D. C. Hine & E. Jenkins (Eds.), *A question of manhood: A reader in U.S. black men's history and masculinity*, pp. 489-501. Bloomington: Indiana University Press.

Dancy, T. E. (2012). *The brother code: Manhood and masculinity among African American men in college*. Charlotte, NC: Information Age Press.

Davis, J. E., & Polite, V. (1999). *African American males in school and society: Practices and policies for effective education*. New York: Teachers College Press.

Delpit, L. (1995). *Other people's children: Cultural conflict in the classroom*. New York: The New Press.

Diamond, B. J., & Moore, M. A. (1995). *Multicultural literacy: Mirroring the reality of the classroom*. New York: Longman.

Du Bois, W. E. B. (1903/2005). *The illustrated souls of black folk*. Boulder, CO: Paradigm.

Dyson, M. E. (2001). When you divide body and soul, problems multiply: The black church and sex. In R. P. Byrd & B. Guy-Shetfall (Eds.), *Traps: African American men on gender and sexuality*. Bloomington: Indiana University Press.

Evans-Pritchard, E. E. (1971). *The Azande: History and political institutions*. Oxford: Clarendon Press.

Estes, S. (2005). Am I not a man and a brother? In S. Estes (Ed.), *I am a man! Race, manhood, and the civil rights movement*. Chapel Hill: The University of North Carolina Press.

Ferguson, A. A. (2000). *Bad boys: Public schools in the making of black male masculinity*. Ann Arbor: The University of Michigan Press.

Franklin, J. H., & Moss, A. A. (1994). *From slavery to freedom: A history of African Americans* (7th ed. Vol. 1). New York: McGraw-Hill.

Frazier, E. F. (1939). *The Negro family in the United States*. Chicago: The University of Chicago Press.

Gay, G. (2000). *Culturally responsive teaching: Theory, research, and practice*. New York: Teachers College Press.

Gossett, T. (1965). *Race: The history of an idea* (2nd ed.). New York: Schesdam.

Graham, L. O. (1999). *Our kind of people: Inside America's black upper class*. New York: Harper Collins Publishing.

Harris, F. (1995). Psychosocial development and Black male masculinity: Implications for counseling economically disadvantaged African American male adolescents. *Journal of Counseling Development, 73*, 279–287.

Hine, D. C., & Jenkins, E. (2001). *A question of manhood, volume II: A reader in U. S. black men's history and masculinity in the United States*. Bloomington: Indiana University Press.

Hoch, P. (1979). *White hero, black beast: Racism, sexism, and the mask of masculinity*. London: Pluto.

hooks, b. (2004a). *The will to change: Men, masculinity, and love*. New York: Atria Books.

hooks, b. (2004b). *We real cool: Black men and masculinity*. New York: Routledge.

Hunter, A., & Davis, J. E. (1992). Constructing gender: An exploration of Afro-American men's conceptualization of manhood. *Gender and Society, 6*(3), 464–479.

Johnson, C. A. (2001). Hearing voices: Unearthing evidence of homosexuality in precolonial Africa. In D. Constantine-Simms (Ed.), *The greatest taboo: Homosexuality in black communities* pp. 132–148. Los Angeles: Alyson Books.

Jones, D. M. (2005). *Race, sex, and suspicion: The myth of the black male.* Westport, CT: Praeger.

Junod, H. A. (1962). *Life of a South African Tribe.* New York: University Books.

Lareau, Annette. (2000). *Home Advantage* (2nd ed.) Lanham, MD: Rowman & Littlefield.

Lee, C. C. (1992). *Empowering Young Black Males.* Ann Arbor, MI: ERIC Counseling and Personnel Services Clearinghouse.

Marable, M. (2001). Groundings with my sisters: Patriarchy and the exploitation of black women. In R. P. Byrd & B. Guy-Shetfall (Eds.), *Traps: African American men on gender and sexuality.* Bloomington: Indiana University Press.

Mercer, K. (1994). *Welcome to the jungle: New positions in black cultural studies.* New York: Routledge.

Montejo, E. (1968). *Autobiography of a runaway slave.* London: The Bodley Head Ltd.

Moynihan, D. P. (1965). *The Negro family: The case for national action.* Washington, DC: Government Printing Office.

Murray, S., & Roscoe, W. (1998). *Boy-wives and female husbands: Studies in African homosexualities.* New York: St. Martin's Press.

Ouzgane, L., & Morrell, R. (2005). *African Masculinities: Men in Africa from the Late 19th Century to the Present.* Palgrave Macmillan: New York.

Perkins, W. E. (2000). Matriarchy, Malcolm X, and masculinity: A historical essay. In M. C. Brown & J. E. Davis (Eds.), *Black sons to mothers: Compliments, critiques, and challenges for cultural workers in education.* New York: Peter Lang.

Summers, M. (2004). *Manliness and its discontents: The black middle class and the transformation of masculinity, 1900–1930.* Chapel Hill: University of North Carolina.

Wallace, M. (2002). *Constructing the black masculine: Identity and ideality in African American men's literature and culture, 1775–1995.* Durham, NC: Duke University.

Weber, M. (1958). The Chinese literati. In H. H. Gerth & C. W. Mills (Eds.), *From Max Weber: Essays in sociology.* New York: Oxford University Press.

Part One

Educational Contexts

Chapter Two

Questions from the Soul/Sole

Examining the Critical Work in Educational Practice

Roland W. Mitchell

> Teachers are not adequately prepared to actively address the problems which exist in society. This silence encourages the propagation of the status quo. . . would-be learners are relegated to the corners and alleys where their voices are but cacophonous echoes which fill the dark void, night air of society.
> —Bell, 2000, p. 117

In "Education 101: Thoughts on Teaching and Race" it appears that Karl Bell (2000) seeks to expand the responsibilities of a professor (college/university educator) to include characteristics traditionally associated with a teacher (K-12 educator). Through this response I specifically set out to highlight the implicit distinctions between the status and often gendered categorizations of professors (professionals/higher-status/men) and teachers (practitioners/lower-status/women) to both illustrate and problematize the significant contributions that Bell's chapter makes. Bell's claim that he is concerned about his students who are members of "this generation of welfare reform, homelessness and hopelessness" (p. 113) is a far cry from characterizations of college professors who are singularly concerned with the transmission of subject-matter knowledge to the blank slates of their students' minds (Freire, 1970). Hence, Bell's reflection on the way that outside influences (home life, levels of anxiety, institutional racism, and comfort in schooling in general) inform a student's encounters of learning is typically associated with the nurturing dispositions of teachers as opposed to the more reserved dispositions often attributed to professors. Further, Bell's primary focus on the added nuances of being a teacher of color attempting to negotiate the ways that his gender and race inform his obligations to and expectations of his students sets the stage for a timely discussion. Taking up Bell's position in this chapter, the following critique suggests that it is time to redefine the parameters of what it is to be a college-level teacher to include the development of the whole student as opposed to narrowly focusing on the objective transmission of discrete factoids. And, for African American students in particular, there is a dire need for professors to take account of life lessons that address the pervasive influence of race and racism on their experiences of formal schooling (Jones, Castellanos, & Cole, 2002).

Bell (2000) astutely argued that "teachers in effect have the ability to create or destroy intellectual life [and as such] this skill cannot be haphazardly utilized or handled by the unprepared or disingenuous" (p. 117). By thinking of teaching in this manner, status-quo visions of professors who only address the academic needs of students are challenged. Bell instead calls for professors to guide their practice with understandings that are referred to in Brown and Davis's (2000) volume, *Black Sons to Mothers,* as being identified with being *teacher-mothers.* Analogies between teaching and mothering hold many productive and challenging possibilities for higher education. The aspects of these possibilities that make a mother's ability to give life analogues to the work of teaching are powerful. However the diminished role of women—and as a result mothers—in a patriarchal society calls for further development of the concept and subsequently its application to Bell's work. Therefore, through our response, we aim to do the delicate work of excavating race, gender, schooling, and the overall responsibility associated with an educator from the legacy of systemic racist and patriarchal oppression that Bell set out to challenge in his chapter.

Teaching Through "Mother Wit"

Mother wit is commonly thought of as innate intelligence, common sense, or sound practical judgment. However, as it specifically relates to African American women, Toni Morrison described mother wit as, "A knowing so deep that the lesson has been instilled and distilled to its essence. . . Collectively these words are a gift—from your own mother, or anyone's mother. They are wise words for life's journey"(O' Reilly, 2004 p.12). Joy Kinnon's (1997) article "Mother Wit: Words of Wisdom from Black Women," provides numerous additional examples from notable Black women. For example, quoting educator Johnnetta Cole, Kinnon selects, "When you educate a man, you educate an individual, but when you educate a woman, you educate a nation" (p. 2). When considering the ebb and flow of power, Alice Walker states, "Nothing of value is given up voluntarily" (p. 2). Consequently in the opening of the article when Bell lamented that his students were done a disservice by never encountering a college-level teacher whose practice was explicitly informed by mother wit, regardless of a student's race or gender, the wisdom associated with such assertions is apparent. Further, this wisdom seems to be greatly needed considering the admittedly dismal performance of a large segment of students who are currently participating in U.S. higher education.

The positives associated with this approach to teaching include meaningful teacher/student interaction (Tinto, 1993; Pascarella, 1996; Pascarella & Terenzini, 2005) opportunities for students to see the relevance of the information they are learning for their everyday lives (Gay, 2000), and ultimately the establishment of an active learning environment (Freire, 1970; hooks, 1994; Delpit, 1995; Delpit & Dowdy, 2003). In a basic sense the benefits move beyond the walls of the classroom and demonstrate that the professor cares about his/her students. If the professor does indeed care about his/her students, then the information and the learning in general move beyond passing on abstract and objective facts to actually becoming a dialogical engagement of meaningful knowledge informed by sound practical judgment. Further, it is no coincidence that each of the aforementioned positives attributed to mother wit is greatly supported by higher education literature as a means for improving graduation rates, retention numbers, and overall student satisfaction (Kuh, Kinzie, Schuh, & Whitt, 2005).

Armed with this information one may question why a *mother-centric* approach to teaching has not swept the postsecondary pedagogical landscape. And when specifically recognizing the plight of African American students who tend not to experience the same levels of success as their European American counterparts (Chang, 2000; Fries-Britt & Turner, 2002; Brown, 2009; Freeman, 1998), it appears that an appeal to teaching informed by mother wit would be extremely beneficial. I personally believe the reason that mother-centric teaching has not been more readily accepted lies in the complex and gendered distinctions often associated with being a postsecondary educator (professor) when compared to K-12 level educators (teachers). In fact, as I will elaborate on in the following section, where K-12 educators are framed as mothers away from home, charged with a more holistic approach of actually nurturing the entire student, by the time students enter higher education they are viewed as adults. And subsequently if one seeks to understand the challenges of teaching through mother wit in current higher education contexts, thoughtful inquiry is needed into the transition from child to adult in which both the student and the teacher are forced to re-negotiate the educational terrain.

The Distinction between K-12 and Postsecondary Teachers: Mother vs. Professor

As the previous section suggested, learning in college classrooms could be greatly enhanced by taking the more holistic approach to teaching that Bell succinctly characterized as teaching through mother wit. However, there are also challenges in using this approach to teaching in the current higher education contexts. Specifically, rigid constructions of gender and professionalism complicate a full-on merger of the roles of professor and mother. For instance, typically professors have more years of education (often with a terminal degree), greater respect from the general public, higher pay, and a staunchly guarded legacy of academic freedom. Also, the profession overall is numerically and discursively masculine as compared to K-12 education (Thelin, 2004). Teachers (K-12), on the other hand, are often thought of as possessing fewer years of education (bachelors and additional certification that rarely includes terminal degrees), less respect among the public, lower salaries and high attrition rates, and are numerically and discursively conceptualized as a feminine profession (Cochran-Smith & Lytle, 1999; Tozer, Senese & Violas, 2008).

These distinctions amount to similar debates within other professions in which the occupation becomes narrowly defined around gendered binaries such as nursing, social work, and counseling. There is substantive literature that discusses professions like these as being *feminized* or women's work (Solomon, 1986; Ropers-Huilman, 2003), and with this categorization comes a lower valuing of these professions within the general population. An anecdotal illustration of this phenomenon that I often use in my own teaching is that, as a result of the majority of the U.S. population having spent thirteen years, more or less, in school, there is a belief that everybody can be a teacher. So I often hear individuals outside of education claim, "I went to school for 13 years and you get summers off, so how hard can teaching be. . . anyone can be a teacher." However, it would seem absurd to state, "Well I've had teeth for 37 years, so I can be a dentist," or "I've had a heart for 41 years, so I can be a cardiologist." Clearly all of these professions are greatly needed, but teachers are so undervalued that (just as we connect mothering to its taken-for-granted biological functions) we link the profession of educating minors to a similar type of natural innate ability. Dentists or doctors, on the other hand, are held in higher esteem as experts in greatly valued professions who are highly educated and skilled.

Against this backdrop, professors prefer to be recognized as experts in their disciplines as opposed to being linked to K-12 educators. And professors vehemently oppose being thought of as exclusively working with adolescents and being viewed as little more than professional care-givers or mothers. In fact, the highest rewards and status are often afforded to researchers. And in many ways the day-to-day work of teaching, and particularly teaching undergraduates, is devalued. Recognizing this trend, the Carnegie Foundation established the Scholarship of Teaching initiative specifically to address the devaluing of pedagogy and ultimately raise the status of teaching among the professoriate. Scholarship of

Teaching proponents Mary Huber and Sherwyn Morreale (2002) describe the Scholarship of Teaching as:

> [B]eing concerned with an invitation to mainstream faculty to treat teaching as a form of inquiry into student learning, to share research and inquiry with colleagues, and to critique and build on one another's work. This critical analysis of professors' teaching seeks to envision the way that pedagogy is improved when teachers look closely at their own teaching practice and share their findings with their colleagues. (p. 12)

Consequently, the attempt by the Carnegie Foundation to raise the status of teaching provides additional proof that even within a profession that supposedly equally recognizes the significance of teaching, research, and service there is still a clearly structured hierarchy that undervalues teaching and the daily work of teachers.

The Value of Teaching: Race, Gender, and Scholarship

Valuing the work of teachers at any level is important, however, college teaching in the manner supported by the Carnegie Foundation's Scholarship of Teaching initiative still relies on a conception of teaching driven by the desire to peer review teaching in the way that researchers assess their research. Hence, one may ask, is this the only way that we can get colleges and universities to take teaching seriously—to make teaching fit into the existing research paradigm? This approach to pedagogy is not necessarily antithetical to teaching through mother wit, but it is rooted in a school of thought that challenges the education of the entire student. Now let me be clear, I acknowledge the significant contributions and innovations made possible by university-based researchers and subsequently understand the value of the research-dominated paradigm in which college teaching exists. But I also recognize that if the work of teaching has to be thought of as another means of producing research to be valued, no funding sources will ever provide a similar level of support to teaching as to national defense research or the development of new pharmaceuticals. Plainly stated, the profit is just not there, and if teaching has to look like *experimental research* to be taken seriously, then it will continue to be thought of as I once heard one of my colleagues say "*women's* or *nigger's* work." Further, we believe that it is no coincidence that these derogatory ways of framing teaching—as less than—just so happens to directly address Bell's over-arching aim of providing a racial and gendered analysis of the issues that students and faculty of color face in U.S. classrooms.

Even after one takes account of the challenges that gender and professionalism cause for a full-on merger of mother wit with college teaching, the lack of racial and cultural diversity in the U.S. professoriate portends a major challenge.

For example, despite the fact that American higher education has been struggling to increase the number of faculty of color for nearly half a century, only about 5 percent of U.S. faculty are African Americans compared to 21 percent of the college student population ("Black Faculty in Higher Education," 2006). Although we do not believe that only Black teachers can teach Black students, research suggests that professors of color enhance the learning environment for students of color (Davis, Dias-Bowie, Greenberg, Klukken, Pollio & Thomas, et al., 2004). A particularly telling example of the disparity exists at my home institution where the Black population of the state exceeds 33 percent of the total, but only 3 percent of the faculty at the flagship institution of the state are African American ("Black Faculty in Higher Education," 2006).

Taking account of these demographics, it may very well be the case that even if we all agree that teaching so as to educate the entire student is ideal, it may be that centuries of systemic racial, cultural, and gender-based discrimination have limited our ability to provide the richest education for *ALL*. Therefore, lacking a racially and culturally diverse teaching force, the existing statistics suggest that we have two options—either 1) wait another 150 years for the U.S. educational system to live up to the nation's claim of equity for all and start employing more equitable employment practices or 2) adjust our definitions of teaching and nurturing to reflect our current higher education environment and expect professors, regardless of their racial, cultural, or gender identity to familiarize themselves with the communal experiences of the student population that they are serving.

As one may expect, I argue for the latter solution—that the existing professoriate must expand its definition of an effective teacher to include racial and gender-specific understandings. As Bell suggested, men must become more readily recognized as nurturing pedagogues, and all teachers, regardless of their race, must learn to teach across racial and cultural boundaries. This approach calls for a move from viewing the insights attributed to mothers or K-12 teachers as purely instinctual or biological to seeing such insights as a learned type of pedagogically meaningful knowledge. So as an academic search committee would argue that a good math teacher needs a knowledge of mathematics that was learned as opposed to innate, so too, the practical insight that Bell describes as mother wit can be studied and acquired. Hence, mother wit can be both epistemic and intrinsic in nature and, if used wisely, significantly enhances professors' ability to address the holistic needs of *all* of their students. Clearly men or majority populations will come to these insights in a different manner than women or people of color, but in the end the understandings associated with teaching across racial and or gendered boundaries can be learned. Further, when conducting searches, we believe evidence of the ability to provide this type of service should be sought out just as disciplinary and research competence are.

Consequently, the unique aspect of Bell's work and the aim of the text in general of carving out a space for responsible teachers to be both pedagogues in the traditional sense and nurturers in a progressive sense are powerful. In fact, by making this claim Bell and the text take seriously the charge of philosopher and critic Cornel West's (1993) that U.S. society is improved when we sift out the best of the western tradition of education and teaching. Therefore Bell challenges the academy to hold on to existing considerations of relating to college students as autonomous adults with different needs than adolescents, while forwarding the idea that the nurturing aspect attributed to teaching through mothering (K-12 teachers) is a powerful pedagogical tool regardless of the grade-level of the student or gender of the teacher. Hence, both male and female educators are challenged to tap into the nurturing aspects of teaching typically associated with being the teacher-mother, specifically applying traditionally women's ways of knowing to the educational venture. The problem arises however along two significant fractures. First, women, people of color, and non-western cultures have traditionally been characterized as singularly depending on intuition over rationality (women); being essentially connected to nature (Native American or Aboriginal cultures); and exotic and mystical (peoples of Asia and Africa). Europeans have historically been framed as the rational creators of science and masters of the natural world (McClintock, 1995). The end result of these racist and patriarchal characterizations has historically found White men to be more human than any other group and, therefore, naturally suited to be professors.

In the end we believe prevailing racial and gendered binaries comprise a significant challenge to Bell's approach to teaching. However, we do believe that the power of Bell's expansion of what college teachers can be amounts to what critical educator Nancy Scheper-Hughes termed as—"life boat ethics or the morality of triage"(1993)—for students of color in an educational system steeped in a legacy of inequitable practices. Hence, against the challenges to mother-centric teaching we hold on to the aspect of Bell's response that we consider to be akin to idiomatic proverbs, or shall we say colonized communal wit, concerning establishing and maintaining a viable community. Examples of this include "it takes a village," that is, socialization into the village calls for village members to act as "their brothers and sisters' keepers." There is significant anecdotal and historical precedence to support Bell's assertion in the Black community that is still fragmented as a result of the lingering effects of surviving centuries of chattel slavery. However what I personally would add to Bell's argument is that professors are challenged to transition from mothering to fathering, acting as siblings, colleagues and even teachers and students of the communal experiences of education of their students. A key aspect of the nuances to Bell's argument that I appeal to here is directly related to expectations of educators or accountability and the responsibility associated with being an educator. In the following sections I will re-conceptualize the roles of accountability and responsibility in higher education contexts to bolster Bell's discussion of college teaching informed by mother wit.

Accountability to Be Both Teacher and Nurturer

> How precious is your unfailing love, O God! All humanity finds shelter in the shadow of your wings. You feed them from the abundance of your own house, letting them drink from your rivers of delight. For you are the fountain of life, the light by which we see.
>
> —Psalm 36:7–9

I am not so bold as to place teachers on the same plane as a higher power or greater force; however, it is clear that in our current educational system teachers are seen as the rivers of delight, the fountain of life from which knowledge flows and thirst for education is quenched. In this context, a parallel comparison using the scripture from the book of Psalms appears appropriate. However, those like Bell who have long viewed teachers as these fountains of life never expected an educational system where accountability would jeopardize the abundance of knowledge and education shared in our classrooms and spaces of learning. This force has become so misunderstood that it seeks to dry up our rivers, wreak havoc on our shelter, and dim the light and progress of our educational future.

In transposing the concept of teacher-mother from a K-12 context to a higher education context, Bell astutely brings along the accountability conundrum that is currently plaguing our K-12 educational system. I am not urging the demise of accountability but rather a greater understanding of its components in a way that creates an accountability framework incorporating system, teacher, student, and family. The very mention of accountability in education yields a wide range of responses from fear of the unknown to the appreciation of a set of benchmarks for "success." Measures of accountability have become and will remain a critical component in the evaluation of student, teacher, and school performance. Given this realization, how then, can this model fit into a higher education context? And to what degree is it appropriate to do so?

Bell confounds this argument by placing most of the accountability on the college-level teacher. This is perhaps the most scrutinized piece of the current accountability model in any educational context. And while this may be a starting point, Bell fails to take into account the shared responsibility that the current accountability system dictates and that he ultimately advocates for in higher education. Too often we continue to blame those in the teaching profession for the shortcomings of our educational systems. And while teachers/professors are the most easily identifiable components of the system, it does not resolve Bell's views on accountability as it relates to race, teaching, and learning. In any educational setting, teaching should lead our accountability—whether we are discussing a set of goals and benchmarks or a personal accountability to provide a space where all students can reach their highest potential. From this perspective race, teaching, and learning become a shared responsibility. Yet, in many instances the quest for accountability leads our teaching and the practices that take place within our classrooms. It is from this perspective that race, teaching, and learning lose the ability to become important catalysts for change. If race, teaching, and learning are to become part of the foundation of our educational system, a new river of delight by which the thirst for equity, social justice, and mutual respect are quenched, we must acknowledge the delicate balance between accountability and responsibility to include both the teacher/professor and the educational system.

A Redefinition of Accountability Through Holistic Teaching as the Norm

In *Whose University Is It, Anyway: Power and Privilege on Gendered Terrain,* theorist Maria Martimianakis (2009) suggests that "Accountability is a process, a technique of management and governance, which forces institutions to reduce very complex processes into objective measures" (p. 53). These remarks signify a crucial component for an application of Bell's challenge to the problems currently facing students and professors of color. Bell's work pushes the boundaries of accountability, which have long been an uncomfortable yet persistent part of K-12 teaching and are slowly but surely making inroads into the work of college-level teachers as well. Typically the argument goes that teachers are significantly responsible for the learning that occurs and that there is a one-size-fits-all model that ensures that measurable learning outcomes will be achieved. If one doubts this statement, please see such policy reports and studies like the Tucker Report and the ongoing ramifications associated with the Spellings Commission.

Through these and similar initiatives the public has called for a greater sense of accountability for educators to prove that learning is actually occurring. I concede that measuring learning outcomes is a very complicated venture and in many ways is akin to counting the number of angels that will fit on the head of a needle. To continue to argue that college-level teaching is too complex to be reduced to discrete measurable outcomes ignores the significant influence of the current accountability debates. The hesitance by college-level educators to seriously participate in these discussions may be read as simply retreating to the infamous "Ivory Tower" and remaining above the fray of an extremely important conversation. This line of thought will cause educators to remain on the margins of a very important conversation that, whether we like it or not, is gaining momentum. Putting our heads in the sand only gives credence to the popular conception by the public that educators are out of touch with the needs of society in general and students in particular.

Further, I believe the hesitance to fully participate in these on-going discussions by K-12 teachers has led to the growing perception that politicians are better suited to set educational standards than teachers. Recognizing this trend in the K-12 setting, college-level educators must be both vigilant and proactive in the accountability debate. Consequently, I believe that a central part of the measure of what a good teacher should do, and be, must include what Bell describes as a mother-centric pedagogy—or what I sought to frame through this response as a nurturing professor who is concerned with the holistic education of all students. I make this claim fully recognizing that the very nature of accountability and standardization has historically been antithetical to the detail and attention that Bell calls for from educators. But in the end if the aim of accountability is to establish a norm, a norm that recognizes that college-level students can benefit from nurturing is better than emphasizing "Best Practices" over the education of the entire student. Consequently, taking account of the struggles that are currently occurring at the K-12 level should force college-level educators to read the writing on the wall and embrace and define what good teaching looks like before it is determined for them by policy makers. In conclusion, I believe a central part of that educational revision must include the thoughtful nurturing of the entire student as a means to provide service to the diverse student population to which Bell is deeply committed.

References

Bell, K. (2000). *Education 101: Thoughts on teaching and race*. In M. Christopher Brown II and James Earl Davis (Eds.), *Black sons to mothers: Compliments, critiques, and challenges for cultural workers in education,* pp. 93–102. New York: Peter Lang.

Black faculty in higher education: Still only a drop in the bucket (2006). *The Journal of Blacks in Higher Education*. Retrieved 1 Dec, 2009 http://www.jbhe.com/features/55_blackfaculty.html

Brown, C. (2009). *Broken cisterns: African American education fifty years after* Brown. Charlotte, NC: Information Age.

Brown, M. C., & Davis, J. E. (2000) *Black sons to mothers: Compliments, critiques, and challenges for cultural workers in education.* New York: Peter Lang.

Chang, M. J. (2000). Improving campus racial dynamics: A balancing act among competing interests. In E. Whitt (Ed.), *ASHE reader on college student affairs administration* (2nd ed., pp. 347–361). Boston: Pearson Custom Publishing.

Cochran-Smith, M., & Lytle, S. L. (1999). Relationships of knowledge and practice: Teacher learning in communities. *Review of Research in Education, 24*, 249–305.

Davis, M., Dias-Bowie, Y., Greenberg, K., Klukken, G., Pollio, H. R., Thomas, S. P., et al. (2004). "A fly in the buttermilk": Descriptions of university life by successful black undergraduate students at a predominantly white southeastern university. *The Journal of Higher Education, 75*(4), 420–445.

Delpit, L. (1995). *Other people's children: Cultural conflict in the classroom.* New York: The New Press.

Delpit, L.,& Dowdy, J. (2003). *The skin that we speak: Thoughts on language and culture in the classroom.* New York: The New Press.

Freeman, K. (1998). *African American heritage and culture in higher education research and practice.* Westport, CT: Praeger.

Freire, P. (1970). *Pedagogy of the oppressed.* New York: Continuum Publishing.

Fries-Britt, S., & Turner, B. (2002). Uneven stories: Successful Black collegians at a Black and a White campus. *Review in Higher Education, 25*(3), 315–330.

Gallien, L., & Peterson, M. (2004). *Instructing and mentoring the African American student: Strategies for success in higher education.* New York: Allyn & Bacon.

Gay, G. (2000). Culturally responsive teaching: Theory, research and practice. New York: Teachers College Press.

Gregory, S. (2000). Strategies for improving the racial climate for students of color in predominately White institutions. *Equity and Excellence in Education, 33*(3), 9.

Harper, S. R., & Quaye, S. J. (Eds.). (2009). *Student engagement in higher education: Theoretical perspectives and practical approaches for diverse populations.* New York: Routledge.

hooks, B. (1994). *Teaching to transgress.* New York: Routledge.

Huber, M., & Morreale, S. (2002). Situating the scholarship of teaching and learning: A cross- disciplinary conversation. www.carnagiefoundation.org/elibrary/docs/situating.htm

Jones, L., Castellanos, J., & Cole, D. (2002). Examining the ethnic minority student experience at predominantly White institutions: A case study. *Journal of Hispanic Higher Education, 1*(1), 19–39.

Kinnon, J. B. (1997). Mother wit: Words of wisdom from black women. *Ebony.* FindArticles.com. 01 Dec, 2009. http://findarticles.com/p/articles/mi_m1077/is_n5_v52/ai_19201537/

Kuh, G. D., Kinzie, J., Schuh, J. H., & Whitt, E. J. (2005). *Student success in college: Creating conditions that matter.* San Francisco, CA: Wiley.

Martimianakis, M. (2009). Reconciling competing discourses: The University of Toronto's equity and diversity framework. In A. Wagner, S. Acker, & K. Mayuzumi, (Eds.), *Whose university is it, anyway? Power and privilege on gendered terrain,* (pp. 44–60). Toronto, ON: Sumach Press.

McClintock, A. (1995). *Imperial leather: Race, gender and sexuality in the colonial contest.* New York: Routledge.

O'Reilly, A. (2004). *Toni Morrison and motherhood: A politics of the heart.* New York, NY: SUNY Press.

Pascarella, E. (1996). Influences on students' openness to diversity and challenge in the first year of college education. *Journal of Higher Education, 67,* 174–195.

Pascarella, E., & Terenzini, P. (2005). *How college affects students: A third decade of research.* San Francisco, CA: Jossey-Bass.

Perna, L. W., Milem, J., Gerald, D., Baum, E., Rowan, H., & Hutchens, N. (2006). The status of equity for Black undergraduates in public higher education in the south: Still separate and unequal. *Research in Higher Education, 47*(2), 197–228.

Ropers-Huilman, B. (2003). *Gendered futures in higher education: Critical perspectives for change.* New York: SUNY.

Scheper, N. (1993) "Life Boat Ethics." Republished in *Gender in Cross-Cultural Perspective,* pp. 31–37. C. Brettell & C. Sargent (eds.), Englewood Cliffs, N.J.: Prentice Hall.

Solomon, B. (1986). *In the company of educated women.* New Haven, CT: Yale University Press.

Thelin, J. R. (2004). *A history of American higher education.* Baltimore, MD: Johns Hopkins University Press.

Tinto, V. (1993). *Leaving college: Rethinking the causes and cures of college attrition* (2nd ed.). Chicago: University of Chicago Press.

Tozer, S., Senese, P., and Violas, P. C. (2009). *School and society: Historical and contemporary perspectives* (6th ed.). New York: McGraw-Hill.

West, C. (1993). *Prophetic thought in postmodern times.* Monroe, ME.: Common Courage.

Chapter Three

Understanding Social Capital and the African American School Experience

George L. Wimberly

Researchers have used various theoretical perspectives to examine social mobility from adolescence to adulthood. Status attainment research (Sewell & Hauser, 1980; Sewell, Haller, & Portes, 1969) has examined the role social class plays in the educational process of children and their educational outcomes. These studies conclude that social class has a strong positive effect on student achievement in school and the likelihood that high school students will go on to college. However, these findings are inconclusive specifically with respect to African American students. Times have changed and the status attainment process of a generation ago may not apply to children today. Students graduating from high school or attaining a GED is much more common today than in the past, yet a high school diploma does not have the same market value it once had. High school graduates' job opportunities are often limited to low-wage service positions. College is theoretically more accessible to students, but college entry and completion rates are markedly low for African Americans. Overall, African Americans today complete high school at about the same rate as their White counterparts. Among African American high school graduates, those transitioning immediately to college grew from 44.4% in 1976 to 55.7% in 2007, yet Whites saw an increase of 48.8% to 69.5% during the same years. Roughly 39% of African American students complete a bachelor's degree within 6 years, compared to 60% of their White peers (U.S. Department of Education, 2009). African American adolescents continue to lag behind Whites in terms of educational achievement and attainment and in the labor market.

Several education policies and school-based initiatives have been designed and implemented to increase social mobility for African American and economically disadvantaged people. Since the 1960s programs such as Title I have provided federal funds to improve reading and math skills for poor youth. Head Start programs have helped poor preschoolers develop social and academic skills to prepare them for the rigors of school. The No Child Left Behind initiatives are currently helping schools across the country attain high academic standards. Other school-based programs, such as Upward Bound and later GEAR-UP, emerged to help low-income and minority students achieve in school and the labor market. Affirmative Action initiatives have demanded that employers and institutions actively seek race and gender diversification.

Social capital theories address the status attainment process, moving beyond traditional notions of race and social class. Social networks play a significant role in helping people learn about educational information, providing access to middle-class norms, people, and culture, and enhancing one's broader life chances in society. Using social capital theories to explain a student's school experiences and educational attainment is relatively new in the research community. Coleman (1988) first examines the impact of social capital on children, focusing on the structure of social capital, not the process. Changes in communities through social programs, partnerships between schools and private businesses, and changes in the school climate have altered students' social networks, creating relationships that support education. Research shows that low-income and minority students rely on their relationships with teachers and school administrators to achieve school success; however, there is a paucity of research linking social capital and educational outcomes, particularly among African American youth (Epps, 1995; Stanton-Salazar, 1997, 2001; Wimberly, 2004).

As institutions schools play a significant role in students' educational outcomes. Schools have the potential to provide the social capital which can instill educational values and give students information and skills to succeed. African American youth particularly must rely on social capital—the resources and the relationships they glean from the school. Through a review of social capital theories and school relationships, this chapter discusses how school social capital impacts African American adolescents' school experiences, including their educational expectations and educational attainment, and how social capital can help students make the transition from high school to college and other postsecondary education.

Social Capital Defined

Coleman (1988) defines social capital by its function, existing in the structure of relations between actors and among actors, not in the actors themselves or in the physical implements of production. He states:

> It is not a single entity but a variety of different entities, with two elements in
> common: they all consist of some aspect of social structures and they facilitate

certain actions of actors—whether persons or corporate actors within the structure. Like other forms of capital, social capital is productive, making possible the achievement of certain ends that in its absence would not be possible. (p. S108)

The relationships which foster social capital are constructed for creating resources. These relationships form social networks that allow one to obtain resources by virtue of social network membership. These relationships are the social capital, not the resources themselves, as social capital inheres in the social structure.

Drawing on Coleman's definition I define social capital as the resources one gains through interpersonal relationships and connections with institutions. One acquires social capital through a recursive process that is rooted in these relationships and developed through trust, obligations, and reciprocity. Social capital is found in relationships in the school, the family, and the community. The effects of social capital include legitimizing a set of norms and values of a specific group, channeling information between individuals and groups, and providing access to opportunities. In the school context, social capital increases educational expectations and attainment through student relationships with teachers, parents, peers, and the school community itself. School social capital can reinforce norms and values associated with an education orientation, pass on information about postsecondary education, and provide students access to educational opportunities.

Social Capital Formation

The elements that go into creating social capital include trust, social mores, and the norms of the social system, which help form individual and institutional relationships. First, the foundation of social capital lies in the relationships an actor has with other people or social institutions. These relationships can be between individuals, between individuals and institutions, or among institutions.

Second, for social capital to be most effective individuals need to be free to pursue their life chances. Oppressive social systems limit one's social capital development. In Marxian terms, the bourgeoisie and the proletariat both possess social capital. Yet, the social capital of the bourgeoisie is more expansive than the proletariat's because the former are free to form relationships with various people and institutions that can affect their social development. The proletariat's social capital does not have the same power or potency as that of the bourgeoisie because they lack the freedom to pursue their life chances. When liberty is restricted social capital is only generated and used in a narrow playing field. Social capital without liberty is not transferable. Moreover, social capital is least effective among oppressed people (Putnam, 2000).

Third, a sense of trust must exist between individuals and institutions for effective social capital development. Trust relationships are a key feature of social capital, underlying the group membership. Through trust, individuals and groups can function without the use of formal or institutional doctrine. Trust involves a set of rewards and sanctions which are tied to group membership. It allows for an exchange of resources between people connected to the same social network and operating in the same social context. When trust does not exist, effective social capital cannot develop.

Fourth, social capital comes from relationships in which individuals or institutions have a moral or social obligation. Morality can be a driving force in many relationships as these moral or social obligations may be the common thread that connects people based on a shared ideology or circumstance. People behave in a moral manner which involves adhering to rules based on attachment to social groups. Moral or social obligations exemplify how social capital is a form of social control. People do not deviate from these obligations without facing sanctions from the group.

Social capital develops through a recursive process in which social obligations and trust cause relationships to develop among actors and institutions. These relationships support the transmission of social capital and are maintained by social capital. Through these relationships, people are able to use social capital to legitimate social norms and values, funnel information, and create opportunities.

Information channels from social relationships are key to the social capital process. This information is the basis for providing action. For example, some may get information about important events in their community through conversations with those in their social network rather than by reading the newspaper, searching the Internet, or watching television. Common interactions with others can provide information about things from the trivial, such as which basketball team has the leading scorer, to the more serious, such as how to change your diet to avoid a heart attack. In the high school setting students interact with their classmates and teachers to obtain educational information such as what classes to take to get into college, how to apply to college, which colleges offer the best academic environment, what jobs are available in the community, and how to succeed in school.

These functions of social capital feed back into the loop to develop more social capital. The information, norms, values, and opportunities that manifest from social capital generate or are part of the process of creating social capital. Thus, the more social capital one has the more social capital one is able to create.

Social Capital and Other Forms of Capital

In general, capital is a resource that is used for production to obtain a specified end. Each form of capital has a specific role that can be valuable in one situation yet can prove harmful in another context. The social context defines the worth of capital. Some capital is in a very tangible form such as economic capital in one's bank account or physical capital in tools and machinery. Less tangible capital includes human capital in one's skills or knowledge, and cultural capital inherent in one's lifestyle and actions. Social capital is probably one of the least tangible capital forms because it exists in relationships. The boundary between each form of capital is often unclear. Each of these forms of capital deserves further explanation.

Human capital is essentially talent, ability, and knowledge that people possess. Human capital development involves an investment of time, money, and energy in order to enhance or develop skills and knowledge within individuals (Becker, 1993). The investment process begins in the family, as parents teach and mold their children into productive citizens. The most common example of human capital is through formal education and training. Schools are the center for human capital development among youth. Laws mandate that children be enrolled in our nations' public or private schools during their early years. Here they learn the fundamentals of reading, mathematics, and science, while being socialized to the world around them. Education is an investment in the future of the children in the hope they will develop into adults who participate fully in the labor market and pay taxes that help support the nation's infrastructure. Through education, people forgo present earnings in order to enhance their future earning potential. College education and graduate and professional studies further enhance individuals' skills and make them competitive in the labor market. Employers purchase these skills as they use their employees to fulfill certain tasks in the labor market. Apprenticeship programs and on-the-job training are other means in which people seek to improve their human capital. Employers invest in human capital in the hope that their employees will be able to help them make more money through the skills, knowledge, and abilities they use in their job.

Economic capital includes one's financial assets and resources. Basically, economic capital is money that can be traded for goods and services. Often the most common forms of economic capital come from one's income, the money received from working. People use their economic capital to purchase material goods such as homes, cars, and products needed for basic survival. Economic capital also enables one to maintain a lifestyle or social class and the privileges and accoutrements that go along with it. In addition, economic capital encompasses one's wealth, the assets one has that can be converted into monetary resources. Many families leave a legacy of wealth that is passed on across generations, ensuring financial stability and social status for years to come.

Cultural capital entails knowledge and appreciation of the fine arts including music, art, dance, and literature. This knowledge or "high-status culture" is often valued by the dominant group in society. Bourdieu (1977a, 1977b) speaks of cultural capital in terms of *Habitus*, a system of lasting transposable dispositions which, while integrating past experience, function at every moment as a matrix of attitudes, perceptions, appreciations, and actions. The attitudes, beliefs, and experiences of those inhabiting one's social world influence them. These valued attitudes likely manifest in high socioeconomic groups or the dominant social class. In the educational arena schools reflect the cultural capital of the dominant class. Students' family and community provide high-socioeconomic-status students with the cultural capital, namely, attitudes, preferences, knowledge, and behaviors, which contributes to academic success (Lamont & Lareau, 1988; Lareau & Horvat, 1999; Morgan & Sorensen, 1999; Perna & Titus, 2005). These internalized values define an individual's attitude toward school. Low-socioeconomic-status students must acquire these cultural tools to negotiate the school terrain, yet they can never fully catch up with their high-socioeconomic-status peers. Students develop educational expectations and other educational outcomes through their *Habitus*. Cultural capital thus inheres in an individual's actions, ideology, norms, values, and lifestyle.

Social capital is embedded in interpersonal relationships, such as between students and teachers or children and parents, and within institutions, such as schools, churches, and communities. Social capital differs from other types of capital in that it is totally a product of relationships. These relationships can be developed through interactions that are rooted in other forms of capital. Social capital is often created or triggered through an indirect process in which others are united based on their human, economic, or cultural capital. Thus as Coleman (1994) argues, social capital can be a by-product of social interactions and other forms of capital.

Social Capital in Schools

Schools provide social capital through interpersonal relationships between students and school personnel as well as between students and their peers. As an institution the school is made up of students, teachers, and administrators all operating in a unified social setting. The school can be conceived of as a social system with its own culture, objectives, and rules. Students extract social capital from the schools' social structure, from peer interactions, and from relationships one develops with teachers and other school personnel. This social capital can affect students' educational expectations and educational attainment. The school can be fertile ground for developing social relationships which influence students' educational expectations and educational attainment. Social capital from school relationships can be manipulated to enhance educational expectations and increase college attendance among all students. Because the social capital predictors can increase the variance in educational attainment and educational expectations, we can alter the level of school, peer, and parent social capital to change educational outcomes.

Schools provide social capital in two ways. First, in an ideal situation students bring capital to the school that is aligned with the capital the school deems worthy. Schools are institutions which unite students with similar values, interests, backgrounds, and resources available to them. Social capital enhances other forms of capital by bringing homogenous people together through either institutions or interpersonal relationships. Students bring to the school their human and cultural capital, and they subsequently form relationships with the school and their peer group.

The school develops social capital based on the cultural, human, and economic capital students bring to the school. The nature of this capital contributes to the strength of the relationship with the school. The social capital is thus a by-product of these other forms of capital. The social capital that students get from the school can be influenced by the social capital they bring to the school. The school is a social system that multiplies students' individual, peer, and parent social capital. Schools reflect the communities or the members of the group. Schools do a good job at reproducing the socioeconomic status of their students (Bowles & Gintis, 1976). In some ways social capital is another means of social reproduction, yet it may mitigate socioeconomic disadvantages and increase educational expectations and educational attainment.

Second, students can accumulate social capital from resources within the school. Social capital exists in the school's curriculum, the physical resources on the campus, and the relationship with teachers, counselors, coaches, principals, and other school personnel. The general structure of the school thus contributes to its educational endowment and generates social capital.

Teachers, principals, counselors, and other school personnel serve as gatekeepers of information about school success, college placement, and labor market entrance for adolescents. These school personnel can provide access to educational opportunities which can increase a student's life chances. Low-income and working-class students may especially rely on school personnel to transfer educational information because their parents may lack much of the information that contributes to academic success and college entrance (Hrabrowski, Maton, & Greif, 1998; Stanton-Salazar, 2004).

A teacher primarily instructs students in specific academic areas; yet, along with other school personnel, teachers are a source of information about what courses the students should take to get into college. Through interactions with students, school personnel can help them learn how to study effectively and how to maintain good grades. School personnel often write letters of recommendation for students pursuing jobs as well as for those seeking scholarships and college admission (McDonough, 1997). The more cohesive the student–teacher relationship, the more social capital students are able to glean from relationships with school personnel.

Teacher expectations for the student create social capital that can affect students' educational attainment. Teachers and other school personnel play an important role in shaping students' academic progress. Research shows that there is a positive relationship between teachers' expectations and student achievement (Irvine, 1990; Irvine & Irvine, 1995; Polite, 1999). Teachers' expectations for their students are social capital in that it influences the type of information they convey, the opportunities they create for their students, and the values they help perpetuate.

Relationships with school personnel not only provide information about academic success, but they also help strengthen students' educational values. Students who have cohesive relationships with school personnel value the educational process and are often committed to the school. African American students often indicate that they are trying to please their teacher by doing well in school (Casteel, 1998). Teacher expectations often have more influence than parents among African Americans. Some explain this as African American students trying to overcome negative stereotypes of low ability, laziness, and academic failure (Fordham, 1996; MacLeod, 1995/2009; Steele & Aronson, 1998; Horvat et al., 2003). Many of these students value school, work hard to complete their assignments, and have respect for the educational process.

Often these school relationships are developed through participation in extracurricular activities such as sports teams, academic clubs, and social groups (Bidwell, Schneider, & Borman, 1998; Schneider & Stevenson, 1999; Muller & Ellison, 2001; Youniss & Yates, 1997). These activities allow students and school personnel to interact informally. Through these interactions, they develop the trust, habits, and norms that go into social capital development.

Thus students gain social capital through relationships with school personnel. As social institutions, schools are an essential source of information about postsecondary institutions and jobs. Students trust schools to prepare them for college and the labor force. Schools serve as a link between students, colleges, and potential employers. Colleges visit schools searching for prospective students. Working-class and poor children often use their teachers, counselors, and school administrators to gain access to middle-class resources and information about jobs and colleges (Stanton-Salazar, 1997, 2004). Businesses often use schools to find potential employees, to give scholarships, or to offer students workplace training (Smith, 2007).

Academic Emphasis of Schools

Generally, schools' academic emphasis is part of the human capital which students can convert into social capital through their institutional connection to the school. Schools with a high academic emphasis support positive student–teacher relationships and facilitate educational attainment. These schools offer a college preparatory curriculum with advanced placement courses, have a high graduation and college entrance rate, and have a strong academic reputation in the community. Schools with a high academic emphasis generate social capital that leads to high educational attainment. Schools that have a college preparatory curriculum encourage their students to take courses that will ready them for the rigors of college. Schools with a history of sending students to college will have materials and programs in place within the school that help students get into college. Many social programs are channeled through schools to create opportunities to help poor and minority students succeed (Jencks, 1993). Programs such as Head Start, Upward Bound, and GEAR-UP help economically disadvantaged students gain academic skills as well as develop relationships with individuals and other institutions in the educational community.

As an institution schools can connect individuals from various social classes and ethnic backgrounds. Low-income children can theoretically attend the same schools as middle-class and wealthy children, thus broadening the social networks and eventually the social capital for all children. Schools can serve as a medium which links students to social resources in the community and the social world. Students' peer groups can reinforce an education endowment by supporting the norms and values associated with it (Hrabowski, Maton, & Greif, 1998; McDonough, 1997).

However, some of the effects of school social capital can be negative. Just as with any group, the school can have too much control over students, or it can restrict their individual development while supporting group interests. For example, Catholic schools may contain too dense a group, stifling students' individual freedom. Research shows that Catholic schools may do a good job preparing their students academically, but the strong emphasis on discipline, order, and their conservative nature may hinder some students' social development (Ellis, 1996). This may particularly be the case for African American students attending elite Catholic and private schools, where they represent a racial and social class minority (Bryk, Lee, & Holland, 1993; Irvine & Foster, 1996).

Some schools may value social capital that does not increase students' educational expectations, college entrance, and labor market participation. Schools with a low academic emphasis may fail to instill strong educational values. For example, vocational high schools are traditionally designed to teach students a trade so they can begin working after graduation. College preparation is not a vocational school's objective, thus the social capital they generate encourages students to get jobs, not to attend college.

Schools may face economic and social disadvantages that make it difficult for them to have a positive impact on students' educational expectations and educational attainment. For example, some schools are located in neighborhoods with high poverty, crime, and other social ills. Just as schools with strong economic capital can produce strong social capital, schools with limited economic capital can have marginal effects on students' outcomes. Often students have other life events or circumstances, such as a lack of economic capital, weak parental support, or substandard living conditions, which preclude them from establishing a strong school commitment. Students may arrive in high schools underprepared for the rigors of the curriculum. Some or a combination of these factors may limit formation of social capital that supports academic success and college going among such students (McDonough, 1997).

Students who change schools frequently have low levels of social capital because they do not have a chance to develop relationships with other students and school personnel. This limits social capital development and can weaken the social capital effect because the students do not have time to build trust or take advantage of reciprocity norms, the essential elements for social capital formation. Transient students are not able to establish ties with other kids and adults in the community. The potential for effective social capital development diminishes in schools with high student mobility (Coleman, 1988; Peng & Wright, 1994; Swanson & Schneider, 1999).

Nonetheless, school is the one institution that is common to virtually all American adolescents. It provides a social context with educators in leadership roles and is a place where students from various social backgrounds can potentially interact. Schools help adolescents develop skills and knowledge they will use in adulthood. Schools are a controlled environment in which students develop and use their social capital, hence the focus of this study. Adolescents often form peer groups in the school and bring their norms and values from home to the school. The literature reflects that both peers and parents can promote social capital that affects adolescents' educational expectations and educational attainment.

African American Adolescents' School Experiences and Social Capital

African Americans are behind their White peers in student achievement, high school graduation, college entrance, and labor market participation. Researchers have explained much of this achievement and attainment gap by social status and economic differences (Jencks, 1993; Jencks & Phillips, 1998). These educational deficits make it difficult for them to form relationships with people and institutions that have access to educational information and opportunities.

Status attainment research links parental socioeconomic status and students' educational outcomes (Sewell, Haller, & Portes, 1969; Sewell & Hauser, 1980; Sewell, Haller, & Ohlendorf, 1970). Many studies go beyond the traditional status attainment model to show how relationships provide social capital and affect educational expectations and educational attainment (Hill, 2008; Noeth & Wimberly, 2002; Wimberly, 2004). By strengthening these relationships, students can circumvent some of the ill effects of race and social class. Research shows that substandard schools, poverty, and a history of racism and discrimination limit African Americans' educational pursuits. I argue that social capital that supports a strong academic emphasis can mitigate these detrimental effects, leading African American adolescents to pursue postsecondary education.

The school's academic emphasis structures the context for social capital development. Schools plagued by high student mobility, dropouts, and a limited curriculum fail to create an environment where students and teachers or other school personnel can form relationships which generate the type of social capital that increases educational attainment. Many African Americans attend schools of low academic emphasis. Their human capital weaknesses limit the effects of the school's social capital on their educational outcomes and puts them at a disadvantage as to the amount of social capital that they can develop from the school. Even if they have the best relationships in the school, African Americans are behind their White peers in terms of the social capital available from the school itself (Hill, 2008; Kao & Tienda, 1998). White students are better able to convert their parents' social class (economic and human capital) into social capital than African Americans. Parents rich in economic capital can select schools with a strong academic emphasis more easily than poor parents can (Lareau & Horvat, 1999; Mullis, Rathge, & Mullis, 2003; Perna & Titus, 2005).

Student–School Personnel Interactions

School social capital draws from students' perceptions of the expectations of teachers, counselors, and other school personnel. School personnel expectations can have a positive and significant effect on African American students' educational outcomes. When students perceive that their teachers and school personnel expect them to achieve at a high level, their own educational expectations increase as well as their odds of attending a two- or a four-year college (Hill, 2008; Perna & Titus, 2005; Wimberly, 2004). This research suggests that African Americans really do care what teachers, coaches, and other school personnel want for them.

Students who have positive relationships, either strong or weak, with their teachers and other school personnel are more likely to pursue postsecondary education than those who lack these relationships. The cohesion of the relationship is defined by the frequency of interaction and the sentiment between the student and school personnel. These relationships provide resources and information about school success and link students to educational and career opportunities. Social capital's effectiveness varies by students' social status. High-social-status students—based on race, income, and education—are likely to develop cohesive relationships with their teachers, parents, and peers. These relationships encourage them to value education and go to college and reveal a link between academic success and access to educational opportunities. Middle-class or high-social-status African American students will be more likely to develop academic relationships and pursue postsecondary education than their lower-status peers (Horvat, Weininger, & Lareau, 2003).

Research reveals African American and White students vary as to the cohesiveness of student–teacher relationships (Hill, 2008; McDonough, 1997; Wimberly, 2004). However, when students and teachers communicate or have a relationship outside regular instruction, all students' educational outcomes improve. This is social capital at work as teachers provide the information and opportunities to enhance students' educational experience. Students who have these interactions with their teachers use their social capital to increase their educational expectations and educational attainment.

Among African Americans, social capital may compensate for a school's academic shortcomings. Students who are deficient in human or cultural capital can establish social capital through the school that can enhance other forms of capital. For example, poor and working-class students who attend prestigious schools with wealthy student populations can gain positive social capital from the school. These students can enhance their cultural and human capital by establishing relationships with fellow students and teachers and becoming involved in the life of the school. Prestigious or high-academic schools have the economic capital to purchase and maintain their campus with the best facilities and state-of-the-art technology. Teachers with prestigious credentials, knowledge, skills, and experiences make up the schools' human capital. These schools can enrich students' cultural capital by exposing them to literature, the fine arts, and other cultural and educational opportunities. Through relationships with school personnel students develop social capital which legitimates educational values and provides information about academic success and college preparation as well as identifies opportunities that can enhance students' life chances.

Discussion and Conclusion

As a group, African Americans have the potential for developing powerful social capital. Historically Blacks have worked collectively to encourage social change, integrate schools and other public facilities in the South, and insure the passage of voting and civil rights legislation. Generally, racial solidarity outweighs social class differences among African Americans. African Americans tend to exhibit a certain degree of bounded solidarity toward economic, political, and social issues (Dawson, 1994). Many African American communities are connected through social institutions such as churches, schools, political organizations, and families, but do

African Americans possess the type of social capital that is valuable in schools and translates into educational and labor market opportunities?

African Americans claim that they value education and academic success (Kao & Tienda, 1998; Noeth & Wimberly, 2002; Wimberly, 2004). This is the first step on the road to a positive school experience. Their attitude implies that they accept the mainstream norms of hard work and self-determination as the means to success.

Schools have a set of norms or "rules of the game" which facilitate success. As discussed, the social capital and cultural capital students need to survive in this setting may be different from what children find in their families or in their communities. The very social capital that works at home may be detrimental to school success. Students must learn how to play the game and develop the social capital that the school values in order to increase their educational expectations and attainment.

African American students' social capital may not effectively move them from high school to college. The social capital from their neighborhood, peer group, or parents may help them survive and excel in the local high school, but it may not lead them to colleges and universities. African Americans tend to live in racially segregated communities and attend segregated schools. Even when neighborhoods and schools are integrated, they are likely to belong to a racially homogenous social network (Kao & Joyner, 2004; Tatum, 1997). The social capital that is effective in the high school or neighborhood may prove detrimental in the mainstream labor market or anywhere else outside their community.

Social structural issues may prevent African American students from going to college. They may lack the money or the means of obtaining the economic capital to attend college. Their social capital is often not effective: Many lack the cultural, human, or economic capital which is necessary to stimulate social capital development in various social contexts. African Americans just do not have the economic and human capital that White students do to convert into effective school social capital (Conley, 1999; Oliver & Shapiro, 2006).

In order for social capital to flourish in schools, the students and school personnel need to establish relationships based on trust, mutual respect, and reciprocity. These are key ingredients in social capital formation (Coleman, 1988, 1994). Through positive relationships, students can better access social capital resources from their teachers, especially information and opportunity resources. Teachers and school personnel act as gatekeepers of information about the education process (Hill, 2008; Kao & Tienda, 1998; Stanton-Salazar, 1997). Students who establish good relationships with school personnel are likely to learn about what it takes to succeed in school and how to get into college. This is especially the case for poor and working-class students who may not get this type of academic information from their parents or community.

Educational expectations and attainment are higher among students who talk with their teachers and have positive feelings toward them. This contributes to a cohesive student–teacher relationship. Research suggests this is the case for Whites but only marginally true for African Americans (Wimberly, 2004). Students who trust and respect their teachers are more likely to pick up on cultural cues and work hard in the classroom. Social, economic, and cultural gaps between African American students and their teachers may make it difficult for them to form cohesive relationships, which may, in turn, lower students' expectations and attainment.

Schools can develop policies and practices to improve poor and minority students' educational outcomes. These policies should respond to African American students' cultural, economic, and human capital to develop the school social capital that will lead them to academic success. Many African Americans attend schools with a minimal academic emphasis. Schools need to encourage all students to pursue some type of postsecondary education. This not only involves providing information about colleges but also includes providing the curriculum and the resources to prepare students for college. Schools must meet instructional needs and challenge students with a rigorous curriculum which includes advanced placement, foreign languages, and other courses traditionally associated with college-bound students.

References

Becker, G. S. (1993). *Human capital: A theoretical and empirical analysis, with special reference to education*. Chicago: The University of Chicago Press

Bidwell, C., Schneider, B., & Borman, K. (1998). Working: Perceptions and experiences. In K. Borman and B. Schneider (Eds.), *The adolescent years: Social influences and educational challenges*. Chicago: The University of Chicago Press.

Bourdieu, P. (1977a). *Outline of a theory of practice*. Cambridge, England: Cambridge University Press.

———. (1977b). *Reproduction in education, society and culture*. Beverly Hills, CA: Sage.

Bowles, S., & Gintis, H. (1976). *Schooling in capitalist America*. New York: Basic Books.

Bryk, A., Lee, V. E., & Holland, P. B. (1993). *Catholic schools and the common good*. Cambridge, MA: Harvard University Press.

Casteel, C. (1998). Attitudes of African American and Caucasian eighth grade students about praises, rewards, and punishments. *Elementary School Guidance and Counseling, 31*, 262–272.

Coleman, J. (1988). Social capital in the creation of human capital. *American Journal of Sociology, 94*, S95–S120.

———. (1994). *Foundations of social theory*. Cambridge, MA: Harvard University Press.

Conley, D. 1999. *Being black, living in the red*. Berkeley: University of California Press.

Dawson, M. C. (1994). *Behind the mule*. Princeton, NJ: Princeton University Press.

Ellis, K. (1996). Topsy goes to Catholic school: Lessons in academic excellence, refinement, and religion. In J. Irvine & M. Foster (Eds.), *Growing up African American in Catholic schools*. New York: Teachers College Press.

Epps, E. G. (1995). Race, class, and educational opportunity: Trends in the sociology of education. *Sociological Forum, 10*, 593–608.

Fordham, S. (1996). *Blacked out*. Chicago: The University of Chicago Press.

Hill, L. D. (2008). School strategies and the "college-linking" process: Reconsidering the effects of high schools on college enrollment. *Sociology of Education, 81*, 53–76.

Horvat, E. M., Weininger, E. B., & Lareau, A. (2003). From social ties to social capital: Class differences in the relations between schools and parent networks. *American Educational Research Journal, 40*, 319–351.

Hrabowski, F. A., Maton, K. I., & Greif, G. L. (1998). *Beating the odds: Raising academically successful African American males*. New York: Oxford University Press.

Irvine, J. (1990). *Black students and school failure: Policies, practices, and prescriptions*. Westport, CT: Greenwood Press.

Irvine, J., & Foster, M. (1996). *Growing up African American in Catholic schools*. New York: Teachers College Press.

Irvine, J., & Irvine, R. (1995). Black youth in school: Individual achievement and institutional cultural perspectives. In R. Taylor (Ed.), *African American youth: Their social and economic status in the United States*. Westport, CT: Praeger.

Jencks, C. (1993). *Rethinking social policy: Race, poverty, and the underclass*. New York: Harper Perennial.

Jencks, C., & Phillips, M. (1998). *The Black-White test score gap*. Washington, DC: Brookings Institution Press.

Kao, G., & Joyner, K. (2004). Do race and ethnicity matter among friends? Activities among interracial, interethnic, and intraethnic adolescent friends. *The Sociological Quarterly, 45*(3), 557–573.

Kao, G., & Tienda, M. (1998). Educational aspirations of minority youth. *American Journal of Education, 106*(3), 349–384.

Lamont, M., & Lareau A. (1988). Cultural capital: Allusions, gaps and glissandos in recent theoretical developments. *Sociological Theory, 6*, 153–168.

Lareau, A., & Horvat, E. M. (1999). Moments of social inclusion and exclusion: Race, class, and cultural capital in family-school relationships. *Sociology of Education, 72*, 37–53.

MacLeod, J. (1995/2009). *Ain't no makin' it: Aspirations and attainment in a low-income neighborhood*. Boulder, CO: Westview Press.

McDonough, P. M. (1997). *Choosing colleges*. Albany: SUNY Press.

Morgan, S. L., & Sørensen, A. B. (1999). Parental networks, social closure, and mathematics learning: A test of Coleman's social capital explanation of school effects. *American Sociological Review, 64*, 661–681.

Muller, C., & Ellison, C. G. (2001). Religious involvement, social capital, and adolescents' academic progress: Evidence from the National Education Longitudinal Study of 1988. *Sociological Focus, 34*(2), 155–183.

Mullis, R. L., Rathge, R., & Mullis, A. K. (2003). Predictors of academic performance during early adolescence: A contextual view. *International Journal of Behavioral Development, 27* (6), 541–548.

Noeth, R. J., & Wimberly, G. L. (2002). *Creating seamless educational transitions for urban African American and Hispanic students*. Iowa City, IA: ACT.

Oliver, M. L., & Shapiro, T. M. (2006). *Black wealth, White wealth: A new perspective on racial inequality*. New York: Taylor & Francis Group.

Peng, S. S., & Wright, D. (1994). Explanation of academic achievement of Asian American students. *Journal of Education Research, 87*, 346–352.

Perna, L., & Titus, M. (2005). The relationship between parental involvement as social capital and college enrollment: An examination of racial/ethnic group differences. *Journal of Higher Education, 76*(5), 485–518.

Polite, V. C. (1999). Combating educational neglect in suburbia: African American males and mathematics. In V. C. Polite & J. E. Davis (Eds.), *African American males in school and society*. New York: Teachers College Press.

Putnam, R. D. (2000). *Bowling alone: The collapse and revival of American community.* New York: Simon & Schuster.

Schneider, B., & Stevenson, D. (1999). *The ambitious generation.* New Haven, CT: Yale University Press.

Sewell, W. H., Haller, A. O., & Portes, A. (1969). The educational and early attainment process. *American Sociological Review, 34,* 82–92.

Sewell, W. H., & Hauser, R. (1980). The Wisconsin longitudinal study of social and psychological factors in aspirations and achievement. *Research in Education and Socialization, 1,* 59–99.

Sewell, W., Haller, A. O., & Ohlendorf, G. W. (1970). The educational and early occupational status attainment process: Replication and revision. *American Sociological Review, 35,* 1014–1027.

Smith, S. S. (2007). *Lone pursuit: Distrust and defensive individualism among the Black poor.* New York: Russell Sage.

Stanton-Salazar, R. D. (1997). A social capital framework for understanding the socialization of racial minority children and youth. *Harvard Educational Review, 67,* 1–39.

Stanton-Salazar, R. D. (2001). *Manufacturing hope and despair: The school and kin support networks of U.S.-Mexican youth.* New York: Teachers College Press.

Stanton-Salazar, R. D. (2004). Social capital among working-class minority students. In M. A. Gibson, P. Gándara, & J. P. Koyama (Eds.), *School connections: U.S. Mexican youth, peers, and school achievement* (pp. 18–38). New York: Teachers College Press.

Steele, C. M., & Aronson, J. (1998). Stereotype threat and the test performance of academically successful African Americans. In C. Jenks & M. Phillips (Eds.), *The Black-White test score gap.* Washington, D.C.: Brookings Institution Press.

Swanson, C., & Schneider, B. (1999). Students on the move: Residential and educational mobility in America's schools. *Sociology of Education, 72,* 54–67.

Tatum, B. D. (1997). *Why are all the Black kids sitting together in the cafeteria? And other conversations about race.* New York: Basic Books.

U.S. Department of Education. (2009). *The condition of education 2009.* Washington, DC: U.S. Government Printing Office.

Wimberly, G. (2004). African American students' educational outcomes: The role of school relationships. In S. J. Paik (Ed.), *Advancing educational productivity: Policy implications from national databases.* Greenwich, CT: Information Age.

Youniss, J., & Yates, M. (1997). *Community service and social responsibility in youth.* Chicago: The University of Chicago Press.

Chapter Four

Negotiating Masculinity in College

African American Males and Academic Engagement

James Earl Davis

The experiences of African American men in college have become a major source of concern and challenge for policy makers and institutions of higher education.* There is a general consensus that many of these students are not going to graduate from college (Dellums Commission, 2006; Morgan & Bhola, 2006). For instance, recent data indicate that the college graduation rate for African American males at public four-year institutions was 31.4% and 38.6% for those attending private institutions (U.S. Department of Education, 2008). In other words, roughly 65% of African American males drop out before completing the requirements for the bachelor's degree. In fact, the rate at which these students persist in college is consistently reported as the lowest among all race and gender groups. However, recent evidence suggests that institutional context may play an increasing role in persistence rates and quality of the college experience (Dancy, 2012).

Further, Cuyjet (2006) advances the conversations on the engagement, retention, and educational attainment of African American men with findings that generally suggest institutional environment definitely matters for African American male college students who have diverse family backgrounds, precollege experiences, and gender attitudes. The research literature is consistent with findings that show African American males are often marginalized students at predominately White institutions (PWIs) and are generally more satisfied at historically Black

---

* Research for this chapter was conducted and written in collaboration with Terrell P. Lasane from the United States Environmental Protection Agency.

colleges and universities (HBCUs) (Brown & Freeman, 2004; Dancy, 2010). African American male undergraduate persistence and graduation rates are relatively low at PWIs as compared to HBCUs (Allen, Epps, & Haniff, 1991; Davis, 1994). Because both PWIs and HBCUs are important in providing higher educational opportunities for African American students, research in both of these contexts is important.

Discussions of a racial "gender gap" have recently occupied the agenda of many educational research and policy analysts. Currently, Black men make up about 40% of all African Americans enrolled in higher education (Lewis, Simon, Uzzell, Horwitz, & Casserly, 2010). At many historically Black colleges and universities, Black males constitute less than 30% of total enrollments (Cuyjet, 2006). Overall, males account for 3.5% of the total enrollment in college; however, they are disproportionately represented among students who are forced to withdraw, those with relative lower academic performance, and relatively negative college experiences (Dellums Commission, 2006). Gender studies in higher education are generally associated with women's experiences and outcomes, but men are also influenced by gender. Almost without exception, the experience of African American male college students is absent from the mainstream literature of higher educational studies as well as from research that attempts to illuminate differences and commonalties across race and gender. Indeed, gender has a great effect on Black males' social and academic experiences in college. Hence, the purpose of this work is to look more closely at the constructions and presentation of masculinity in different college settings.

Review of the Literature

Previous research has shown that at school, masculine gender roles may create a reward and punishment structure that can undermine academic engagement (Davis, 2006). Through gender role socialization, young boys are usually taught to be independent and active, and these traditional masculine behaviors may contribute to academic difficulties throughout their school years. In elementary schools, teachers often report a unique set of concerns that inhibits the learning potential of boys relative to their female counterparts, as these boys are striving to reach an acceptable level of masculinity. Boys may receive social rewards (i.e., popularity, enhanced social attractiveness) for pronounced masculine behaviors that interfere with academic engagement and instrumental classroom behavior (Pfeifer & Sedlacek, 1974; Silverman & Dinitz, 1974). Moreover, it has been suggested that African American males learn to equate the academic world with femininity, perhaps because elementary school teachers consistently reward behaviors that are traditionally feminine (conformity, quietness, and cooperation) and punish behaviors that are traditionally masculine (independence, adventurousness, and rebellion to authority) (Kagan, 1964; Richardson, 1981).

Research has shown that, based on early socialization experiences, African American males quickly learn the social rewards associated with masculine behaviors and the derogatory name-calling and peer disapproval frequently associated with behaviors perceived as feminine (Davis, 2002, 2003; Adler, Kless, & Adler, 1992; Bernard, 1979; Bernard, Elsworth, Keefauver, & Naylor, 1981; Silvern, 1978). The traditional masculine gender role in our society has been characterized as one of instrumentality, and it has only been relatively recently that the rigidity of this role has been challenged (Bem, 1974). The instrumental orientation that is associated with masculinity has consisted of behaviors, traits, and competencies that lead to the efficient completion of tasks (Kilmartin, 1994). While task completion and efficiency can be considered positive traits, a number of negative traits have also often been associated with the traditional masculine role. In higher educational settings, for instance, the masculine role may sometimes create a reward and punishment structure that can undermine academic engagement.

By the time African American males reach college age, there are a number of well-developed gender roles that may continue to have a negative relationship to their academic engagement. It is plausible, based on the evidence cited above, that these behaviors may evolve from a masculine subculture that places academics at a lower position in a hierarchy of social alternatives. As a result of masculine socialization of "appropriate" gender role norms, in college settings some males may adopt gender-specific beliefs concerning academic activities (i.e., studying, meeting with professors, and using tutors) and regular involvement in social activities (i.e., drinking, partying, and participation in athletics). These gendered social constructions constitute a masculine culture that generally devalues the role of academic engagement and achievement (Lasane, Sweigard, Czopp, Howard, & Burns, 1999). The question of whether the college context influences outcomes is unaddressed in the literature. Differences in masculine gender roles and attitudes due to varying expectations of masculine self-presentation strategies on historically Black campuses and in predominately White college settings are important to understand.

This exploratory study focuses on two different higher education contexts for African American males and explores research on the complexities of Black males' constructions of masculinity. This discussion is framed by one fundamental assumption: there is virtually no race- or gender-neutral schooling context for Black males in higher education. Although this argument may appear inconsistent with the availability of and access to racially desegregated and sex-integrated colleges and universities, even these institutions present challenges for Black males that go beyond the seemingly placid surface harmonies of race and gender relations. Historically Black institutions and, to a much lesser degree, all-male college settings provide another lens through which to more closely examine how campus environments influence the experiences of African American males.

Masculinities Go to College: Research and Theory

African American males' social constructions of masculinity are grounded in a campus culture that intentionally isolates, exploits, and objectifies African American males. The social construction of Black men on college campuses regardless of their athletic status is steeped in the hegemony of Black masculinity and how it frames the experience and affect of African American males enrolled in college. Afrocentric models of masculinity are being proposed as alternatives to European conceptions of masculinity. These "new" conceptions of masculinity seek a shift from Western ideas of male socialization to a cultural awareness grounded in the experiences and history of African people (Akbar, 1991; Jeff, 1994) . The intent of these models is transformative; however, images of a normative masculinity being either unfulfilled or misdirected still dominate. This incongruity between academic engagement and traditional masculine behaviors sets the stage for a potentially disastrous set of outcomes for Black males in higher education.

A general hypothesis is that incongruence occurs between academic engagement and masculine behavior (Majors & Billison, 1992). Cool pose theory states that men demonstrate a cluster of pronounced masculine behaviors in order to show calm, invulnerable reserve in a broad range of social situations. That is, cool pose is a form of strategic self-presentation, a form of impression management whereby individuals seek to maximize rewards and avoid punishments (Tedeschi, 1981). According to cool pose theory, African American males, in particular, do not allow others to observe their vulnerabilities, anxieties, or fear of failure. Majors and Billison (1992) describe the unique cultural aspects of African American experience, but other researchers have adopted the more generic elements of the theory to frame empirical results that describe the accepted masculine roles of several ethnic groups in our society (Doss & Hopkins, 1998; Pleck, 1995).

Research has provided support for the existence of competing aspects of the masculine self-concept that may be present in the culture of college students. Doss and Hopkins (1998) have identified two cofactors of the masculine gender role. Their measure of masculine ideology assesses a cluster of internalized attributes that culturally, socially, and psychologically define maleness in a given society. They use the *Multicultural Masculinity Ideology Scale* to identify these factors. The first of these factors, Hypermasculine Posturing, involves attitudes and beliefs that would reasonably inhibit academic engagement and positive interpersonal functioning (i.e., interpersonal insensitivity, sensation-seeking, and toughness). The second of these factors, Achievement, contains a cluster of attitudes and beliefs that would likely facilitate academic achievement (i.e., persistence, autonomy, confidence, and resiliency).

Based on analysis of data collected from 2,000 undergraduates from diverse racial and ethnic backgrounds, a replication of Doss and Hopkins's (1998) findings was expected. Specifically, the goal was to determine whether specific academic aspects of the masculine gender role that are reinforced throughout male development, particularly in college (i.e., mastery, competitiveness, assertiveness, and independence), would be positively correlated with academic engagement behavior. These aspects of the masculine gender role would have positive instrumental value where student success is facilitated by self-determination and autonomy—traits most closely associated with masculine gender roles (Deci & Ryan, 1991). Conversely, aspects of the masculine gender role that are sometimes exaggerated in order to manage masculine self-presentation (i.e., hypermasculine behaviors that involve toughness, anti-femininity, and impulsive decision-making), would be negatively correlated with academic engagement due to the negative effects they may have on study behaviors (Czopp et al., 1998; Lasane et al., 1999, Majors & Billison, 1992). Effective academic engagement in this study is defined as the process whereby students utilize proximal subgoals and conscientious study behaviors in order to achieve positive outcomes and whereby students carefully determine academic outcomes through effective time management and self-motivation.

In summary, the present study was undertaken to explore the relationship between endorsement of masculine-role constructions and academic engagement behaviors (self-regulated academic learning, completion of academic assignments, and effective time management) in a sample of African American college males. The hypothesis was that academic aspects of traditionally masculine behaviors and social constructions would reduce to two factors: one would be positively correlated with academic engagement and one would be negatively correlated. In addition, the researchers anticipated that these gender factors (a positive masculine factor and a negative masculine factor), in addition to hypermasculinity would, as a set of variables, significantly predict academic engagement behavior. Finally, the researchers also expected that African American males in different college contexts (HBCU and PWCU), as a result of culturally specific gender role socialization experiences, would differ on the aspects of the masculine gender role. This expected difference would be due to varying expectations of the role of and self-presentation strategies for African American men on historically Black campuses versus in predominately White college settings (Davis, 1994).

Methods

Participants and Data Sources

Two colleges are the settings for this research project: a historically Black college in the South and a predominately White university in the Midwest. This sample of

62 African American college males represents diverse socioeconomic backgrounds and high school experiences. The mean age of the participants is 18.85 (SD = 3.86). Each participant in the study provided responses to three instruments: (1) the Index of Masculinity, (2) the Hypermasculinity Index, and (3) the Behavioral Preferences Checklist.

The *Index of Masculinity*, a 19-item questionnaire, was developed to assess the degree to which individuals endorse traditional masculine characteristics of competitiveness that are positively and negatively associated with academic engagement and achievement. The two subscales of the index of masculinity correspond to the researchers' conceptualization of the aspects of traditional masculinity (i.e., competitiveness) that would likely facilitate or inhibit academic engagement: Mastery Competitiveness and Antisocial Competitiveness. Scale items were formed for each of the subscales on the index of masculinity based on a review of literature exploring gender-typed behaviors and a theoretical analysis of the relationships that traditionally gender-typed behaviors might have with academic engagement (Bem, 1974; Best & Williams, 1993; Spence, Helmreich, & Stapp, 1974). The index of masculinity uses a 7-point rating scale ranging from (1) "extremely uncharacteristic of men" to (7) "extremely characteristic of men" for the two subscales. A sample item on the Mastery Competitiveness subscale is "I continuously strive to perform better than others in my classes." A sample item from the Antisocial Competitiveness subscale is "When I force my ideas upon others, it is often perceived as disruptive to the group." The Cronbach alpha of the Mastery Competitiveness subscale (11 items) and the Antisocial Competitiveness subscales (8 items) were .64 and .75, respectively. Test-retest correlations for the Mastery Competitiveness and Antisocial Competitiveness subscales were .76 and .81, respectively. A small exploratory study on the instrument determined that the two subscales were significantly related to the Hypermasculine Posturing and Achievement subscales of Doss and Hopkins's (1998) Multicultural Masculinity Ideology Scale in ways that supported the construct validity of the measure.

Participants then completed a sample of twenty items from the Hypermasculinity Index (Mosher & Sirkin, 1984) and indicated the degree to which they agreed with exaggerated, stereotypically masculine statements using the same 7-point scale. Items were selected from the larger scale that seemed likely to influence student academic outcomes. Items that did not meet this criterion were eliminated. Research cited above suggests that hypermasculinity, characterized by high sensation-seeking, fearlessness, callous attitudes toward women, and a rigid masculine code of beliefs, may be correlated with Black males' frequency of positive academic behavior. Sample items from this scale include the following: "It's natural for men to get into fights" and "After I have gone through a really dangerous experience I feel high." Mosher and Sirkin (1984) report an alpha of .89 for the Hypermasculinity Scale, and there was an alpha of .78 for the 19 items used in the study.

Finally, participants completed the Behavioral Preferences Checklist, an index of academic engagement (Lasane & Jones, 1999). Using this scale, participants rate the frequency with which they perform 17 academic behaviors (e.g., taking detailed notes, doing assigned readings, and studying with others who demonstrate mastery of course concepts) on a 1 to 5 scale with "Always" and "Never" as endpoints. Lasane and Jones (1999) reported an alpha of .81 for this instrument and a test-retest correlation of .86. There was a Cronbach alpha of .84 in the study. After completing all instruments, participants completed a questionnaire of background demographic information. These data sources offer important evidence of traditional masculinity for African American male students attending both historically Black and predominately White institutions of higher education. These data also complement results from larger national databases on the experience of college students and serve as a window to our awareness of how the relationship between race and gender plays itself out in various higher educational settings.

Results

In order to assess the content validity of the Index of Masculinity, the study subjected the 19 items to a principal components analysis with Varimax rotation. Using a combination of the latent root criterion and the scree plot criterion, a two-factor solution was found. The first factor (eigenvalue = 3.52, variance explained = 17.65%) included items that corresponded to the hypothesized factor of Antisocial Competitiveness. The second factor (eigenvalue = 2.40, variance explained = 12.0%) appeared to correspond to the hypothesized factor of Mastery Competitiveness. The weighed regression factor scores were used as the dependent variables in analyses reported below.

To explore the relationship between masculine role precepts and academic engagement, the three masculine gender role subscale scores (Antisocial Competitiveness, Mastery Competitiveness, and Hypermasculinity) were regressed on Academic Engagement. Intercorrelations between subscales ranged from .134 to .343. Variance-inflation factors were computed to assess the multi-collinearity of these three predictor variables, but there was no evidence they were collinear. The three masculinity measures variables together significantly predicted academic engagement, R^2 (3, 269) = .136, $p < .01$. Further, each of the predictors was significantly related to the level of academic engagement reported by the participants.

College type (historically Black and predominately White) differences for each of the masculine gender measures used in the study were examined. Intercorrelations between dependent measures were low (ranging from 0.00 to .32), so the data were examined for college type differences by using t-tests. The data were also examined in 62 cases on the academic engagement, Antisocial Competitiveness, and Mastery Competitiveness factors of the index of masculinity, and in 62 cases on the Hypermasculinity scale.

African American men at the Black colleges had higher scores on the Antisocial Competitiveness factor than their peers on the predominately White campuses, $t(259) = 5.46$, $p < .01$. Black college men also had higher scores than predominately White college men on the Hypermasculinity measure, $t(263) = .2.46$, $p < .05$. There were no college type differences on the Mastery Competitiveness factor on the Index of Masculinity.

Discussion

The major hypotheses were confirmed. An exploration of the stereotypical masculine roles that may be implicated in academic engagement behaviors could be significantly explained by two factors for African American males. The first masculine factor contained items that corresponded to an Antisocial/Competitiveness factor. Items on this factor describe a desire to reflect one's individuality and make one's unique contributions known—even at the expense of denigrating the contributions of others with whom one works. Further, and consistent with previous research on gender roles on Black college campuses, men in the Black college scored higher on this factor than African American men at a predominantly White college. These results suggest that aspects of educational development that require cooperation may be compromised at historically Black colleges by the adherence to stereotypical masculine roles. Since aspects of the college environment require work in groups (i.e., seminar classes, group projects, incorporating class feedback to enhance quality of work, and positive social relationships with fellow students and instructors), further research should address the specific liabilities that may accompany antisocial competitiveness.

The second factor from the Index of Masculinity, Mastery Competitiveness, was positively correlated with academic engagement. This aspect of competitiveness corresponds to a desire to achieve individual levels of excellence that do not seem to be gauged relative to the achievements of others. The finding is consistent with research showing that aspects of masculine gender roles may contribute to positive outcomes in areas of achievement. Doss and Hopkins (1998) found academic achievement to be a major cofactor in their measurement of Masculinity Ideology and this further supports the instrumentality orientation of traditional masculinity that may be beneficial in academic settings. Interestingly, however, there were no significant college differences on this factor. As lines become less clear between Black men on various college campuses and the proportion of androgynous (high on dimensions of both masculinity and femininity) individuals increases, men experiencing very different college experiences in these data express the same level of endorsement of items that correspond to achieving excellence in academic settings while resisting the need to detract from others' accomplishments. Generally, most African American males in this study do not report a relaxed set of standards with regard to asserting the individuality of contributions in collective efforts. Future research should address society's changing gender roles with respect to competition and explore the impact of these changing roles on achievement and interpersonal functioning at historically Black and predominately White colleges.

The data found support for a negative relationship between hypermasculinity and academic engagement. This result is not surprising. The college culture influenced by this exaggerated self-presentation of stereotypical masculine traits is related to an "external" hip-hop culture of high sensation-seeking and impulsive, risky decision-making behavior that may detract from effective academic behaviors (Davis, 2006; Lasane & Jones, 2000). These findings may suggest that African American males who feel normative pressures to conform to an exaggerated masculine gender role standard may be most likely to underachieve academically.

Further research should explore whether students who demonstrate hypermasculine behaviors would regard study behaviors as an admission of a vulnerability to threats of self-concept that is incongruous with masculine role norms. Despite the fact that a number of negative behaviors are associated with hypermasculinity, Czopp et al. (1998) have shown that individuals who adopt certain aspects of a hypermasculine presentation style are more socially attractive on a number of dimensions deemed important to college students. Thus, the hypermasculine behaviors may be reinforced socially and may be resistant to change despite their negative relationship with academic achievement. Future research should explore the social cognitive biases and self-handicapping features of a hypermasculine lifestyle and how they relate to patterns of academic underachievement among African American male college students (especially in social groups that have strong "traditional" gender role norms in place: athletes, fraternity members, etc.).

Implications for Higher Education

In this exploratory study examining the role of gender constructions on the academic engagement behaviors of college students, the data show initial support for the hypothesis that specific aspects of masculinity are related to academic engagement. The specific mechanisms that mediate the relationship between these variables require further research, particularly the role college cultural environment plays. This research represents an ongoing research program that is aimed at uncovering the aspects of masculinity that may compromise the optimal academic achievement and interpersonal functioning of African American males who are already having difficulty in higher education.

Although considerable attention has been directed toward an understanding of gender and racial differences in higher education, we still need to focus on the unique intersection of race and gender. The important and unique collegiate experiences of African American men have been omitted from this discourse. The current plight of African American males in college demands a much sharper focus, both theoretically and methodologically. Given the recent concerns about college enrollment and completion rates, it is rather ironic that scant attention has been given to the perspectives of African American college men concerning issues of masculinity and academic performance.

Findings from this study and other relevant research challenge colleges and universities to reconsider traditional approaches to exclusive race- or gender-based strategies for integrating African American males into the mainstream of academic and social life on campus. Colleges and universities often ignore their aspirations, disrespect their ability to learn, fail to access and cultivate their many talents, and impose a restrictive range of masculine options. Within this overwhelmingly oppressive schooling context, too many African American male college students simply give up—beaten down by a higher education system that places little value on who they are and what they bring to college settings.

Their negative college experiences and relatively poor academic performance are usually viewed as by-products of structural institutional factors and entrenched college culture. However, these experiences may be linked to how African American men construct and adapt to systemic pressures and expectations—usually undermined by maladaptive definitions of masculinity (Hunter & Davis, 1994). These issues are potential points of departure and direction for higher education institutions as they try to provide more responsive academic environments. Both historically Black and predominately White colleges are being held more accountable for providing more conducive learning communities by acknowledging gender's role in the social and academic lives of Black males. Ultimately, truly valuing the presence and perspectives of African American males on campus and supporting them as they learn to negotiate their identities in these environments will result in their success.

Certainly a broader and more diverse definition of acceptable masculinity is needed at the college level (Connell, 2005). Much too often, however, only a narrow conception of masculinity is readily available to African American males. Any thought, action, or response counter to the masculinity norms on college campuses is considered inappropriate and subject to peer punishment. This regulation of masculinity requires a level of gender "know-how" that must be understood by males in order to survive socially and academically in higher education. To be sure, the dynamic nature of negotiating identity categories at college is difficult for all males. Some of these students, because of their nontraditional hypermasculine style or appearance, however, endure a disproportionate level of criticism and social estrangement when more hypermasculine styles are valued.

Ultimately all males are disadvantaged by these strict gender norms and hypermasculinity in college. Conformity to these masculine behaviors not only increases the level of anxiety about being socially ostracized, but it also dictates males' range of social, emotional, and academic experiences in college (Davis, 1999). The inability to explore and embrace other possibilities of manhood reduces the kinds of options and opportunities African American males can have and desperately need in higher education. In turn, a university culture that acknowledges diversity in how men can be men cannot exist unless proactive teaching and socialization are realized.

References

Adler, P. A., Kless, S. J., & Adler, P. (1992). Socialization to gender roles: Popularity among elementary school boys and girls. *Sociology of Education, 65,* 169–187.

Akbar, N. (1991). *Visions of black men.* Nashville, TN: Winston-Derek.

Allen, W. R., Epps, E. G., & Haniff, N. Z. (1991). *College in black and white: African American students in predominantly white and in historically black public universities.* Albany, NY: SUNY Press.

Bem, S. L. (1974). The measurement of psychological androgyny. *Journal of Consulting and Clinical Psychology, 42,* 155–162.

Bernard, M. E. (1979). Does sex role behavior influence the way teachers evaluate students? *Journal of Educational Psychology, 71,* 553–562.

Bernard, M. E., Elsworth, G., Keefauver, L. W., & Naylor, F. D. (1981). Sex-role behavior and gender in teacher-student evaluations. *Journal of Educational Psychology, 73,* 681–696.

Best, D. L. & Williams, J. E. (1993). A cross-cultural viewpoint. In A. E. Beall & R. J. Sternberg (Eds.), *The psychology of gender* (pp. 215–248). New York: Guilford.

Brown, M. C., & Freeman, K. (2004). Black colleges: New perspectives on policy and practice. In B. A. Jones (Ed.), *Educational Leadership in the 21st century.* Stamford, CT: Ablex Publishing Corp.

Connell, R. W. (2005). *Masculinities.* Berkeley: University of California Press.

Cuyjet, M. J. (2006). *African American men in college.* San Francisco: Jossey-Bass.

Czopp, A. M., Lasane, T. P., Sweigard, P. N., Bradshaw, S. D., & Hammer, E. D. (1998). Masculine styles of self-presentation in the classroom: Perceptions of Joe Cool. *Journal of Social Behavior and Personality, 13,* 281–294.

Dancy, T. E. (2012). *The brother code: Manhood and Masculinity among African American males in college.* Charlotte, NC: Information Age Press.

Dancy, T. E. (2010). College manhood and masculinities: Connecting theory and research to practice. In T. E. Dancy (Ed.), *Managing diversity: (Re)Visioning equity on college campus.* New York: Peter Lang.

Davis, J. E. (2006). Research at the margin: Mapping masculinity and mobility of African American high school dropouts. *International Journal of Qualitative Studies in Education, 19,(3),* 289–304.

Davis, J. E. (2003). Early schooling and the achievement of African American males. *Urban Education, 38,* 515-537.

Davis, J. E. (2002). Transgressing the masculine: African American boys and the failure of schools. In B. Mayeen and W. Martino (Eds.) *What About the Boys? Issues of Masculinity in School.* London: Open University Press.

Davis, J. E. (1999). What does gender have to do with the experiences of African American college men? In V. C. Polite and J. E. Davis (Eds.), *African America males in school and society*. New York: Teachers College Press.

Davis, J. E. (1994). College in Black and White: The academic experiences of African American males. *Journal of Negro Education, 63,* 570–587.

Deci, E. L & Ryan, R. M. (1991). A motivational approach to self: Integration in personality. In R. Dienstbier (Ed.) *Nebraska Symposium on Motivation: Vol. 38 Perspectives on Motivation* (pp. 237–288). Lincoln: University of Nebraska Press.

Dellums Commission. (2006). *A way out: Creating partners for our nation's prosperity by expanding life paths of youth men of color.* Final Report. Washington, DC: Joint Center for Political and Economic Studies.

Doss, B. D., & Hopkins, J. R. (1998). The multicultural masculinity ideology scale: Validation from three cultural perspectives. *Sex Roles, 38,* 719–741.

Hunter, A., & Davis, J. E. (1994). Hidden voices of Black men: The social construction of manhood. *Journal of Black Studies, 25,* (1), 20–40.

Jeff, M. F. X. (1994). Afrocentrism and African-American male youth. In R. Mincy (Ed.), *Nurturing young Black males: Challenges to agencies, programs and social policy.* Washington, DC: Urban Institute.

Kagan, J. (1964). Acquisition and significance of sex-typing and sex-role concepts and attitudes. In M. L. Hoffman & L. W. Hoffman (Eds.), *Review of child development research* (vol. 1, pp. 137–169). New York: Sage.

Kilmartin, C. T. (1994). *The masculine self.* New York: Macmillan.

Lasane, T. P. & Jones, J. M. (1999). Temporal orientation and academic engagement: the mediating properties of a motivational self. *Journal of Social Behavior and Personality, 14,* 31–44.

Lasane, T. P. & Jones, J. M. (2000). Temporal orientation and college students' decision-making: When socially induced temporal myopia interferes with academic goal-setting. *Journal of Social Behavior and Personality, 15,* 75–86.

Lasane, T. P, Sweigard, P. N., Czopp, A. M., Howard, W. L., and Burns, M. J. (1999). The effects of student academic presentation on perceptions of gender and sociability. *North American Journal of Psychology, 1,* 229–242.

Lewis, S., Simon, C., Uzzell, R., Horwitz, A., & Casserly, M. (2010). *A call for change: The social and educational factors contributing to the outcomes of Black males in urban schools.* Washington, DC: Council of the Great City Schools.

Majors, R., & Billison, J. M. (1992). *Cool pose: The dilemmas of Black manhood in America.* New York: Lexington Books.

Morgan, L. P., & Bhola, S. (2006). *Creating a culture of success: Black men—steps toward success.* New York: The Children's Aid Society.

Mosher, D. L., & Sirkin, M. (1984). Measuring a macho personality constellation. *Journal of Research in Personality, 18,* 150–163.

Pfeifer, C. M, & Sedlacek, W. E. (1974). Predicting Black student grades with nonintellectual measures. *Journal of Negro Education, 1,* 67–77.

Pleck, J. H. (1995). The gender role strain paradigm: An update. In R.F. Levant & W.S. Pollack (Eds.), *A new psychology of men* (pp. 11–32). New York: Basic Books.

Richardson, L. R. (1981). *The dynamics of sex and gender: A sociological perspective* (2nd ed.). Boston, MA: Houghton Mifflin.

Silverman, I. J., & Dinitz, S. (1974) Compulsive masculinity and delinquency: An empirical investigation. *Criminology, 11,* 498–515.

Silvern, L. E. (1978). Masculinity-femininity in children's self-concepts: The relationship to teachers' judgments of social adjustment, and academic ability, classroom behaviors and popularity. *Sex Roles, 4,* 929–949.

Spence, J. T., Helmreich, R. L., & Stapp, J. (1974). The personal attributes questionnaire: A measure of sex role stereotypes and masculinity-femininity. *Journal Supplement Abstract Service Catalog of Selected Documents in Psychology, 4,* 43. (Ms. No. 617)

Tedeschi, J. T. (Ed.). (1981). *Impression management theory and social psychological research.* New York: Academic Press.

U.S. Department of Education (2008). *Graduation rates component.* National Center for Education Statistics, Integrated Postsecondary Education Data System (IPEDS). Washington, DC.

Chapter Five

A Talk to Teachers about Black Male Students

H. Richard Milner IV

In this chapter, building on and from Baldwin's (1963) important speech "A Talk to Teachers," I "talk" to teachers about Black* male students. In many ways, the issues I explore here are just as prevalent today as they were when Baldwin delivered his speech almost half a century ago. I am not talking to a distinct group of White, Latino, Asian, or Black teachers; I am talking to all teachers because teachers from all racial and ethnic backgrounds need to be better prepared to teach and empower African American male students.

The demographic divide rationale, which emphasizes the divide between the racial background of many students and their teachers, in much of the literature makes a case for the importance of preparing teachers to understand and teach for diversity (see, for instance, Gay & Howard, 2000; Landsman & Lewis, 2006; Zumwalt & Craig, 2005). For instance, I (see, Milner, 2012), along with other researchers, have demonstrated that African American teachers can be successful with African American students because of their outside of school experiences (Foster, 1997). However, here I argue that all teachers need to (re)consider their belief systems and consequently their instructional practices with African American male students. One line of thinking is that Black teachers, for instance, automatically possess the pedagogical skills and mind-sets necessary to teach African American males successfully. However, I agree with Tatum (2001) when she declared,

---

* The terms Black and African American will be used interchangeably throughout this chapter.

In a race-conscious society, the development of a positive sense of racial/ethnic identity not based on assumed superiority or inferiority is an important task for *both* White people and people of color. The development of this positive identity is a lifelong process that often requires unlearning the misinformation and stereotypes we have internalized not only about others, but also about ourselves. (p. 53, italic added)

The point is that teachers of color may have been kidnapped and socialized into believing they are inferior, or they may believe, embrace, or even contribute to some of the inaccurate discourse regarding African American male students and their potential. In this way, teachers of color may have a negative sense of their racial/ethnic identity. They may subconsciously believe that African American students are not as smart or capable as White students. Thus, this talk is designed to help all teachers think seriously about their work with African American male students. What can teachers do to better meet the needs of these students?

This talk to teachers about Black males concerns a serious subject; however, the talk is quite similar to what I have written in the past (see, for example, Milner, 2007, 2009) and similar to what I have read and heard from others regarding the education of all Black students and Black male students in particular (see, for instance, Davis & Jordan, 1994; Howard, 2001; Tatum & Muhammad, 2012. In many ways, I am reiterating and reinforcing the important points I and others have made about what is necessary to educate Black male students who continue to be mis-served and mis-educated in educational institutions across U.S. society (Milner, 2007; Irvine, 1990; Woodson, 1933).

I realize that addressing the instructional needs of Black students goes far beyond the classroom or what teachers can do. Researchers have emphasized the influences of both outside- and inside-of-school variable that shape the experiences of students inside of school (Caldas & Bankston, 1997; Coleman, 1969; Noguera & Wells, 2011). For instance, Coleman (1969, 1988) reported that schools had relatively little influence on the achievement of students and consequently students' life chances. He found outside-of-school factors such as poverty as extraordinarily central determinants of student success.

While research in the out-of-school line of research is persuasive, relying solely on outside-of-school variables and how they impact what happens to students inside of school can make it difficult to empower practitioners, especially teachers, to believe they can indeed make a real difference for all students. Teachers may ponder the following question: how do I meet the needs of African American male students in my classroom or school when they have so many challenges at home/outside the classroom? Evidence has also revealed that teachers and teaching can be the most powerful *inside-of-school* predictors of success for students (Barton, 2003; Gay, 2010; Milner, 2010). To illuminate, Barton (2003) found that curriculum rigor, which is intricately and inextricably connected to teacher expectation, was the strongest inside-of-school predictor of student academic achievement.

The point here is not that outside-of-school factors are not essential elements to consider; they are important. As I reviewed the masses of literature focused on outside-of-school factors, I kept returning to a root, fundamental and what will become a permeating question throughout this chapter: But what about the role of schools—specifically teachers—in being responsive to the outside-of-school realities that influence African American male students? Thus, this chapter is about teachers and teaching—keeping in mind that I realize that variables beyond school are essential points of consideration in the complex maze of meeting the needs of students.

In subsequent sections of this chapter, I provide a snapshot of what literature outlines about African American male students. I then attempt to re-conceptualize and advance some of Baldwin's (1963) ideas, positions, and principles that are relevant to contemporary matters. I frame this section around some of Baldwin's principles because they provide important moral reminders of the kinds of issues that should be considered regarding the education of all students. The discussion then shifts to a picture of the mind-set and practices of an African American male teacher and what he does to teach students successfully in an urban classroom. While this teacher's classroom contains students from different racial and ethnic backgrounds, his decisions and mind-set are especially successful with African American students. I provide examples of the kinds of experiences that can provide insight for practitioners in other sociopolitical contexts, and I conclude with some implications and suggestions for the next steps.

Black Male Students in the Educational System

Some Black male students struggle in the current educational system, but it is important to note that not all of them struggle for academic and social success in schools. On the contrary, some Black male students are successfully navigating and negotiating school expectations. In a cursory review of the literature, however, it is difficult to locate these positive accounts although a thorough review of the educational experiences of African American students reveals some success (see, for instance, Morris, 2004; Milner, 2008) In short, those Black male students who are successful in school appear to understand what Delpit (1995) called the culture of power and have the knowledge and skills to navigate and negotiate educational systems.

Some Black male students have difficulty in schools, and "the" educational system has not been well equipped to meet these students' needs. Black students, for instance, are grossly underrepresented in gifted education and overrepresented in special education. Ford (2006) wrote: "Sadly, I have seen little progress relative to demographic changes—Black and Hispanic students continue to be as under-represented in gifted programs today as they were 20 years ago" (p. 2). Moreover, a report from the Schott Foundation for Public Education (2004) stressed:

> In many school districts, up to 70 percent of black boys who enter 9th grade do not graduate four years later with their peers. In most districts, black boys are disproportionately assigned to special education and nearly absent from advanced placement classes. (Holzman, 2004, p. 2)

The Schott Foundation for Public Education places the urgent nature of teaching Black students at the top of the foundation's agenda in *Public Education and Black Male Students: A State Report Card*. In short, the report card revealed that "in 2001/2002 59% of African-American males did not receive diplomas with their cohort" (p. 4). Moreover, where education is concerned, the report revealed that "New York City and Chicago, for example, enrolling nearly 10% of the nation's Black male students between them, fail to graduate 70% of those with their peers" (p. 4).

Skiba, Michael, Nardo, and Peterson (2002) analyzed disciplinary records of 11,001 students in 19 middle schools in a large urban midwestern public school district during the 1994–1995 academic year. Skiba et al. reported a "differential pattern of treatment, originating at the classroom level, wherein African American students are referred to the office for infractions that are more subjective in interpretation" (p. 317). These data suggest that Black male students in particular are often called to the principal's office more often than their White counterparts. The Skiba et al. (2002) study pointed out that students of color overwhelmingly received harsher punishments for "misbehavior" than did their White counterparts. As an example, the authors described a fistfight at a high school football game in Decatur, Illinois, that resulted in the superintendent's recommendation that all seven of the African American students involved be expelled from school for two years. Apparently, in the same district, weapons were used in a fight involving White students, but less severe punishment was imposed upon those students. Why are some groups of students—particularly Black male students—punished more severely and more frequently than are others?

This is a dismal picture of educational experiences for African American male students that I will not dwell on in this chapter. I want to turn my attention in the remainder of this chapter to what teachers can do to address the needs of African American male students. The principles I conceptualize in the next section are shaped by Baldwin's (1963) insights and supported by my own research and that of others. Before considering these important principles, again, I want to emphasize that although teachers play an essential role in what happens to African American male students in schools across U.S. society, they operate within and through bureaucracies and systems that can make it difficult for some of them to do their best work. Teachers, for instance, often (1) have low expectations for Black male students; and (2) they "teach down" to them. They often "water down" the curriculum because they are too often socialized, encouraged, and trained to do so through hegemonic power structures and systems that hold Black male students in low esteem. When teachers work in unsupportive and repressive environments where the permeating perception is that Black male students are inferior and incapable, it can be difficult for them to see the brilliance and other assets in African American male students. Teachers and administrators often see difference (that is, conceptions, beliefs, convictions, values, and behaviors that are inconsistent with their own) as wrong. Different behaviors are often equated with insubordination: teachers often see Black students as deficits rather than as assets (Ford, 2006).

Principles for Teachers to Remember

Teachers should remember the following important principles when teaching African American male students. These principles are tailored specifically to meet the needs of Black male students although they are transferable to students from other racial and ethnic backgrounds as well as for female students. I have framed the discussion around three ideas that Baldwin would suggest are foundational in working with Black male students: (1) teachers must remember the importance of identity in education; (2) teachers must deeply understand and remember the social context of their work; and (3) teachers must remember the interrelated nature of the mind and heart in education.

Principle 1: Remember the Importance of Identity.
One principle inherent in Baldwin's talk to teachers concerned the teaching and identity intersection. Toshalis (2010) reminded us that teaching really is identity work. Teachers should become intimately aware of their own and their students' multiple and varied identities in order to enhance their classroom practices with African American male students. For instance, teachers have a racial and ethnic identity, a spiritual identity (whether they believe in a higher power or not), a gender identity, and an overall teaching identity that all shape their mind-sets and instructional practices in the classroom. Teachers, like the rest of us, perform and enact their identities depending on the situation and on the type of person they want others to experience and get to know. African American male students also have varied and multiple identities that are critical aspects of the teaching and learning exchange. These students have a racial and ethnic identity, a gender identity, and so forth. At times, these identities act in accord while at other times they are in conflict and are performed through tension.

The identity tensions that sometimes manifest among African American male students are a result of how they have been (and are still) categorized, named, and viewed in U.S. society and within the educational system. Thus, teachers must provide spaces where African American males can develop a keen sense of their identity and how their identities have been shaped in order to avoid "becoming schizophrenic" (Baldwin, 1963, p. 146) because they come to believe some of the identity labels that others have placed upon them. Baldwin states that many Whites in America have been socialized into seeing (male) African Americans as "less than human" (p. 150). The stereotypes and misconceptions that emerge from the media, for instance, can propagate myths and untruths about African American male students; these students themselves may even come to believe the negative ideologies about who they are, their worth, and their capacities for success in education and society.

Thus, this principle demands that teachers work to complement and build on who students are rather then attempting to change them (Ladson-Billings, 2006). In this sense, African American male students may become resentful or frustrated when teachers attempt to change or alter aspects of their identity that are important to them. For instance, efforts to coerce Black male students into speaking a particular (standard) way may be met with opposition from Black male students because they may value their language identity—perhaps nonstandard English (Delpit, 1995). Rather than attempting to change students' language identity, Baldwin suggested that teachers should attempt to complement and add to students' language so that students do not become resentful and so that they can eventually see the worth and value to them for speaking standard English (Delpit, 1995). Explaining to Black students that we live in a system where power structures force people to place values and demands on how one speaks (even when people understand what is being said through nonstandard English) can make it complicated for students to understand why they are being asked to speak in a particular way and change what might be perceived as an important aspect of their identity.

Principle 2: Remember the environment where teaching and learning are occurring.
A second point emphasized in Baldwin's speech concerned that of the marriage between teaching/learning and the social context of education. Teachers and students develop and enact identities in particular locations. For instance, there has been a line of thinking that African American students did not perform well in schools for fear that they would be accused of "acting White" (Fordham & Ogbu, 1986). However, later researchers stressed the necessity for deeper contextual analyses. In other words, the social contexts in which African American students find themselves are critical to academic identity formation and enactment. For instance, it was common in the high school where I taught to have an African American valedictorian and salutatorian, and students were not ridiculed for academic success in that social context. The idea is that teachers and African

American students should not be divorced from the spaces—the environments—in which they teach and learn and that generalities can be dangerous if one does not pay serious attention to the nuances in the space.

Baldwin (1963) suggested that teachers need to promote critical consciousness in the social context to empower an African American male student to "examine the society in which he is being educated" (p. 146). Thus, knowledge and decisions about how the world works need to be critically examined and deconstructed. Such a position is tantamount to critical theorists' (Freire, 1998; Wink, 2000) notions about how knowledge construction and deconstruction should emerge in the classroom and is also consistent with scholars who focus on the culture and teaching nexus (Gay, 2000; Ladson-Billings, 2006). According to Baldwin (1963), African American male students need to be provided space to examine the myths about them that are prevalent in society. Further, I am suggesting that African American male students deserve to be educated in social contexts that allow them to have voice and perspective in the classroom and that also provide them with the tools to critique and analyze what knowledge is, according to whom, and why (Apple & King, 1990). In short, both teachers and students need to consider how broader sociocultural, socioeconomic, sociopolitical, and general social contexts shape the experiences and behaviors of those in education.

Indeed, the social context of schools and communities may reinforce the status quo. For instance, the social context should be considered when examining students' performance and outcomes. Consider, for instance, the following contextually grounded realities that inevitably influence teachers and students. I have adapted many of these examples from Barton's (2003) policy analysis, *Parsing the Achievement Gap: Baseline for Tracking Progress:*

- There is a disproportionate number of new educators in urban and high-poverty schools; students whose teachers have five years of experience or more make three to four months more progress in reading during a school year.

- Teachers are absent from school more often in urban and high-poverty schools in comparison to schools in other locations; as a result, students in urban schools are taught by substitute teachers, many of whom are not trained in subject matter domains or teaching.

- There is often a lack of commitment and persistence among educators in urban and high-poverty schools. Educators graduate from college/teacher education programs, and work in urban and high-poverty schools until another position becomes available in a "more desirable" location.

- There is a disproportionate number of educators teaching outside their field of expertise in urban and high-poverty schools

- Money and resources are unequal in different social contexts (Tate, 2008): numbers of high-need districts where resources are low too often receive the same resources as districts with much greater resources. For instance, some districts distribute "equally funded programs into schools regardless of how many students need them. For example, a district might allocate $100,000 to each school with English-language learners, even though one school might have 200 students with limited English proficiency and another—often a more affluent school—might have only 20 [students]" (Roza, 2006, p. 11):

Thus, it is no secret that urban and high-poverty schools face persistent challenges that put student learning opportunities in jeopardy. Teachers are challenged in this principle to understand not only who they are teaching but also where the teaching and learning occurs.

Principle #3: Teachers' practices should be shaped with both the heart and mind.
Not only did Baldwin's speech focus on the teaching and identity intersection as well as the intersection of teaching and the social context of education, it also emphasized the centrality of mind and heart in teaching. It is clear that teachers of Black male students need to conduct themselves in ways that remember their "minds and hearts" (p. 145) in teaching. Teaching is work that certainly requires the mind: teachers must make rational and urgent decisions on behalf of their students in promoting optimal learning opportunities. With increased attention to standardized testing and predetermined curriculum guides, one might think that teaching is a profession that follows a technical orientation. However, it is the everyday situations—the thinking that teachers engage in during classroom interactions with students—that allow them to make important and informed decisions about how best to develop the learning environment. Thus, teachers of African American male students must be mindful of the various realities that shape their work with students.

In addition, this principle is about approaching the teaching and learning exchange with the heart. However, approaching the work with care, concern, and heart is not enough. It is certainly not enough to care if one does not also provide African American male students with experiences that are rigorous and challenging enough to prepare them to work through hegemonic systems that too often prevent them from achieving academic success. In this sense, teaching with heart is not about teachers being "soft" or forgiving when African American male students do not meet high expectations or when they refuse to reach their full capacity. Teaching with the heart means that teachers do not allow students to just settle or to just get by. Thus, teachers teach with the heart by developing and demonstrating a deep level of care for their students that is grounded in a reality that they want their African American male students to succeed just as they would their own biological children (Foster, 1997). As Irvine (2003) and Foster (1997) declared, teaching with care means that teachers adopt "other mother" and other father roles with their students.

Caring relationships are established, according to Weinstein (1996), by teaching strategies that "draw from a wide range of methods; they are challenging and intensive, flexibly applied, [and] responsive to student obstacles encountered in learning" (p. 18). In describing some common characteristics of care among the 13 teachers in his study, Brown (2003) reported,

> These 13 urban teachers create caring classroom communities by showing a genuine interest in each student. They gain student cooperation by being assertive through the use of explicitly stated expectations for appropriate student behavior and academic growth. And these teachers demonstrate mutual respect for students through the use of congruent communication processes. (p. 282)

Sadly, teachers are sometimes secretly afraid of their African American male students because they have never known anyone who "looked, talked, or acted like" (Weiner, 1993, p. 119) them. It is difficult for teachers to care about individuals they fear. For instance, Ennis (1996) examined issues of confrontation among 10 urban high schools that enrolled approximately 110,000 students from lower- to middle-class families. Her findings revealed some possible outcomes when teachers feel unsupported by their administrators and when they implicitly fear their students. Ennis discovered that some 50% of the teachers in the study reported that they did not teach certain content "because of the confrontations that such topics generate with specific students" (p. 145).

Because these teachers did not want to feel "ganged up on" in their classrooms, students were denied opportunities and access to a curriculum that may better prepare them for society. The teachers in the study avoided teaching content that "they believed students were disinterested in learning. . . students refused to learn or to participate in learning, or. . . generated discussions that the teachers felt unprepared to moderate" (Ennis, 1996, p. 146). The teachers were, in a sense, granting students permission to fail (Ladson-Billings, 2002) because they denied them access to important information that could impact their current and future opportunities. In classrooms where fear takes precedence over care, teachers provide information, ask questions (if students are lucky), give directions, provide assignments, give tests, assign homework (that they sometimes do not grade/read), punish noncompliance, and grade papers (Haberman, 1991).

The question remains: What happens when teachers exhibit fear of instead of care for their African American male students?

So far, I have provided a picture from the research literature of African American male students. I have emphasized that although some African American male students succeed, the literature, in large measure, presents their experiences in negative terms. I then discussed some general principles, drawn from Baldwin's speech, regarding a good approach to teaching Black male students. I want to now showcase an African American teacher and his practices in an urban school. While this teacher, Mr. Jackson, taught students from different racial and ethnic backgrounds, he was especially successful with African American students. Other teachers may want to employ some of his insights into their own practices as they work to meet the needs of Black male students.

Mind-set and Practice of a Black Male Teacher

Mr. Jackson (*pseudonym*) was an African American mathematics and science teacher who had been certified for seven years but had been in the district for ten years as an assistant or substitute teacher. Mr. Jackson always wore glasses, a shirt and tie, and, most of the time, a suit jacket. He could be found standing in front of his classroom door between classes. He often reminded passing students to "be mindful of the time" so as not to be late for their next class. He had a deep love and appreciation for music, which filtered down into his curriculum development and teaching. In particular, Mr. Jackson enjoyed jazz, pop, rhythm and blues, classical, and hip-hop music; music was almost always playing softly during his mathematics and science classes. I want to focus on four recurrent themes that seem to capture Mr. Jackson's mind-set and practices: (a) the value of learning; (b) targeting power and image among students; (c) immersion in the students' world(s); and (d) the intersection of music and learning.

The Value of Learning

Mr. Jackson stressed that his pedagogy and classroom were shaped by the idea that he needed to help his students find the value and relevance of school for their lives. In other words, because students often "cared most" about impressing their friends and because students were often more interested in what was happening in other aspects of their lives (such as dating, sports, and other hobbies), Mr. Jackson realized that it was essential to help them see school as a "hip" and "cool" place to be. He wanted his students to see the value of school and the value of learning: According to Mr. Jackson,

> [T]he biggest struggle in most urban schools is getting over the "It's not cool to learn" factor. Once you break those barriers and you get your classroom manage-

ment in check everything rolls pretty smooth[ly]. But that [the idea that school is not cool] is a microcosm of our society.

Mr. Jackson felt that entertainment is a number one priority in society, and, "[I]t's like that in the school system. The biggest struggle would be getting. . . the children to understand how important education is and that it is ok to act cool and be smart and intelligent" at the same time. In class, Mr. Jackson would target and "hook" the students whom other students in the school viewed as "cool" or hip.

There was a power structure among the students at Bridge Middle School. In some schools, the student athletes are at the top of the hierarchy. In other schools, the valedictorian could be considered the cool, popular, and powerful student in the context. At Bridge Middle School, according to Mr. Jackson and based on my observations, the athletes and cheerleaders were often held in the highest esteem among their peers: Mr. Jackson worked to get these students, those considered popular and cool, on his "side" in the classroom and to engage them in learning. In this way, Mr. Jackson created a classroom setting that stressed the importance of learning and doing well in school. He believed that once students witnessed the cool students being actively involved in learning opportunities that the majority—even those who might not normally be actively engaged in learning—would get connected as well. Mr. Jackson was fostering the value of learning by targeting the most powerful students in his class to serve as implicit role models for their classmates.

Targeting Power and Image among Students
Mr. Jackson believed that targeting particular students was critical from the very beginning of the school year, and it was necessary to use such power as an anchor for the engagement and learning of all students. He wanted to get the popular students to embrace his vision for the class so that other students would follow their lead:

> I try to target the coolest. I try to target the toughest. I try to target the most popular students, and I get them to understand and follow my vision. And once I get them, the rest of the class usually follows.

Mr. Jackson believed that he needed to create a classroom context where students were committed to learning and engaging in classroom learning opportunities. So, when Mr. Jackson mentioned that he wanted students to follow his vision, he was suggesting that he wanted students to follow a vision of valuing learning and perceiving school as a cool and hip place to be.

Mr. Jackson could not stress enough the power and influence that students have on each other. In many respects, students' peers are more important to them than their teachers or even their parents. The most popular students at the school have a great deal of power and influence, and Mr. Jackson understood that he had to get those students on his side.

> You have to get the people who have the most influence—the peer influence is very big in their world, very big. So if you get the toughest kids, the strongest kids, the most powerful kids, you get them to buy in, then you have got it [for the entire class].

In class, it was obvious that Mr. Jackson had gotten the buy-in from the entire class—even the students who were considered the most popular and/or the toughest. Still, Mr. Jackson stressed that consistency was very important in the context:

> I don't care what your [power] status is—you are going to get consequences. I don't care if you are the big linebacker bully in the school, or if you are the quiet little girl who is eighty pounds and never does anything. I want you serious about your work [engaging in learning]. So, you have to be careful not to let some people off because kids are watching you do that.

So, in a sense, Mr. Jackson was consistently pointing to issues of image and perceptions between and among students as well as between the teacher and the students. He believed that students were watching what happened in the classroom, how he handled situations—whether he was being "fair, firm, and consistent." Thus, Mr. Jackson was ever mindful of this and worked to make sure his students had a positive image of him and what was going on in the classroom.

Although Mr. Jackson stressed how important it was for him to target the "powerful" students to create a solid classroom context, he also stressed that he had to be fair, equitable, and consistent among his students. Image and perception played a role in his wearing of a shirt and tie each day, for instance. His life story—his experiences with other, more seasoned teachers in other schools—led him to believe that his clothing was an important part of his own "image" and power as a teacher. The students were watching him. In Mr. Jackson's words, "Teachers should dress for where they are going not necessarily where they are currently." It was this statement that really connected to one of the missions of his teaching: He wanted his students to envision life beyond their current situations. Mr. Jackson aspired to become a principal at some point in the future, and he was dressing for where he was going, not necessarily where for his present position. Indeed, as Mr. Jackson explained, students talked to one another and let others know what was happening in the classroom, and image and perception were central to the decisions Mr. Jackson made in the classroom.

Targeting the most popular students—at least in terms of the images students had of themselves and others—was an important feature of the classroom context created by Mr. Jackson. Additionally, Mr. Jackson immersed himself in his students' worlds, and this immersion was evident in his success as a teacher.

Immersion in Students' Worlds

Mr. Jackson had a deep interest in, knowledge about, and connections to the life experiences of his students. He was conscious of what was going on in the students' lives both inside and outside of the classroom, and he worked very hard to make sure he "remained current" about what was happening in the students' worlds. In his words,

> [I want to] implement things from their world into their academic setting. So, if I am doing math problems, I am going to have problems with stuff that comes out of the rap world or the video game world . . . Just recently, our basketball team was doing really well, and I used the players in the math assignments, and that gets them engaged.

And Mr. Jackson was not talking about just incorporating "their world" experiences from time to time in the learning that took place. Rather, he was referring to teachers' actually "keeping their worlds" in the curriculum and teaching—consistently. I saw that the students looked forward to word problems or examples with "real-world" relevance. They would often correct minor errors made about the number of points a player scored, for instance; their corrections may have seemed to be insignificant or trivial to others but were a big deal to the students because it was their reality—a reality that was important to them: they wanted and expected the examples to tell the truth about their life worlds (from a phenomenological perspective).

I wondered how Mr. Jackson was able to stay so current about what was happening with the middle school students with whom he worked. He was able to quote versions of hip-hop songs, list names of the most popular professional athletes, and had an idea of the latest movies that were out—he was, in a sense, immersed in pop culture. Mr. Jackson explained why he was so connected to the world of his students:

> The reason I know what is happening in their world is that I live in their world. I have a fourteen-year-old; I have an eleven-year-old; I have an eight-year-old. I know the world they came from with my eight-year-old, and I know where they are with my eleven-year-old . . . I know where they are going with my fourteen-year-old. Because I teach in middle school, I am right around eleven- and twelve-year-old range [students] . . . And I am a D.J.—I like the rap music myself. I play rap music. I feel like a kid at heart sometimes, so I kind of stay in touch with them in that way too.

It is important to note that Mr. Jackson did not believe that it was impossible for other teachers to immerse themselves in students' worlds—even if they did not have children around the same age as the students at Bridge Middle School. To the contrary, he believed that teachers could learn about the world of their students and use what they learn to enhance the learning that took place in the classroom:

> You have to immerse yourself in their world in some form or fashion. I am just lucky to come from the world that I teach in. I came from that world. I truly live in that world, so I am immersed already in my natural life. So if I were in a system where the students came from a different world, I would just have to immerse myself in their world.

In other words, he did not believe that teachers should make excuses for why they could not learn about and engross themselves in the worlds of their students. He asserted: "You have to understand their desires, wants, and needs and dislikes . . . You have to implement that in your academics because if they are not interested, then they are not going to learn." Clearly, there is a direct connection between the immersion of a teacher in the world of students and the learning opportunities that are available in a classroom.

As previously mentioned, Mr. Jackson had a genuine interest in and affection for music, and he used this in his teaching. Mr. Jackson believed that teachers should use what they have (themselves) as assets just as he believed teachers should allow students to use what they have in the classroom as assets. One asset that Mr. Jackson brought into the classroom was knowledge of and an interest in (hip-hop) music.

Intersection of Music and Learning

Another important feature of Mr. Jackson's mind-set and teaching had to do with the intersection of music and learning. Music was almost always playing in Mr. Jackson's room, and students from other classes would stop by his classroom—just to see what was being played on any particular day. When asked about the relevance and reasoning behind his implementation of music in the classroom, Mr. Jackson said:

> Well, it's nothing new. It was actually used in ancient Egypt where they used drums and instruments in the classroom. I do it for a couple reasons. Number one reason is kind of selfish—I like it. . . [I]t's like people like to go take smoke breaks or eat chocolate—I like to listen to music. And, it soothes me. It's usually jazz, sometimes some soft rock, [or] some soft R & B, but it's usually jazz, occasionally classical. The research states that when you play soft music, it calms students down and if you continue to play it, it kind of works as association—when students take tests, and you play the same songs [as what was played when covering the material] they can remember something about the assignment [or content] through the sound of the song—through association.

The students enjoyed the class perhaps because the teacher offered something different than what typically happened in some classrooms where students come in, sit down, listen to a lecture, do worksheets, and are dismissed (Haberman, 1991). I would hear the students in the hallway or in the cafeteria report that they were ready to "get to Jackson's class." They were eager to find out what was going to happen on any given day.

One learning opportunity that the students really enjoyed was what Mr. Jackson called Science Feud. During these feuds, Mr. Jackson would not play soft music; he would play music that students could dance to—music that was relevant and responsive to student interests. And the students loved it! Mr. Jackson explained the structure and relevance of the game. Similar to the popular game show *Family Feud*, the students would essentially answer questions that he would pose about some aspect of science that had already been covered in the class. The game served as a form of review for upcoming examinations. The "hook" was not necessarily that Mr. Jackson was playing music during the game, as was the case on the game show, where they played a violin version of square-dance music. The hook was the particular type of music being played. It was the kind of music that the students wanted to hear; it was consistent with what they listened to during their free time at school and also what they listened to outside of school. It was the kind of music that made the students want to be in the teacher's class. As the students walked up to the front of the room to answer the "survey" question during Science Feud, Mr. Jackson played some music that the students enjoyed, typically rhythm and blues or hip-hop. In Mr. Jackson's words,

> I'll stop the music, and I'll ask a question and they [the students] have to hit the table. The first one to hit the table and get the answer correct, gets a point. And the team that wins, I'll let them leave class early or get to leave first or whatever. The sixth graders I had who are now in seventh or eight grade—they'll still come by when I have it going on and they say, "I wanna play, I wanna play." They like it.

So, while the students enjoyed playing the game because they wanted to listen to the music, Mr. Jackson told me that they actually studied the material and tried to answer the questions correctly. The hook was the incorporation of the genre of music into the activity that the students appreciated and found relevant and responsive to them. In essence—finally—the students felt like they could relax a bit while still working hard to answer the questions and learn the content that had been covered.

Summary and Conclusions

In this "talk" to teachers about Black male students, I have asked that teachers remember some of Baldwin's wisdom in his important speech in 1963. In particular, I stressed several important matters: (1) teachers must remember the importance of identity in education; (2) teachers must deeply understand and remember the social context of their work; and (3) teachers must remember the interrelated nature of the mind and heart in education. I also briefly reviewed the state of Black male students in education and noted that much of the literature paints a very negative portrait of the group. I shifted the discussion to a Black male teacher, Mr. Jackson, and how he thought about and implemented lessons to maximize student learning opportunities in an urban school with a large number of African American students. I am hopeful that my focus on Mr. Jackson's practices will provide important practical meaning and insight into how other teachers, too, can change (or at best improve) their mind-sets and practices to better meet the needs of African American male students. Other mind-sets and practices have been identified in the research literature that have important implications for teaching Black male students that I did not completely capture in the three principles identified, the snapshot of Mr. Jackson's work, or Baldwin's insights. I conclude with a summative list and explanations (see Table 1 below) of other perspectives that may prove useful to teachers serious about better meeting the needs of Black male students. This list draws from my research with Black male students as well as others' research (see, for instance, Gay, 2000, 2010; Ladson-Billings, 2006; Milner 2010).

Table 1: Summary of Transferable Mind-sets and Practices to African American Males

Stressed the value and importance of learning: Teachers explicitly conveyed the importance and value of education and learning to students. They helped students understand and embrace the reality that one can be smart and intelligent and, at the same time, cool and hip.

Immersed themselves in students' worlds: Teachers attempted to understand what it meant to live in the world of their students through music, sports, film, and pop culture. They incorporated this knowledge and understanding into the learning opportunities in the classroom.

Incorporated pop culture: Teachers understood the multiple layers of popular culture that students were interested in outside of school. They incorporated this understanding in developing relevant and responsive lessons for students.

Did more with fewer resources: Teachers did not allow what they did not have to hinder their efforts, goals, and visions for their students. They did whatever it took to succeed and for their students to succeed; they never gave up.

Rejected deficit notions: Teachers concentrated on the assets that students brought into the classroom and built on those assets in the learning contexts. They also understood their own assets as teachers and used those as a foundation to bridge learning opportunities in the classrooms.

Understood equity in practice: Teachers understood the difference between equality and equity. They worked to meet the needs of individual students and realized that their curriculum and instruction might not be exactly the same among all students at all times, but would depend on the particular needs of each student.

Built and sustained relationships: Teachers understood that students needed to get to know them and that they needed to get to know their students. They saw their teaching as a family affair and viewed their students as their own. In other words, they engaged in "other mothering" and "other fathering."

Understood power structures among students: Teachers understood that there were power structures among the students. They recruited popular students to embrace the vision of learning and engagement in the classroom in order to get other students engaged and motivated to learn.

Understood the self in relation to others: Teachers assembled knowledge and understood points of intersection and convergence between themselves and their students. They used this knowledge and understanding to build and sustain relationships in the classroom.

Granted students entry into teachers' worlds: Teachers allowed students to learn things about them and made connections to demonstrate the commonalities that existed between students and teachers. They shared stories with their students and allowed students to share theirs in order to build community and collective knowledge.

Conceived of school as a community with family: Teachers conceived of school as a community that was established by all those in the environment. They allowed students to have voice and perspectives in how the community would be defined. Teachers respected and cared about those in the community as if they were family members.

Dealt with race: Teachers rejected color-blind and culture-blind ideologies. They saw themselves and their students as racial and cultural beings.

Perceived teaching as mission and responsibility: Teachers cared deeply about their students and developed mission-minded approaches that allowed students to reach their potential.

Developed critical consciousness: Teachers critiqued the knowledge and information available. They consciously fought against injustice; they spoke out against inequity both inside and outside of the classroom, and empowered students to do the same.

Teachers must have the mind-set to succeed, coupled with a vision for success. Baldwin (1963), quoting the *Holy Bible*, reminded teachers that "where there is no vision the people perish" (p. 152). Indeed, our visions shape our practices—that is, what we do. I am hopeful that this talk has provided for some serious reflection and (re)visioning of what needs to happen if African American male students are to succeed in education.

References

Apple, M. W., & King, N. (1990). Economics and control in everyday school life. In M.W. Apple (Ed.), *Ideology and curriculum*. New York: Routledge.

Baldwin, J. (1963). A talk to teachers. Delivered October 16, 1963, as "The Negro Child—His Self Image"; originally published in *The Saturday Review*, December 21, 1963.

Barton, P.E. (2003). *Parsing the achievement gap: Baseline for tracking progress*. Princeton, NJ. Educational Testing Services.

Brown, D. F. (2003). Urban teachers' use of culturally responsive management strategies. *Theory into Practice, 42*(4), 277–282.

Caldas, S. J., & Bankston C. III (1997). Effect of school population socioeconomic status on individual academic achievement. *The Journal of Educational Research, 90*(5), 269.

Coleman, J. S. (1988). Social capital in the creation of human capital. *The American Journal of Sociology, 94,* 95–120.

Coleman, J. S. (1969). *Equality and achievement in education*. Boulder, CO: Westview Press.

Davis, J. E., & Jordan, W. J. (1994). The effects of school context, structure, and experiences on African American males in middle and high school. *Journal of Negro Education, 63*(4), 570–587.

Delpit, L. (1995). *Other people's children: Cultural conflict in the classroom*. New York: New Press.

Ennis, C. D. (1996). When avoiding confrontation leads to avoiding content: Disruptive students' impact on curriculum. *Journal of Curriculum and Supervision, 11*, 145–62.

Ford, D. Y. (2006). Identification of young culturally diverse students for gifted education programs. *Gifted Education Press Quarterly, 20*(1), 2–4.

Fordham, S., & Ogbu, J.U. (1986). Black students' school success: coping with the burden of "acting White." *Urban Review 18*, 176–206.

Foster, M. (1997). *Black teachers on teaching*. New York: New Press.

Freire, P. (1998). *Pedagogy of the oppressed*. New York: Continuum.

Gay, G. (2010). *Culturally responsive teaching: Theory, research, and practice*. 2nd edition. New York: Teachers College Press.

Gay, G. (2000). *Culturally responsive teaching: Theory, research, and practice*. New York: Teachers College Press.

Gay, G., & Howard, T. (2000). Multicultural teacher education for the 21st century. *The Teacher Educator, 36*(1), 1–16.

Haberman, M. (1991). The pedagogy of poverty versus good teaching. *Phi Delta Kappan, 73*(4), 290–294.

Holzman, M. (2004). *Public education and Black male students: A state report card*. The Schott Educational Inequity Index, Cambridge, MA: The Schott Foundation for Public Education.

Howard, T. C. (2001). Telling their side of the story: African American students' perceptions of culturally relevant teaching. *Urban Review, 33*(2), 131–149.

Irvine, J. J. (2003). *Educating teachers for diversity: Seeing with a cultural eye*. New York: Teachers College Press.

Irvine, J. J. (1990). *Black students and school failure: Policies, practices and prescriptions*. New York: Greenwood.

Ladson-Billings, G. (2006). "Yes, but how do we do it?": Practicing culturally relevant pedagogy. In J. Landsman & C. W. Lewis, *White teachers/diverse classrooms: A guide to building inclusive schools, promoting high expectations and eliminating racism.* Sterling, VA: Stylus.

Ladson-Billings, G. (2002). Permission to fail. In L. Delpit & J.K. Dowdy (Eds.), *The skin that we speak: Thoughts on language and culture in the classroom* (pp. 107–120). New York: The New Press.

Landsman, J., & Lewis, C. W. (2006). *White teachers/diverse classrooms: A guide to building inclusive schools, promoting high expectations and eliminating racism.* Sterling, VA: Stylus.

Milner, H. R. (2012). Challenging negative perceptions of Black teachers. *Journal of Educational Foundations, 26*(1–2), 27–46.

Milner, H. R. (2010). *Start where you are, but don't stay there: Understanding diversity, opportunity gaps, and teaching in today's classroom.* Cambridge, MA: Harvard Education Press.

Milner, H. R. (2009). Preparing teachers of African American students in urban schools. In L. C. Tillman (Ed.), *The handbook of African American education* (pp. 123–140). Thousand Oaks, CA: Sage.

Milner, H. R. (2008). Disrupting deficit notions of difference: Counter-narratives of teachers and community in urban education. *Teaching and Teacher Education, 24*(6), 1573–1598.

Milner, H. R. (2007). African American males in urban schools: No excuses—teach and empower. *Theory into Practice, 46*(3), 239–246.

Morris, J. E. (2004). Can anything good come from Nazareth? Race, class, and African American schooling and community in the urban south and Midwest. *American Educational Research Journal 41*(1), 69–112.

Noguera, P. A. & Wells, L. (2011). The politics of school reform: A broader and bolder approach for Newark. *Berkeley Review of Education, 2*(1), 5–25.

Roza, M. (2006). *How districts shortchange low-income and minority students.* Washington, DC: The Education Trust.

Skiba, R. J., Michael, R. S., Nardo, A. C., & Peterson, R. L. (2002). The color of discipline: Sources of racial and gender disproportionality in school punishment. *The Urban Review, 34*(4), 317–342.

Tate, W. F. (2008). Geography of opportunity": Poverty, place, and educational outcomes. *Educational Researcher, 37*(7), 397–411.

Tatum, B. D. (2001). Professional development: An important partner in antiracist teacher education. In S. H. King & L. A. Castenell (Eds.), *Racism and racial inequality: Implications for teacher education* (pp. 51–58). Washington, DC: AACTE Publications.

Tatum, A. W., & Muhammad, G. E. (2012). African American males and literacy development in contexts that are characteristically urban. *Urban Education, 47*(2), 434–463.

Toshalis, E. (2010). The identity-perception gap: Teachers confronting the difference between who they (think they) are and how they are perceived by students. In H. R. Milner IV (Ed.), *Culture, curriculum, and identity in education* (pp. 15–36). New York: Palgrave Macmillan.

Weiner, L. (1993). *Preparing teachers for urban schools: Lessons from thirty years of school reform.* New York: Teachers College Press.

Weinstein, R. S. (1996). High standards in a tracked system of schooling: For which students and with what educational support? *Educational Researcher, 25*(8), 16–19.

Wink, J. (2000). *Critical pedagogy: Notes from the real world.* (2nd ed.). New York: Longman.

Woodson, C. G. (1933). *The mis-education of the Negro.* Washington, DC: Associated Publishers.

Zumwalt, K., & Craig, E. (2005). Teachers' characteristics: Research on the demographic profile. In M. C. Smith & K. M. Zeichner (Eds.), *Studying teacher education: The report of the AERA panel on research and teacher education* (pp. 111–156). Mahwah, NJ: Lawrence Erlbaum.

 Part Two

Educational Practices

Exploring the Property Rights and Liberty Interests of African American Males in Public Schools

Confronting the Denial of Education under the Guise of Maintaining Order

Mark A. Gooden

Polite (2000) conducted a case study of Metropolitan High School (MHS), located in a predominantly African American suburban community outside a major city. There he interviewed 115 African American males, teachers and staff members, parents, and other leaders over a three-year period. He also conducted 600 hours of observations and reviewed documents. He analyzed his data using qualitative research strategies. Although he did not use chaos theory to analyze his data originally, he maintained that chaos theory holds promise in explaining the challenges that African Americans faced at MHS. Consequently, he used chaos theory to reexamine these data.

Specifically, Polite (2000) set out to "show how actions, policies, and procedures, viewed at the time as innocuous and insignificant, resulted in poor academic preparation and an overall chaotic school environment that adversely affected African American males" (p. 219), by highlighting the ecology of resistance to schooling. He notes that the relationships between the various central components responsible for the education of African American males at MHS thus emerge as critically important. Polite (2000), as a participant-observer, who at the time was an administrator in the district and a researcher, takes advantage of being within the system and works through the challenges this presents.

Polite (2000) lays out six theoretical concepts of chaos theory and argues that it applies to school systems and how they operate to impede the progress of African American males. He summarizes these from work by Blair in her argument that chaos theory applies to educational administration. She uses the butterfly effect and the onset of turbulence, which is followed by *dissipative structures and random shocks*, two constructs that can specifically describe the nonlinear nature of chaos-ridden schools and school districts. She extrapolates the concept of *strange attractors* from chaos theory to refer to the central components of a system that seem to be the focal points from which disastrous events evolve. For a full discussion of chaos theory and how it relates particularly to the schooling of African American males, please review the chapter.

I certainly appreciate Polite's approach: he makes a convincing argument that chaos theory can be useful in describing factors that impact the educational environment for African American males. Much of what he found in his 2000 research holds true now from the perspective of chaos theory. However, I would respectfully expand his argument to note that some aspects are explained better by more of a systematic (organized, methodical), systemic (universal, of the larger system), and historic deprivation of the rights of African American males, which has been going on for several decades on a larger level. This, of course, results in a tragic loss of hope of succeeding in schools on the part of African American males, which is then followed by the "ecology of resistance" to schooling that Polite (2000) noted. I argue that this ecology is not limited to the students.

Polite (2000) examined the changing demographics of the "excellent" suburban school and how the teachers and the system made no provisions to adjust for the increase in African American males, and indeed were found wanting because they had not. For example, African American males were allowed to take larger numbers of elective courses without challenge, and they were allowed to avoid attending classes without real consequences. Moreover, several teachers, some of whom had seen the school's "glory days" when the school was less ethnically diverse, were so unresponsive that they were perceived not to care. Such actions, I would argue, are tacitly approved by a system that places no legal or ethical burden upon educators to do more. Indeed, such actions do little to shock the consciousness of educators who should be at least curious about the high incidence of "failure."

The Challenge

In the past three decades, African American males have had a difficult time in schooling and in life. Norwood (2008) notes:

> Over the last 25 years, the social, educational and economic outcomes for Black males have been more systemically devastating than the outcomes for any other racial or ethnic group or gender. Black males have consistently low educational attainment levels, are *more* chronically unemployed and underemployed, are less healthy and have access to fewer health care resources, die *much* younger, and are

many times more likely to be sent to jail for periods *significantly longer* than males of other racial/ethnic groups. (p. 23, italics in original)

On average, Black males are more likely to attend the most segregated and least resourced public schools (Schott Report, 2008). As if attending these schools were not bad enough, they are more likely to be suspended, expelled, or placed in special education within these schools (Brown, 2011a, 2011b). The evidence is clear that the African American male is having a very difficult time in America, especially in the area of education. To be clear, other groups are facing challenges, but none approach the African American males' plight. Moreover, there is no concerted interest in addressing these issues by implementing a national solution.

Two Storied Experiences Calling upon Black Assistant Principals

When I was teaching mathematics at a high school, I noted the racial makeup of the leadership team. The school's racial makeup was at least 90% African American. The principal was a White man and there were four assistant principals. The first assistant principal was a White woman and she was in charge of curriculum matters, the master schedule, and other things but not discipline. Then there was the African American woman principal in charge of the seniors. Lastly, there were two administrators, a Black man and a Black woman, and they handled all discipline issues for the students in grades 9–11. In fact, we sent discipline referral forms to them according to the student's last name as they each covered roughly half of the alphabet. While I had a good working relationship with all of them, I was closer to the Black male assistant principal. I also aspired to work as an assistant principal, and as part of course work in a leadership program I interviewed him on more than one occasion. He had been a very good secondary mathematics teacher at the school who had really helped students succeed academically. He often lamented the fact that now his role was mostly that of disciplinarian, and most of his interactions with the students revolved around discipline issues and how he was expected more often than not to suspend students, at least for a day or two.

The experience left me with questions about the role of Black principals in protecting the rights of students. This issue came up for me again about 10 years later when I was observing and interviewing an African American principal in a technical high school that had a majority African American population. This principal was having a difficult time as he clashed philosophically with many on his teaching faculty. He was expected to discipline Black children at the cost of all else. For example, teachers insisted students be suspended for "minor infractions" like using profanity. He was roundly criticized for not maintaining order because he was approaching discipline in a way that kept more students in school. Still, many of the teachers concluded he simply was not suspending enough students.

I asked about the most common rule students were breaking for which teachers, many of whom were Black, strongly felt the need to suspend them. The teachers and the principal noted the major issue was students were freely using profanity, which was regarded as disrespectful. Second, the teachers thought the students talked back too much.

Essentially then, majority of the teachers wished to repeatedly suspend students for discipline and disrespect. The principal noted that this was a challenge because many of the students he saw struggling academically were Black males, but they were also the ones sent to the office more often. One last interesting note to this story is that this principal was hired as an assistant principal several years earlier, and he realized that part of the reason he got that job was the perception that he would be a good disciplinarian for students in this urban district. In fact, he admitted that he even answered questions in the interview in a way that made him seem like someone who would be tough and keep kids in order.

He continued this philosophy and mode of operating as an assistant principal after he was hired. However, when he became a principal, he changed his approach because he thought that the denial of an education outweighed the discomfort of tolerating profanity and even disrespect at times. He essentially went against how the system had defined him as a leader. This change of philosophy is instructive because it will take a huge effort to get African Americans males interested and keep them engaged, and it is going to take new approaches that add excitement to the curriculum, given all the resistant forces.

That idea is the basis for this chapter. Why is suspension the common response to Black males who are disinterested in school and the dry content that teachers often focus on so heavily in the test? What are our expectations when it comes to Black males fully participating in their education? Do we really expect to provide access to this benefit in the context of manufactured discipline issues, or are we always secretly aiming to exclude them from the education process altogether through placement in special education, suspension, or even expulsion? In fact, even when the Black male is present in class, he is the least likely student to gain from an education if we use test scores as one indicator. Do all of these factors amount to a failure of the educational system or of African American males in the school setting? Do they amount to a denial of the due process of life, liberty, and property as guaranteed by the Fourteenth Amendment—a response that can be system based, systemic, and historic in nature?

Although we could argue that the failure is primarily the result of the students' behaviors, and, indeed, some scholars have argued that black students opposition to education is the issue (Ogbu, 2003) or the result Black anti-intellectualism (McWhorter, 2000), this does not capture the entire picture. The arguments proffered by these two researchers are more complex than can be represented by a couple of sentences. Indeed, an examination of either in detail can present a plausible argument for underachievement of African Americans in general, and African American males in particular. However, focusing exclusively on students' personal challenges and shortcomings detracts from the root issue of institutional racism of the system. Though pointing to racism presents a real challenge that might appear at the macro-level and insurmountable, it is necessary to explore as it surfaces behaviors of other actors instead of just the responses of African American males to the educational system, which is a secondary root issue. The root issue is racism and it has spurred responses from civil rights leaders and civic leaders of many dedicated individuals focused on improving education before and beyond the *Brown v. the Board of Education* (1954) case. Just the knowledge that racism is really a present actor casts a different light on how it should be interrogated in education, especially as it has impacted the growth of African American males. As pioneers seeking to address the education of African American males directly, Georgia & Maryland, among other states, have each have launched initiatives focused addressing the plight of the African American males (Board of Regents, 2003; Maryland State Department of Education, 2007).

The System Is Not Neutral

What if the real reason for the failure of African American males is that the school system has not prepared itself to integrate them since desegregation? What if the system even becomes hostile to African Americans because they are perceived as a threat to its efficiency? What if African Americans were prohibited from learning to read and write earlier in the history of this country? To be sure, states seem to operate under the ostensibly egalitarian assumption that education is available to all and African American males, like others, should take advantage of it. Although this premise sounds deceptively simple, there are some problems with it. First, if we explore the history of education in America, we find that it is in fact built on a philosophy that made it initially available only to White males with property (Harris, 1995; Tyack, Anderson, Cuban, Kaestle, & Ravitch, 2002). We also note that for much of the nineteenth century it was illegal to teach enslaved African Americans to read in Southern states (see, e.g., the Black Codes).

Hence, if we have a system that emanates from a society that has tried to control African Americans by socializing them more to assimilate than to achieve, then it is no wonder that we have an institutional system that has done more to exclude African American males from the educational environment. For those who would argue that the past has no bearing on current circumstances, I would urge them to consider the following as evidence. The most cogent proof that the history of slavery and desegregation reaches into the present is that we still have segregated and racially isolated schools in this country (Anderson, 1988). As noted above, we also are witnessing an exclusion of African American males from the educational environment or a high placement rate of those students in special education classes. Racism is still the institutional basis for much of what is happening in schools, which are organized around housing options. Redlining heavily impacted where African Americans could live in this country. In fact, in offering his concept of interest convergence, Bell (2004) has successfully argued that racism is a permanent fixture of this society, and its effect on schooling has brought about a number of unsavory outcomes, including a lack of resources and low levels of achievement.

As further proof, I offer the post-Reconstruction years. Educating African Americans, and males in particular, is something this country has not seriously considered as a policy. Polite (2000) illustrates this on the microcosmic level when he notes that students who have the promise for succeeding are being defeated by a chaotic school system. However, it represents where this country was 10 years ago, and where it is even now for the education of African American males. Elsewhere, I have been joined by other scholars in arguing that the road to desegregation was slow, and that even after it was legally implemented, the path to equity was thwarted by local school boards (Brown, 2004; Gooden, 2004; Tillman, 2004). If we think of the current state of education and how few policies have followed to address what happened after *Brown*, we see that the result is analogous to what happened to African Americans in this country after slavery. The country was ill prepared to address issues of African Americans, having been a slave-owning nation for 200 years. Du Bois (1903/1997) gives a gut-wrenching account of what African Americans experienced post-Emancipation. Anderson (1988) joins him in making the case that essentially African Americans were set free and left to their own devices and even charged with creating their own education system in the South to increase their upward mobility.

Singer (2009) notes that William Tecumseh Sherman promised "forty acres and a mule" to African Americans during Reconstruction, wherein the government promised the loan of a federal government mule to plow that land. Some African Americans took advantage of these programs and either bought or leased parcels of land. Due to a lack of interest and failed government policy, most African Americans in the South did not receive the promised 40 acres and a mule. Indeed, sharecropping after the Civil War, combined with a failure to give 40 acres and a mule to the freed slaves, came close to reproducing slavery (Singer, 2009).

However, President Andrew Johnson soon vetoed a bill to enlarge the powers and activities of the Freedmen's Bureau, thereby reversing many of the policies of the bureau. This proved to wipe away what could have resulted in real property wealth for some African Americans. To be clear, if such a benefit of property would have been granted during Reconstruction as intended by Sherman, it could have made a significant difference in African American males' access to education, as then and even now, we recognize a correlation between property wealth and education (Harris, 1995). Indeed, emancipating African American men via the Thirteenth Amendment but providing no property essentially created a right with little power and social capital to effectively exercise it. The same is true wherein the Fifteenth Amendment provided suffrage rights to African American men while Southern state legislators preempted this federal right, making it illegal for them to exercise this right unless they owned property, thus thwarting their full participation as a citizen in this democracy. Additionally, Whites visited violence upon those African Americans in the South who would dare exercise their right to vote.

Historically, there has been a correlation between property and education, so not presenting freed slaves with property, among other things, left them victims of the most invidious discrimination imaginable, and thus left them essentially powerless to fend for themselves. Such a lack of enforcement as a national policy gave rise to the Civil Rights movement and the eventual passage of the Voting Rights Act of 1965, which essentially barred the use of literacy tests, grandfather clauses, and other requirements to own property prior to voting. However, the damage imposed during slavery was amplified when it was followed by such blatant deprivation of rights, which lasted easily one hundred years, as noted below.

We see that even when the system is not as blatant as Southern legislators blocking progress, it is slow when it moves in the name of progress. A prime example is the *South Carolina v. Katzenbach* (1966) case. Although the justices noted the slowness of granting African American men their rights and were critical of it, there was no definitive effort to change it.

> Congress had found that case-by-case litigation was inadequate to combat widespread and persistent discrimination in voting, because of the inordinate amount of time and energy required to overcome the obstructionist tactics invariably encountered in these lawsuits. After enduring nearly a century of systematic resistance to the Fifteenth Amendment, Congress might well decide to shift the advantage of time and inertia from the perpetrators of the evil to its victims. (*South Carolina v. Katzenbach*, 383 U.S. 301, 1966, pp. 327–328)

This excerpt captures much of the challenge of the legal approach to addressing educational issues. In fact, this pattern of protracted legal approach is eerily analogous to the path of *Brown v. Board of Education* (1954) being decided and the separate but equal principle being struck down, followed by no real educational "forty acres and a mule" property rights ever manifesting. If there is a property right in education, then African Americans have been denied full benefit of it by state resistance, among other things, especially in the South. Just as above, the tactic of using a "case-by-case litigation approach to combat wide-spread and persistent discrimination" is going to prove to be inadequate, and nearly fifty-five years after the decision, we see the African American male having a really difficult time navigating through under-resourced schools.

While the Southern perpetrators created nearly a century of blatant, systematic resistance to the Fifteenth Amendment, the resistance to *Brown*'s original purposes is not so blatant and therefore it is harder to track, as there are no obvious state laws that explicitly deny an education to Black males. However, to be sure, while there are no laws, the history of dis-educating, mis-educating, or not educating at all has created a climate that is conducive to a denial of their education, albeit absent explicit policies. In other words, it is not de jure denial of their education, but certainly it amounts to de facto denial. Consider that the country had slavery for more than 200 years and then Blacks were free with no real way to integrate into society except with whatever they could come up with after being denied education for so long. Even Blacks who were free would be affected by the policies and thinking toward African Americans in general. The same is true in the post-*Brown* era. *Brown v. Board of Education* held that the maintaining of separate but equal schooling was a violation of the equal protection clause of the Fourteenth Amendment, but that is about it. There was no strict nationwide enforcement of this national policy.

Defining Due Process in the Context of Property Rights and Liberty Interest

In the Supreme Court decision of *Goss v. Lopez* (1975), several Columbus, Ohio, middle and high school students brought a class action to review their suspensions without hearings. School officials were acting under the authority of an Ohio statute which permitted the suspension of pupils for misconduct for up to 10 days. The students were arguing that this was a violation of their Fourteenth Amendment due process rights. The U.S. Supreme Court held that the students facing temporary suspension from public school were entitled to protection under the due process clause. Moreover, because the denial of an education even for a brief period of time is not de minimis (insignificant), the court noted that due process required school officials who were suspending students for up to 10 days to give notice of the charges and an opportunity for the students to present their version to authorities. Ideally, this notice would come prior to removal from school except when this was not feasible due to safety concerns. In such cases, educators have latitude to immediately remove the student and provide necessary notice of the hearing as soon as is practicable.

Although *Goss* was decided in 1975, it holds some interesting implications for today's students in general, but for Black males in particular. First, within the text of the case, there is a compelling argument for how the court has legally defined property rights and liberty interests relative to education. Black males are suspended more often than any other group. While many act as if the answer is to blame these students and conclude that they have problems behaving in school which leads to being disciplined, others have refuted these arguments and pointed out that the consequences of continually suspending these students are counterproductive and negatively impact their life chances (Meiners, 2007; Noguera, 2009).

Although not recognizing education as a fundamental right, federal courts have still regarded it as important. For example, in the landmark *Brown* case, the Supreme Court noted that "education is perhaps the most important function of state and local governments" (*Brown v. Board of Education*, 1954, p. 493). The *Goss v. Lopez* (1975) court added that

> the total exclusion from the educational process for more than a trivial period, and certainly if the suspension is for 10 days, is a serious event in the life of the suspended child. Neither the property interest in educational benefits temporarily denied nor the liberty interest in reputation, which is also implicated, is so insubstantial that suspensions may constitutionally be imposed by any procedure the school chooses, no matter how arbitrary. (p. 737)

So students facing temporary suspension from a public school have property and liberty interests that may be entitled to protection under the due process clause of the Fourteenth Amendment.

Initially in the *Goss* case, Columbus public officials contended that because there is no constitutional right to an education at public expense, the due process clause does not protect against expulsions from the public school system. The Supreme Court disagreed and refuted this position citing its prior decisions. The Court pointed out that the Fourteenth Amendment forbids states from depriving any person of life, liberty, or property without due process of law. Indeed, protected interests in property are typically not created by the constitution but by an independent source such as state statutes or rules entitling the citizen to certain benefits.

As the logic goes, states have endeavored to offer an education to their citizens, including African American males. This is indicated in their state constitutions and statutes. Having chosen to extend the right to an education to students generally, Ohio, like other states, may not withdraw that right simply on the grounds of misconduct, absent *fundamentally fair procedures* to determine whether the misconduct has occurred. The state must recognize a student's legitimate entitlement to a public education as a property interest that is protected by the due process clause of the Fourteenth Amendment. Therefore, the first point of the *Goss* case is that this right may not be taken away arbitrarily or capriciously, without observing minimum procedures required by that clause. But, the often implied, but no less important, question is whether the system is fundamentally fair in its application of these procedures. Arguably, in light of the high incidence of suspensions and expulsions of African American males relative to their percentage in the school population, this is a systemic, systematic, and historic problem where the answer to this question is most likely "No." Students in *Goss* plainly had legitimate claims of entitlement to a public education on the basis of state compulsory laws, so a property interest in education existed for those students. The same is true for all African American males.

The due process clause also forbids arbitrary deprivations of liberty, and *Goss* (1975) confirms that liberty interests are implicated "[w]here a person's good name, reputation, honor, or integrity is at stake because of what the government is doing to him, [and] the minimal requirements of the Clause must be satisfied" (p. 736). School officials in *Goss* suspended students from school for periods of up to 10 days based on charges of misconduct. The court maintained that if the suspensions were sustained and recorded,

> those charges could seriously damage the students' standing with their fellow pupils and their teachers as well as interfere with later opportunities for higher education and employment. It is apparent that the claimed right of the State to determine unilaterally and without process whether that misconduct has occurred immediately collides with the requirements of the Constitution. (*Goss v. Lopez,* 1975, p. 736)

Suspending a student can seriously impair his reputation so minimum procedures must be in place before this happens. Because African American males are suspended more than other groups, a Black student's reputation has been damaged in school and society, and this has resulted in decreased access to education (Civil Rights Project, 2001). In fact, educators who wish to focus on academics and develop their students' skills in this area face an uphill battle, or, as Polite (2000) termed it, "an ecology of resistance." Moreover, sincere educators face students with low expectations of their academic abilities, treating them as suspects in the educational environment and in America. We are constantly bombarded with messages that they are dangerous and not interested in education. Moreover, we forget the effect of these many messages on the ability to teach these students and truly value their contributions.

The consequences of these actions are not minor. African American males are particularly targeted by a number of public school practices that result in severe racial disparities in several key areas that run counter to helping them succeed in school. For example, these include a nationwide higher density of African American boys referred to special education, in many cases for behavioral problems; and the disproportionate assignment to alternative school placements and corporal punishment with Black males (Fitzgerald, 2009; Gregory, 1997; Grossman, 2002; Meiners, 2007; Civil Rights Project 2001). Fitzgerald (2009) noted how significant a role subjective practices play in placing students in special education. He noted that these methods were far from perfect and oftentimes resulted in African Americans males being disproportionately and inaccurately targeted. Research from the Civil Rights Project (2001) found Blacks 2.9 times more likely to be referred than their White counterparts.

Procedural due process is supposed to ensure a fundamentally fair process. That means, legally, if students violate a rule, school officials will employ a process that is not arbitrary or capricious. In general, the Fourteenth Amendment regulates such a process in that specific rules and guidelines are put in place to inform students beforehand of what will happen if they break certain rules. In the context of the law, informing the students gives them adequate notice before they violate a rule. But what if the rule, as applied, is different for different groups, resulting in different results for some groups? While *Goss v. Lopez* (1975) has outlined important procedures that should be followed when disciplining all students, the procedures really change when the student is an African American male. Indeed, we have been reminded that that law is limited when it is, like our educational system, a part of an institution founded upon oppression and social control (Fitzgerald, 2009; Watkins, 2001). We may have good intentions of serving African American males on a fair and equitable basis, but we are operating within a framework that assumes the punisher is applying the rules without bias. We may be doing our best but we are in a system of barriers set up to work against our best work. We are working to overturn a powerful history that constantly questions whether these students can be successful in school, by first assuming they are suspects from the start who have little interest in learning.

Take, for example, the fact that the majority of African American students in this country are still relegated to under-resourced urban schools within districts that struggle with systematically higher teacher turnover rates, less-qualified teachers who are tend not to be culturally proficient. So, these Black boys start with potential in schools that are low performing and under-resourced and somewhere in elementary school they start to lose interest in education early (Brown, 2011a). Next, Black males continue this course and collide hard with the system and its restrictively applied procedures, and too often they lose by ending up suspended from a school that keeps them in a substandard, draconian, test-driven, high-pressure environment. Noguera (2009) points out how many of the teachers in these schools work hard to keep the environment engaging, but the challenges are many. In his work, he also found that Black boys are punished twice as often as others (Noguera, 2009).

Conclusion

Polite (2000) spends a large part of his discussion pointing out the avoidance of schooling by African American males and the decreasing academic achievement at Metropolitan High School. We can see that early exclusion can clearly contribute to low performance, which can impact interest in school, especially if these Black males are not seeing themselves succeed. Polite maintains, though, that these students have the potential but make decisions that run counter to their true academic potential. For example, he found that the African American males in his study selected large numbers of electives that left them ill prepared for college or work even though they met the graduation requirements. Some avoided engaging in school by not applying themselves, and others just pretended to attend but instead spent time outside of school with their peers.

On one hand, Polite (2000) notes that the predominantly White teaching force and the Black teachers at the schools all seemed to reflect upon the school's glory days (when the student body was mostly White) and how motivated those students and parents were compared to the parents and students in the school at the time of the study. They essentially thought student failure and teacher burnout were due to unmotivated parents, deficient home value systems, and academically unengaged African American students who did not understand the value of an education. On the other hand, the African American male students, including the successful ones, found many of the teachers to be uncaring and aloof, and less than interested in their education. As a response to this attitude, African Americans males, who often are on the brink, continued to lose interest in schooling, and this led to a host of other related, though not surprising issues, including school violence.

Although Polite (2000) does not intend for the results of his study to be generalized broadly, I think they present a familiar context, which we are "seeing in schools," but we are not really comprehending or analyzing this phenomenon in the context of the overall picture. For example, far too many teachers take the myopic view of the teachers at MHS. Sadly, though not surprisingly, many leaders, including African American assistant principals, adopt the aloof approach of the leaders in the study. Polite notes problems at the school level, but I would argue that these phenomena of failure are more universal than we sometimes consider at first glance. They are systemic, systematic, and historic. In other words, though many of our African American male students need to focus, be held accountable, and get the work done, institutional racism still plays a huge role.

Several scholars have noted how when we start to talk about the education of the African American male, we start with deficit thinking (Brown, 2011a; Brown, 2011b; Milner, 2010; Howard, 2010). This is systemic. Our methods are rooted in a one-size-fits-all paradigm, except for Black boys, whose place is somewhere other than the classroom. It might be because of their parents, their environment, or their intelligence, but we are reluctant to believe it is because of our teaching models and negative beliefs about their abilities in the classroom. Gregory (1997) sums it up, indeed, when he says that some students arrive with three strikes against them: Black, poor, and male. These are systemic issues and we have to earnestly address them throughout the system or we will continue to have pockets of chaos and success.

Our way of doing things is systematic and rooted in a history that is often repeated. As Polite illustrates, and other scholars have supported, African American males have been victims of deficit thinking of the past and their opportunities are truly impacted by this reality. Schooling was supposed to be done one way, and since White students of the past could followed this model better and have continued to do so at a more successful rate, then African American males were expected to adopt this model, regardless of cultural influences, and carry out learning the same way. That is how things work in a meritocracy—all should be treated equally. Well, history and law also teaches us that there are problems with this kind of thinking because of a history of discrimination in education and in other arenas in this country.

Although the law will provide some limited relief, it will avoid privileging African American males in any way, even in the context of the Fourteenth Amendment. There is the belief that the law was built on a set of race-neutral approaches, but as history and the need for the Fourteenth Amendment confirm, this is not true. However, affirmative action in K-12 and higher education settings makes it appear this way (Gooden & Downing, 2009; Daniel & Gooden, 2010). Berne and Steifel (1999) accurately note that equity is not the same as treating people equally; indeed, equity, which is different from equal educational opportunity, focuses on educational outcomes and results, and because children have different needs and come from different circumstances, we cannot treat them all the same.

If we start with this as our premise, then we have a chance at being successful in approaching the difficult job of educating African American males who might resist schooling because they just might doubt that it can be designed to actually work for them. They might even operate as part of an "ecology of resistance" and present multiple ways to avoid schooling altogether. However, these are not reasons to count them out of the educational environment. I would argue that in light of these reasons and the incredibly powerful systemic, systematic, and historic forces that crush their hopes and dreams, we must work very hard to convince them that despite these forces they have a chance and we will work hard to support them and their education.

References

Anderson, J. D. (1988). *The education of Blacks in the south, 1860–1935*. Chapel Hill: The University of North Carolina Press.

Bell, D. (2004). *Silent covenants: Brown v. Board of Education and the unfilled hopes for racial reform*. New York: Oxford University Press.

Berne, R., and Steifel, L. (1999). Concepts of school finance equity: In H. S. Ladd, R. S. Chalk, & J. S. Hansen (Eds.), *Equity and adequacy in education: Issues and perspectives* (pp. 7–33). Washington, DC: National Academy Press.

Board of Regents of the University System of Georgia, African American Initiative. (2011). Recruiting, retaining and graduating African American male students. Retrieved from http://www. usg.edu/aami/

Brown, A. L. (2011a). Pedagogies of experience: A case of the African American male teacher. *Teaching Education, 22*(4), 363–376.

Brown, A. L. (2011b). "Same old stories": The Black male in social science and educational literature, 1930s to the present. *Teachers College Record, 113* (9). 2047–2079.

Brown, F. (2004). The first serious implementation of *Brown*: The 1964 civil rights act and beyond. *Journal of Negro Education, 73*(3), 182–190.

Brown v. Board of Education, 347 U.S. 483 (1954).

Civil Rights Project at Harvard University. (2001). *Opportunities suspended: The devastating consequences of zero tolerance and school discipline policies.* Report by the Advancement Project and the Civil Rights Project. Cambridge, MA. Retrieved December 10, 2009, from http://www. civilrightsproject.ucla.edu/research/discipline/cover_tableofcontents.pdf and http://www. civilrightsproject.ucla.edu/research/discipline/final_report.pdf.

Daniel, P. T. K. & Gooden, M. A. (2010). Conflict on the United States Supreme Court: Judicial confusion and race-conscious school assignments. *Brigham Young University Education & Law Journal, 1*, 81.

Du Bois, W. E. B. (1903/1997). *The souls of Black folk.* Boston: Bedford Books.

Fitzgerald, T.D. (2009). Controlling the Black school-age male: Psychotropic medications and the circumvention of public law 94-142 and section 504. *Urban Education 44*(2), 225–247.

Gooden, M. A. (2004). A history of Black achievement as impacted by federal court decisions in the last century. *Journal of Negro Education, 73*(3), 230–237.

Gooden, M. A. and Downing, S. (2009). Affirmative action: Leveling the playing field. In D. Cleveland (Ed.), *When "minorities are encouraged to apply": Diversity and affirmative action in higher education* (pp. 225–239). New York: Peter Lang.

Goss v. Lopez, U.S. 95 S.Ct. 729 (1975).

Gregory, J. (1997). Three strikes and they're out: African American boys and American schools' responses to misbehavior. *International Journal of Adolescence and Youth, 7,* 25–34.

Grossman, H. (2002). *Ending discrimination in special education.* Springfield, IL: Charles C. Thomas.

Harris, C. I. (1995). Whiteness as property. In K. W. Crenshaw, N. Gotanda, G. Peller, & K. Thomas (Eds.). *Critical race theory: The key writings that formed the movement* (pp. 276–291). New York, NY: The New Press.

Howard, T .C. (2010). *Why race and culture matters in schools: Closing the achievement gap in America's classrooms.* New York: Teachers College Press.

Maryland State Department of Education, Maryland Task Force on the Education of African American Males (2003). Retrieved from http://www.google.com/search?q=Task+Force+on+t he+Education+of+African-American+Males&ie=utf-8&oe=utf-8&aq=t&rls=org.mozilla:en-US:official&client=firefox-a

McWhorter, J. H. (2000). Explaining the Black education gap. *Wilson Quarterly,* Summer 2000, *24*(3), 72–92.

Meiners, E. R. (2007). *Right to be hostile: Schools, prisons and the making of public enemies.* New York. Routledge.

Milner, H. R. (2010). What does teacher education have to do with teaching? Implications for diversity studies. *Journal of Teacher Education, 61*(1–2), 118–131.

Noguera, P. (2009). *The trouble with Black boys.* San Francisco: Jossey-Bass.

Norwood, K. J. (2008). Adult complicity in the dis-education of the Black male high school athlete & societal failures to remedy his plight. *Thurgood Marshall Law Review, 34,* 21–82.

Ogbu, J. U. (2003). *Black American students in an affluent suburb: A study of academic disengagement.* Mahwah, NJ: Lawrence Erlbaum.

Polite, V. C. (2000). When "at promise" Black males meet the "at-risk" school system: Chaos! In M. Christopher Brown and James E. Davis (Eds.). *Black sons to mothers: Compliments, critiques, and challenges for cultural workers in education* (pp. 219–245). New York: Peter Lang.

Schott Foundation for Public Education (2008). Given half a chance: The Schott 50 State Report on Public Education and Black Males. Retrieved from http://www.Blackboysreport.org/

Singer, J. W. (2009) Democratic estates: Property in a free and democratic society. *Cornell Law Review* 94 CNLLR 1009–1051.

South Carolina v. Katzenbach, 383 U.S. 301 (1966).

Tillman, L.C. (2004). (Un)intended consequences? The impact of the *Brown v. Board of Education* decision on the employment status of Black educators. *Education and Urban Society, 36*(3), 280–303.

Tyack, D., Anderson, J., Cuban, L., Kaestle, C., & Ravitch, D. (2002). *School: The story of American public education.* Boston: Beacon.

Watkins, W. (2001). *The White architects of Black education: Ideology and power in America, 1865–1954.* New York: Teachers College Press.

Chapter Seven

And Their Own Received Them Not

Black Gay Male Undergraduates' Experiences with White Racism, Black Homophobia

Terrell L. Strayhorn

In the preface to *We Real Cool: Black Men and Masculinity*, bell hooks (2004) states, "When [people] get together and talk about men, the news is almost always bad news. If the topic gets specific and they focus in on black men the news is even worse" (p. ix). Consider the national trends and often-cited statistics that illustrate the "bad news" about Black men in America. First, one-fourth of all Black Americans live below the federal poverty level, which is about twice the national rate; poverty rates are even higher among African American men, whose rate is three times that of non-Hispanic White men (Thompson & Parker, 2007). Black men are also disproportionately represented among the unemployed and undereducated. Specifically, 50% of Black men in their 20s are unemployed, and Black males have the highest high school dropout rate of both sexes and all racial/ethnic groups (Knaus, 2007). Less than 50% of Black males who start high school graduate within four years, compared to 75% of White males (Bridgeland, Dilulio, & Morison, 2006; Toldson, 2008).

Similarly, more than two-thirds of Black men who start college do not graduate within six years, which is the lowest completion rate among all groups (U.S. Department of Education, 2007). And since high-paying jobs typically require prior work experience or higher levels of education, Black men also tend to earn less in the labor market. For instance, Thompson and Parker (2007) calculated a median earnings index of 0.74, indicating that Black men are paid approximately $12,374 less annually than their White counterparts. Faced with limited, or at least restricted, opportunities for upward social mobility and economic prosperity in America, it may come as little surprise that Black males have the highest death rate of any other group and report low scores on most indices of overall well-being with the exception of obesity and exercise (Thompson & Parker, 2007). Indeed, as hooks (2004) concludes, the weight of evidence suggests that "despite all the advances in civil rights in our nation, feminist movement, sexual liberation, when the spotlight is on Black males the message is usually that they have managed to stay stuck, that as a group they have not evolved with the times" (p. ix).

In similar fashion, research has tended to emphasize the problems and predicaments of Black men but neglects and virtually omits a discussion of their successes. Recent scholarly treatments on Black men can be organized into two major categories: (a) those that examine the structural constraints on the chances of Black male success and (b) those that highlight behavioral barriers to Black male progress. An example of the former is *Race Matters* by Cornel West (1993). Dr. West's cogent contemplation of the moral and cultural crisis facing Black life in America reveals how stiff competition for jobs due to the entrance of new workers (i.e., immigrants and White women) into the labor force has limited the employment opportunities of Black (male) workers. In fact, he cites a statistic that 15% of Black men, aged 25–46, reported to the Census Bureau that they had earned $0 in the previous work year. All too often, West concludes, "the only option for such young Blacks is military enlistment" or lawless consumeristic tactics that promise temporary gain and disproportionately longer jail sentences (p. 81).

West's (1993) incisive analysis of what Myrdal (1944) termed the "Negro Problem in America" and Du Bois (1961) labeled the "problem of the color line" unmasks a sobering irony about Black male life in this country—just as Black men are unemployed, dropping out, imprisoned, and being killed in record numbers, their styles have become powerfully influential in pop culture. And despite their undeniable influence on the historical and present positioning of the "Land of the Free, Home of the Brave," very little is done systematically to redress (and address) the savage inequities that cascade over time, yielding long-term inequalities that profoundly affect Black male life in America. Indeed, most sociopolitical responses—whether produced by the media or politicians—seem to downplay the social nightmares faced by Black male youth while praising the viability of the "American Dream," a political ideology to which few Black men subscribe (Hochschild, 1995; Isaacs, 2007).

Another example of scholarship that casts a critical gaze at the structural constraints on Black male progress is Ann Arnett Ferguson's (2000) *Bad Boys: Public Schools in the Making of Black Masculinity*. Ferguson draws upon three years of fieldwork and reveals how "school labeling practices and the exercise of rules operated as part of a hidden curriculum to marginalize and isolate Black male youth in disciplinary spaces and brand them as criminally inclined" (p. 2). She explains how school practices and socialization processes track African American male children into prison through punishment. In her study, African American boys represent only one-fourth of students at Rosa Parks Elementary School, yet they accounted for nearly 50% of students sent to the Punishing Room. Her statistics reflect the predicament of Black male youth nationally in schools; I have noted elsewhere that Black male youth are overrepresented among those suspended or expelled from school (Strayhorn, 2008e).

Moreover, Ferguson (2000) points out that it is not the behaviors of Black males that distinguish them from their peers; she acknowledges that *some* Black male youth talk out of turn, yell at teachers, and use profanity like all other kids. Rather it is the meanings assigned to and consequences of such acts that are different, greater, more severe for young Black men. Essentially, school professionals, teachers, and peers do not give Black boys the same latitude afforded their non-Black and female counterparts when it comes to "acting up," "playing around," "goofing off," "acting White," or "just being a boy." Under such pressures, "many [Black] Schoolboys disidentify with school and join the ranks of the Troublemakers by the time they get into high school because of this tug of war [between proving one's masculinity to peers while demonstrating one's academic prowess to teachers]" (Ferguson, 2000, p. 215). And the author problematizes the demotion from Schoolboy to Troublemaker by pointing out that "there are serious, long-term effects of being labeled a Troublemaker that substantially increase one's chances of ending up in jail" (p. 230). Once a boy is labeled a Troublemaker, he is more likely to be banished from the classroom, to be expelled from school, or to drop out of high school, which increases the likelihood of being unemployed, dependent on social welfare, and, ultimately, imprisoned, or so the cycle goes (Martin & Halperin, 2006).

To be sure, I understand the importance of documenting the "bad news" and indelible scars left by lack of adequate social and policy attention to the crisis facing Black male youth (The College Board, 2010) as some of my own research has done that work (e.g., Strayhorn, 2008c, 2008d, 2009). Still, we must not confine or restrict our conversations to the "problems" and "pathologies" vocabulary. Such a paralyzing framework shines light on the issues that Black men face in America (as if they were the only ones with issues) yet suffocates the successes and, perhaps most important, the underlying conditions that give rise to the "bad news" which is often talked about but rarely alleviated. Structuralist arguments also tend to treat Black men as a monolithic group of individuals whose experiences are more similar than different. Yet, not all Black men are unemployed, hail from low-income urban families, or drop out of high school. Not all Black men identify with enactments of hegemonic, patriarchal notions of (Black) masculinity or identify as heterosexual (Harper & Nichols, 2008; Majors & Billson, 1992; Staples, 1982); some identify as Black gay men (BGM) although the presence and experiences of BGM are virtually silent in the existing literature on Black male life in America. For example, with the exception of his abbreviated mention of the predicament of Black gay men whose rejection of normative Black masculinity leaves them marginalized in White America and ridiculed in Black America, West's (1993) analysis in *Race Matters* proceeds without any specific mention of BGM.

Purpose of the Chapter

Much more information is needed about the experiences of BGM in American society and within educational contexts, particularly insights that can be used to identify new or improve existing policies and programs that address the critical needs of Black male youth. To do this, research findings are needed that both unearth the academic and social challenges that BGM undergraduates (BGMUs) face in various contexts and unpack the possible ways educators can support such students. This chapter was designed with these purposes in mind. Before describing the study and presenting its major findings, I review the extant literature on BGMUs in the next section.

Prior Research on Black Gay Male Undergraduates

Since there is comparatively little written specifically about BGMUs, literature on lesbian, gay, bisexual, and transgendered (LGBT) persons in general was drawn upon to inform this study. Research on LGBT adolescents and college students is largely theoretical, with particular accents on "constructed" identities (Abes & Jones, 2004; Dilley, 2005; Fassinger, 1998) and developmental experiences of such students (Fassinger, 1991; Renn & Bilodeau, 2005). Still others have focused on the process by which individuals come to understand themselves as gay or "homosexual" and how such understandings are reconciled with previously held perceptions of self (Cass, 1979, 1984; D'Augelli, 1994). For example, Cass (1979) identified six stages through which gay individuals struggle to resolve conflicts and tensions between perceptions of self and others when forming a homosexual identity: (a) identity confusion, (b) identity comparison, (c) identity tolerance, (d) identity acceptance, (e) identity pride, and (f) identity synthesis. All of this research, however, has proceeded without giving specific attention to the experiences of Black men who identify, privately or publicly, as gay.

As I have noted elsewhere (Strayhorn, in press), only recently have scholars turned a critical gaze to the lived experiences of BGM in general and BGMUs in particular. For instance, some books and chapters that estimate the number of BGM in America describe the challenges they face being "Black, gay, and male" as well as highlight the factors that lead some BGM to lead public lives as "assumed heterosexuals" and privates *lives of quiet desperation*, quoting Henry David

Thoreau (1971), as men on the down low or "DL" (King, 2004). Other publications document Black males' experiences with social pathologies (e.g., racism, homophobia)—negative experiences that often stymie development (Harris, 2003; Washington & Wall, 2006).

Black gays face racism within the broader gay community, which tends to be predominantly White (Boykin, 1996). For example, Black gays report race-based discrimination among White LGBT people in gay bars, clubs, social parties, and even online dating sites (Adams & Kimmel, 1997; Brown, 2008). Consequently, Boykin (1996) said plainly, "The dirty little secret about the homosexual population is that White gay people are just as racist as White straight people" (p. 234).

Also, Black gays encounter covert and overt forms of homophobia or negative beliefs about homosexuality within the African American community, which tends to subscribe to conservative views about gender expression, religion, and sexuality (Greene, 1994; Herek & Capitanio, 1995). This is especially true for Black gay men (Icard, 1986), although African Americans' attitudes toward gay men vary by gender with Black females expressing more positive feelings than Black males (Battle & Lemelle, 2002). hooks (1989) rightly concluded, "Often Black gay folk feel extremely isolated because there are tensions in their relationship with the larger, predominantly White gay community created by racism and tensions within Black communities around issues of homophobia" (p. 125).

Another segment of research consists of empirical studies centering on several major foci related to BGM and BGMUs. One group of studies examines issues of sexual orientation and racial identity (Brown, 2008; Icard, 1986) and whether and how BGM identify sexually (Brown, 2005). For instance, Brown (2005) employed a case study approach to analyze qualitative data from 110 African American men in Atlanta. And although all of his male participants indicated that they have sex with men, relatively few identified as gay (37%); 13% identified as "down low bisexual," 9% as bisexual, 7% as homosexual, and even 17% as straight. He rightly concluded that Black gay men cannot accept a gay identity for three reasons: homophobia, heterosexism, and constructions of Black masculinity. Scholars of BGMUs have tended to focus on factors influencing their college choice (Strayhorn, Blakewood, & DeVita, 2008) and their social experiences at predominantly White institutions (Strayhorn, 2012). For instance, Strayhorn, Blakewood, and DeVita (2008) conducted an exploratory qualitative study of African American gay male undergraduates at a single predominantly White institution. Semi-structured interviews with 7 self-identified BGMUs revealed that they went to college to "come out" and, therefore, considered the location of the school when choosing a college. Additionally, participants identified supportive relationships with peers and family members, self-determination, and independence as critical to their success in college.

Given the importance of personal/individual and social factors to the developmental experiences of LGBT persons, it seemed important to consider how such factors relate to the lived experiences of LGBT adolescents in general and gay men in particular. To do so, I employed D'Augelli's (1991, 1994) gay identity development model, which provided constructs for talking about the experiences of BGMUs in the study upon which this chapter is based.

Theoretical Framework

Recent research adds empirical evidence supporting the fact that sexual identification is a complex, dynamic process, which is inextricably influenced by social psychological factors such as gender, gender identity, culture, and environment (Renn & Bilodeau, 2005). Thus, theoretical models that descibe the (homo)sexual identity formation process as separate from the psychosocial and/or sociocultural context are insufficient for describing the development of such individuals over a lifetime. One plausible alternative, however, is D'Augelli's (1994) model of gay identity development.

D'Augelli (1994) identified six developmental processes by which individuals come to assume a homosexual identity. The six processes are: (a) exiting heterosexual identity (i.e., acknowledging the self as non-heterosexual and understanding one's attractions); (b) developing a personal LGBT identity (i.e., learning how to be non-heterosexual from LGBT persons and challenging internalized myths about homosexuality); (c) developing an LGBT social identity (i.e., developing a network of people who know one's orientation and upon whom one can rely to provide support); (d) becoming LGBT offspring (i.e., focusing on the nature of family relationships and the role of "coming out"); (e) developing an LGBT intimacy status (i.e., establishing a meaningful relationship where emotional intimacy is expressed); and (f) entering an LGBT community (i.e., [re]development of a commitment to political and social action; the process of challenging social barriers). D'Augelli's model is rooted in a human development "life span" perspective that is context-contingent. Consequently, no two people travel the same developmental path and developmental processes may occur simultaneously or more independently. The model holds significant assumptions about the ways in which individuals come to understand and accept their LGBT identity, and I examine these assumptions below.

The Study

This chapter draws upon data from an ongoing study of BGMUs at predominantly White institutions (PWIs). Although the larger study consists of responses from a multi-institutional sample of BGMUs at PWIs and historically Black colleges and universities (HBCUs), this chapter is based upon a single institution for which complete data were readily available. The campus is best described as a large, public research-extensive land grant university that offers multiple venues for student involvement on campus, ranging from student government to intramural sports, fraternities to an LGBT student association. At the time of the study, the university enrolled approximately 30,000 students, 49% of whom were men; and just under 8% were African American according to the university's institutional research unit. More information about the study has been published elsewhere (e.g., Strayhorn, Blakewood, & DeVita, 2008).

A total of nine participants provided information that formed the basis of this chapter. All participants were enrolled full-time; academic majors ranged from Spanish to opera, finance to psychology. Participants were involved in a number of campus organizations: dance, cheerleading, college Democrats, to name a few. To elicit information about BGMUs' experiences, I worked with members of my research team to develop an interview protocol that consisted of several major questions and a few minor probes. For instance, participants were asked, "What has college been like for you?" Probes encouraged participants to "describe a time when. . ." or "tell us more about. . .," in consonance with techniques recommended by qualitative experts (Kvale, 1996). Semi-structured one-on-one interviews were the primary method of data collection; each interview lasted 90 to 120 minutes, on average. Data analysis proceeded in several stages using the constant comparison method outlined by Glaser and Strauss (1999). In short, the analytic process consisted of identifying a preliminary set of codes using a form of open coding, comparing and contrasting initial codes to determine whether different words or phrases could be combined or collapsed into similar categories, and then sorting categories and codes into major themes (for more, see Strayhorn, Blakewood, & DeVita, 2008).

Key Findings

Three major themes were identified: establishing a sense of belonging, coming out in college, and experiencing racism and homophobia. Supportive relationships with peers, family members, and particular educators were identified as a vital source of the support needed to manage the challenges that BGM face in college contexts. These findings are discussed briefly here, using verbatim quotes from participants to illustrate the meaning and significance of each theme. In all cases, self-selected pseudonyms are used in the place of real names to ensure confidentiality of all participants.

Establishing a Sense of Belonging

Almost all participants noted that it was difficult to feel a sense of belonging to the institution at which they were enrolled. Due to negative social experiences, most participants reported a sense of "betweenness" as a BGM attending a PWI. For instance, BGMs in our study did not necessarily feel strong ties to the university or to their gay or same-race peers. Desmond, a 19-year-old psychology and public relations double major, provided an explanation that reflects the essence of what other participants shared:

> I guess. . . it's like I came here expecting college to be this life-changing experience. . . and it was or it is. And, I expected to get away from [my hometown] where I would be around more open-minded people and feel free to be myself. But. . . . Well, for starters, the people here are not necessarily more open-minded.

Not only did study participants describe their peers as close minded, but several participants reported difficulty finding friends who share their interests and experiences. Desmond said:

> It's just difficult to find friends that are like you. . . Black, gay men who want to do more than have sex. And that's been the most difficult challenge. . . but I've made friends with Black females and tried to focus on other things like [involvement in ethnic student organizations] and stuff.

Coming Out in College

"Coming out" was another challenge expressed by participants, although all said they went to college to "come out" and live out (i.e., live openly as gay men). Lawrence said: "Coming to college was basically coming out for me because back home only a select few knew." Similarly, Desmond explained further:

> I mean I came here to be out to myself and my close friends. . . I was out a little in high school but I couldn't be myself at home in [my hometown] around my mom and godmom and all of them. I knew I needed to get away—far away—to be comfortable being me. But it's hard being Black and gay at [this college].

These statements reflect perspectives held by several others in our study—that college is a time of self-discovery, new beginnings, and self-disclosure of one's sexual identity (i.e., coming out), although the campus environment may pose challenges that must be overcome for one to assume his sexual identity.

Experiencing White Racism and Black Homophobia

Lastly, a major finding of this study was that participants described two social pathologies that negatively influenced their collegiate experiences—(White) racism and (Black) homophobia. Participants described enduring racist comments (e.g., "Black people are lazy") or hearing racist slurs (e.g., "nigger jokes") when interacting with their White peers, White *gay* peers, or associates of their White friends. Participants also experienced sexual harassment and violence (i.e., verbal or physical) by same-race, heterosexual peers because of their sexual orientation. Consider the following:

I had a bad experience here when I was sort of dating a White guy. He was like I can't date you anymore and I was just like, why? He said because you're Black. I was just like, okay, this is really bad, like, I'm going to ruin your reputation. . . so I mean that's been like a negative side of my dating. (Betsy)

First of all, because I've not been around a lot of other Black people, it's like I'm normally attracted to White guys only. . . but that doesn't mean all of them are attracted to me. One time I was dating this White guy and we went to hang out with his friends one night. When they met me, his one friend said, "Hey Chuck, I didn't know you were dating niggers now." Then, he tried to laugh it off and say he was only kidding. (Blake)

I can't count them all right now but easily almost all of my friends are White. . . and if they aren't they certainly aren't Black guys because most Black guys are ignorant about hanging out with gay guys. . . thinking you're always trying to date them (laughing). (Leon)

There were other examples of Black homophobia. Quinn became quite emotional when describing how other Black men on campus "act a little undignified toward [him]"; he said:

People might make a comment like people saying I'm gay. But yeah, from Black people, it's been, like mad snide comments. Because gay in the African American community, it seems, to most Black people, it's even like greater fault than. . . I don't know. Black guys really don't take too well to it. And they're really heinous sometimes about it. They always say stuff like "You fu*king faggot."

Desmond's earlier quote goes on to address this issue as well:

I guess. . . it's like I came here expecting college to be this life-changing experience. . . and it was or it is. And, I expected to get away from [my hometown] where I would be around more open-minded people and feel free to be myself. But. . . . Well, for starters, the people here are not necessarily more open-minded. You're mistreated sometimes if you're Black and then you're threatened or something if you're gay.

Despite experiences with White racism and Black homophobia, BGM in our study tended to be more comfortable with White gay men and Black straight women than their same-race male counterparts. For instance, Lamont shared how his White gay friends helped him:

Like, I've got lots of White gay friends. . . I have quite a few friends that came [to this college] from home. I came knowing a lot of people, a good amount, and I know people that don't go to the university, but they live in [the local area]. And they've been to the university so they understand what it's like. And I've got some friends that I've met here and they're part of my support group.

Some participants in our study, however, confessed having Black heterosexual female friends who they were "really close with." Quinn's remark reflects the spirit of comments made by others:

> But yeah, during like, my scholarship meetings and we'd have to do community service projects and what not. You know, I would find a Black girl to hang out with. I'd attach myself to a girl and we'd have fun and, you know, buddy up.

Perhaps surprisingly, very few participants reported having other Black gay male friends and only two claimed to know another BGMU on campus. Still, having White gay male and Black straight female friends with whom they could communicate about their experiences and upon whom they could rely for advice was a necessary source of support for BGM in the present study.

Implications for College Educators and Cultural Workers

It has been said elsewhere (Brown & Davis, 2000) that educators are mothers and the act of mothering is a form of cultural work (Freire, 1998). Thus, what is needed is a lens for viewing teaching as mothering and mothering as cultural work. To this end, I borrow the concept of othermothering or cultural guardianship, found in African American feminist literature, to illuminate the nurturing and cross-familial habits of care found largely in the African American culture (Case, 1997; Collins, 2000). Othermothering has three major components: (a) the manner in which the *ethic of care* is transmitted, (b) *cultural advancement* or a shared responsibility to improve the lives of African American children through individual actions, and (c) *institutional guardianship*, which refers to the pervasive belief that Black institutions should be protected and preserved at all times (Case, 1997). Although the concept of othermothering originally focused on women's relationships with young children in the Black community, it has evolved over time to be a useful interpretive frame for understanding the ways in which both men and women form relationships with Black collegians (e.g., Fries-Britt & Turner, 2002) and HBCU students (e.g., Hirt, Amelink, Bennett, & Strayhorn, 2008). Here I apply the concept of othermothering to the findings presented in the section above to offer three recommendations about the roles that educators can play as cultural workers when helping BGMUs succeed in college.

First, BGM participants expressed difficulty establishing a sense of belonging on campus as a result of feeling "betwixt and between" (Strayhorn, 2008a) two worlds, neither in which they were able to integrate fully. Previous research suggests that sense of belonging is an important determinant of success, as students with a more developed sense of belonging are more likely to persist in college, less likely to experience depression, and report higher degrees of social and psychological functioning (e.g., Hagerty, Williams, Coyne, & Early, 1996; Sargent, Williams, Hagerty, Lynch-Bauer, & Hoyle, 2002). Thus, educators might act as *guardians* to BGMUs. By helping BGMUs resolve some of the tensions they feel as they negotiate two very different "worlds," educators can fulfill their roles as protectors or advisors who facilitate the academic achievement of their academic offspring, translated "students." Additionally, it is important for educators to make time for students, in this case BGMUs, which may help them feel included in the campus community. No matter how busy they get, educators should carve out room on their calendars for such students to talk about their experiences in college, identify challenges they face, and help them find support, if necessary, to balance the competing demands with which they wrestle.

Second, managing the "coming out" process was another challenge cited in the study that formed the basis of this chapter. And although almost all participants indicated that they went (away) to college to come out, more than half talked about moving away from biological family members (e.g., parents) to disclose their sexual orientation to close friends, other LGBT people, and significant others; the last three groups, in a few instances, served as a new "gay family"—individuals upon whom BGM could rely for advice and support. That some BGM establish family-like relationships with other LGBT people, most of whom are White, after moving away from their biological family makes intuitive sense, especially when considered in light of the fact some Black parents reject or sever ties with their LGBT children at the moment of disclosure or discovery (Battle & Bennett, 2000). Educators and cultural workers should consider this information when working with BGMUs and LGBT students who are struggling to assume their gay identity. Without an *ethic of care* that gives attention to their concerns and lived experiences, BGM are left to go it alone, thereby greatly increasing the odds of their leaving college.

Lastly, BGMUs reported experiencing racial discrimination from White gay peers and homophobia (i.e., unwarranted antagonism due to their sexual orientation) from Black male peers. In fact, this finding inspired the title of this chapter, which reflects the notion that BGMUs in our study were rejected by "their own" on two fronts. Though gay, they faced rejection (i.e., racism) from White gays and, though Black, BGMUs faced rejection (i.e., homophobia) from Black males. Literally, their own received them not. Encountering racism and homophobia breeds feelings of isolation, loneliness, and lack of support (Sutton & Kimbrough, 2001), thereby inhibiting students' performance, which may lead to attrition (e.g., Clewell & Ficklen, 1986; Strayhorn, 2008b). Thus, educators and cultural workers might engage in a constellation of activities to assist BGMUs in their development. For instance, by helping BGMUs filter racist and/or homophobic messages, educators can challenge negative stereotypes, interrupt misinformed perspectives, speak out against injustice, and promote positive identity formation while working with students. Educating the broader campus community on issues of sexual identity development, LGBT populations, and LGBT communities of color; implementing policies that seek to eliminate racism and other forms of discrimination on campus; as well as building spaces on campus where BGMUs can engage with their LGBT and/or same-race peers in educationally meaningful ways will likely improve the climate conditions on campus. In this way, educators can demonstrate their abiding commitment to *cultural advancement.*

In *The State of Black America,* President Barack Obama (2007) states, "The failure of our policies to recognize black men as husbands, fathers, sons, and role models is being acknowledged, and we need a new ethic of compassion to break the cycle of educational failure, unemployment, absentee fatherhood, incarceration, and recidivism" (p. 11). Indeed, this chapter was designed to give voice to the experiences of BGMUs, who are often unacknowledged in the literature and unaddressed in our policies. Adopting educational practices consistent with othermothering and understanding their role as cultural workers, educators can break the cycle of "bad news" about Black men by replacing a checklist of complaints with a catalog of compliments, an ethos of confusion with an ethic of compassion, and a gloomy past riddled by troubling statistics with a bright and promising future.

References

Abes, E. S., & Jones, S. R. (2004). Meaning-making capacity and the dynamics of lesbian college students' multiple dimensions of identity. *Journal of College Student Development, 45,* 612–632.

Adams, C. L., & Kimmel, D. C. (1997). Exploring the lives of older African American gay men. In B. Greene (Ed.), *Ethnic and cultural diversity among lesbian and gay men* (pp. 132–151). Thousand Oaks, CA: Sage Publications.

Battle, J., & Bennett, M. (2000). Research on lesbian and gay populations within the African American community: What have we learned? *African American Research Perspectives, 6*(2), 35–47.

Battle, J., & Lemelle, A. J., Jr. (2002). Gender differences in African American attitudes toward gay males. *Western Journal of Black Studies, 26*(3), 134–139.

Boykin, K. (1996). *One more river to cross: Black and gay in America.* New York: Bantam Doubleday Dell.

Bridgeland, J. M., Dilulio, J. J., Jr., & Morison, K. B. (2006, March). *The silent epidemic: Perspectives of high school dropouts.* Washington, DC: Civic Enterprises, LLC.

Brown, C. E., III. (2008). *Racism in the gay community and homophobia in the Black community: Negotiating the gay Black male experience.* Unpublished master's thesis, Virginia Tech, Blacksburg, VA.

Brown, E., II. (2005). We wear the mask: African American contemporary gay male identities. *Journal of African American Studies, 9*(2), 29–38.

Brown, M. C., II, & Davis, J. E. (Eds.). (2000). *Black sons to mothers: Compliments, critiques, and challenges for cultural workers in education.* New York: Peter Lang.

Case, K. I. (1997). African American othermothering in the urban elementary school. *The Urban Review, 29*(1), 26–39.

Cass, V. C. (1979). Homosexuality identity formation: A theoretical model. *Journal of Homosexuality, 4*(3), 219–235.

Cass, V. C. (1984). Homosexuality identity formation: Testing a theoretical model. *Journal of Sex Research, 9*(1–2), 105–126.

Clewell, B. C., & Ficklen, M. S. (1986). *Improving minority retention in higher education: A search for effective institutional practices.* Princeton, NJ: Educational Testing Service.

Collins, P. (2000). *Black feminist thought: Knowledge, consciousness, and the politics of empowerment* (2nd ed.). New York: Routledge.

D'Augelli, A. R. (1991). Gay men in college: Identity processes and adaptations. *Journal of College Student Development, 32,* 140–146.

D'Augelli, A. R. (1994). Identity development and sexual orientation: Toward a model of lesbian, gay, and bisexual development. In E. J. Trickett, R. J. Watts & D. Birman (Eds.), *Human diversity: Perspectives on people in context* (pp. 312–333). San Francisco: Jossey-Bass.

Dilley, P. (2005). Which way out? A typology of non-heterosexual male collegiate identities. *Journal of Higher Education, 76,* 56–88.

Du Bois, W. E. B. (1961). *The soul of Black folk: Essays and sketches.* Greenwich, CT: Fawcett Publications.

Fassinger, R. E. (1991). The hidden minority: Issues and challenges in working with lesbian women and gay men. *Counseling Psychologist, 19,* 157–176.

Fassinger, R. E. (1998). Lesbian and bisexual identity and student development theory. In R. L. Sanlo (Ed.), *Working with lesbian, gay, bisexual and transgender college students: A handbook for faculty and administrators* (pp. 13–22). Westport, CT: Greenwood Press.

Ferguson, A. A. (2000). *Bad boys: Public schools in the making of Black male masculinity.* Ann Arbor: The University of Michigan Press.

Freire, P. (1998). *Teachers as cultural workers: Letters to those who dare to teach.* Boulder, CO: Westview.

Fries-Britt, S., & Turner, B. (2002). Uneven stories: Successful Black collegians at Black and White campuses. *Review of Higher Education, 25,* 315–330.

Glaser, B. G., & Strauss, A. L. (1999). *The discovery of grounded theory: Strategies for qualitative research.* New York: Aldine De Gruyter.

Greene, B. (1994). Ethnic-minority lesbians and gay men: Mental health and treatment issues. *Journal of Consulting and Clinical Psychology, 62,* 243–251.

Hagerty, B. M. K., Williams, R. A., Coyne, J. C., & Early, M. R. (1996). Sense of belonging and indicators of social and psychological functioning. *Archives of Psychiatric Nursing, 10*(4), 235–244.

Harper, S. R., & Nichols, A. H. (2008). Are they not all the same? Racial heterogeneity among Black male undergraduates. *Journal of College Student Development, 49*(3), 199–214

Harris, W. G. (2003). African American homosexual males on predominantly White college and university campuses. *Journal of African American Studies, 7*(1), 47–56.

Herek, G. M., & Capitanio, J. (1995). Black heterosexuals' attitudes towards lesbians and gay men in the United States. *The Journal of Sex Research, 32,* 95–105.

Hirt, J. B., Amelink, C. T., Bennett, B. R., & Strayhorn, T. L. (2008). A system of othermothering: Relationships between student affairs administrators and students at historically Black colleges and universities. *The NASPA Journal, 45*(2), 210–236.

Hochschild, J. L. (1995). *Facing up to the American dream: Race, class, and the soul of the nation.* Princeton, NJ: Princeton University Press.

hooks, b. (1989). *Talking back: Thinking feminist, thinking Black.* Boston: South End Press.

hooks, b. (2004). *We real cool: Black men and masculinity.* New York: Routledge.

Icard, L. (1986). Black gay men and conflicting social identities: Sexual orientation versus racial identity. *Journal of Social Work and Human Sexuality, 4*(1–2), 83–93.

Isaacs, J. B. (2007, November). *Economic mobility of Black and White families.* Washington, DC: The Pew Charitable Trusts.

King, J. L. (2004). *On the down low: A journey into the lives of "straight" Black men who sleep with men.* New York: Harlem Moon.

Knaus, C. (2007). Still segregated, still unequal: Analyzing the impact of No Child Left Behind on African American students. In S. J. Jones, L. B. Malone, R. Jefferson-Frazier, V. R. Wilson, R. V. Sharpe & M. McArdle (Eds.), *The state of Black America 2007: Portrait of the Black male* (pp. 105–121). New York: Beckham Publications Group, Inc.

Kvale, S. (1996). *InterViews: An introduction to qualitative research interviewing*. Thousand Oaks: Sage.

Majors, R., & Billson, J. (1992). *Cool pose: The dilemmas of Black manhood in America*. New York: Touchstone.

Martin, N., & Halperin, S. (2006). *Whatever it takes: How twelve communities are reconnecting out-of-school youth*. Washington, DC: American Youth Policy Forum.

Myrdal, G. (1944). *An American dilemma: The Negro problem and modern democracy*. New York: Harper.

Obama, B. H. (2007). Foreword. In S. J. Jones, L. B. Malone, R. Jefferson-Frazier, V. R. Wilson, R. V. Sharpe & M. McArdle (Eds.), *The state of Black America 2007: Portrait of the Black male* (pp. 9–12). New York: Beckham Publications Group, Inc.

Renn, K. A., & Bilodeau, B. L. (2005). Leadership identity development among lesbian, gay, bisexual, and transgender student leaders. *The NASPA Journal, 42*(3).

Sargent, J., Williams, R. A., Hagerty, B. M. K., Lynch-Bauer, J., & Hoyle, K. (2002). Sense of belonging as a buffer against depressive symptoms. *Journal of the American Psychiatric Nurses Association, 8*, 120–129.

Staples, R. (1982). *Black masculinity: The Black male's role in American society*. San Francisco: Black Scholar Press.

Strayhorn, T. L. (2008a). *Betwixt and between: To be young, gifted, gay, and Black at a White institution*. Paper presented at the National Conference on Race and Ethnicity in American Higher Education (NCORE), Orlando, FL.

Strayhorn, T. L. (2008b). Fittin' In: Do diverse interactions with peers affect sense of belonging for Black men at predominantly White institutions? *The NASPA Journal, 45*(4), 501–527.

Strayhorn, T. L. (2008c). Influences on labor market outcomes of African American college graduates: A national study. *The Journal of Higher Education, 79*(1), 29–57.

Strayhorn, T. L. (2008d). The invisible man: Factors affecting the retention of low-income African American males. *National Association of Student Affairs Professionals Journal, 11*(1), 66–87.

Strayhorn, T. L. (2008e). Teachers' expectations and urban Black males' success in school: Implications for academic leaders [Electronic Version]. *Academic Leadership Journal, 6*. Retrieved June 1, 2008 from http://www.academicleadership.org/emprical_research/Teacher_Expectations_and_Urban_Black_Males_Success_in_School_Implications_for_Academic_Leaders.shtml.

Strayhorn, T. L. (2009). Different folks, different hopes: The educational aspirations of Black males in urban, suburban, and rural high schools. *Urban Education, 44*(6), 710–731.

Strayhorn, T. L. (2012). *College students' sense of belonging: A key to educational success*. New York, NY: Routledge.

Strayhorn, T. L. (in press). Coming out, fitting in: Interrogating the social experiences of black gay males at white cholleges. In M. E. Dancy and M. C. Brown (Eds.) *African American males and education: Researching the convergence of race and identities*. Charlotte, NC: Information Age.

Strayhorn, T. L., Blakewood, A. M., & DeVita, J. M. (2008). Factors affecting the college choice of African American gay male undergraduates: Implications for retention. *National Association of Student Affairs Professionals Journal, 11*(1), 88–108.

Sutton, E. M., & Kimbrough, W. M. (2001). Trends in Black student involvement. *NASPA Journal, 39*(1), 30–40.

The College Board. (2010, January). *The educational crisis facing young men of color: Reflections on four days of dialogue on the educational challenges of minority males*. New York: Author.

Thompson, R., & Parker, S. (2007). The National Urban League Equality Index. In S. J. Jones, L. B. Malone, R. Jefferson-Frazier, V. R. Wilson, R. V. Sharpe & M. McArdle (Eds.), *The state of Black America 2007: Portrait of the Black male* (pp. 17–58). New York: Beckham Publications Group, Inc.

Thoreau, H. D. (1971). *Walden*. Princeton, NJ: Princeton University Press.

Toldson, I. A. (2008). *Breaking barriers: Plotting the path to academic success for school-age African American males*. Washington, DC: Congressional Black Caucus Foundation, Inc.

U.S. Department of Education, National Center for Education Statistics. (2007). *The condition of education 2007* (NCES 2007). Washington, DC: U.S. Government Printing Office.

Washington, J., & Wall, V. A. (2006). African American gay men: Another challenge for the academy. In M. J. Cuyjet & Associates (Eds.), *African American men in college* (pp. 174–188). San Francisco: Jossey-Bass.

West, C. (1993). *Race matters*. New York: Vintage Books.

Chapter Eight

Barriers to Persistence for Black Male Collegians at an Historically Black University

An Exploratory Study

Robert T. Palmer

A strong body of research has shown that historically Black colleges and universities (HBCUs) provide a family-oriented environment (Allen, Jewell, Griffin, & Wolf, 2007; Brown & Davis, 2001; Fleming, 1984; Fries-Britt & Turner, 2002; Palmer & Gasman, 2008), facilitate cultural empowerment (Fleming, 1984; Freeman, 2005; Freeman & Thomas, 2002), engender interest in attending graduate or professional school (Allen 1992; Brown & Davis, 2001; Perna, 2001; Roebuck & Murty, 1993; Wenglinsky, 1996), and foster academic success (Brown & Davis, 2001; Davis, 1994; Fleming, 1984; Fries-Britt & Tuner, 2002; Palmer & Gasman, 2008). For these reasons, many have praised the positive impact that HBCUs have on Black students. In fact, Pascarella and Terenzini (1991) explained:

> Much evidence. . . suggests that Black students who attend predominantly White colleges and universities experience significantly greater levels of social isolation, alienation, personal dissatisfaction, and overt racism than their counterparts at historically Black institutions. . . Given this evidence, one might hypothesize that attendance at historically Black colleges enhances the persistence and educational attainment of Black students, and indeed most evidence supports this hypothesis. (p. 462)

Some research has shown that given the chronic funding disparities between HBCUs and their predominantly White institutional counterparts (PWIs), the impact that HBCUs have on Black students is particularly compelling (Allen et al., 2007; Brown & Davis, 2001; Palmer & Gasman, 2008; Kim, 2002).

Notwithstanding the effect that HBCUs have on Black students, recent research has shown a gender disparity between Black males and females as it relates to the number of students attending HBCUs as well as PWIs (Dancy & Brown, 2008). While data from the National Center for Education Statistics (NCES) show that this gender disparity is applicable to other racial and ethnic groups, it is more severe among Black students. For example, according to the NCES in 2004, the postsecondary enrollment gender gap of Blacks reached 28.6%, compared to a gap of just 8.7% in 1976 (NCES, 2007). Over the same time period, the gender gap was substantially smaller among other racial and ethnic groups. Specifically, among White, Asian, and Hispanic males and females, the gender gap in college enrollment was 11.8%, 7.5%, and 17.1% in 2004, and 4.7%, 8.6%, and 7.6%, in 1976, respectively (NCES, 2007).

Not only are HBCUs experiencing a gender disparity among enrolled students, but some are grappling with low graduation rates and persistence rates among Black students. Interestingly, an article in *Diverse Issues in Higher Education* noted that according to analysis of government data by the Associated Press of 83 federally designated four-year HBCUs, 37% of Black students graduate within six years, which is 4% percent lower than the national graduation rate for Black students. Research indicates that Black males are a major reason for HBCUs' dismal graduation rate, with only 29% completing a baccalaureate degree within six years (Pope, 2009). Other scholars (e.g., Dancy & Brown, 2008; Harper & Gasman, 2008; Roach, 2001) have highlighted the low persistence rates among Black males at HBCUs. More specifically, Kimbrough and Harper (2006) noted that Black females are graduating from HBCUs at rates two to three times higher than their male counterparts. Given this issue, many HBCUs are intently focused on investigating ways to increase retention and persistence rates for their Black male collegians. To this end, this chapter seeks to provide an additional resource to positively impact Black male retention and persistence. Specifically, this chapter will discuss barriers to retention and persistence of Black males and discuss tactics that student affairs could employ to enhance outcomes.

Purpose of the Study

The contemporary literature provides only a few studies of the experiences of Black men at HBCUs. Interestingly, while numerous researchers have focused on the experiences of Blacks at PWIs (Bonner & Bailey; 2006; Brown, 2006; Dancy & Brown, 2008; Fries-Britt, 1997, 1998; Fries-Britt & Griffin, 2007; Fries-Britt & Turner, 2001; Griffin, 2006; Guiffrida, 2003, 2004, 2005; Harper, 2005, 2006a, 2006b, 2008, 2009; Harper & Nichols, 2008; Harper & Quaye,

2007; Patton, 2006; Strayhorn, 2008), recent research on Black male collegians is lacking (e.g., Harper, Carini, Bridges, & Hayek, 2004; Harper & Gasman, 2008; Kimbrough & Harper, 2006; Lundy-Wagner & Gasman, 2011; Palmer, Davis, & Hilton, 2009; Palmer & Gasman, 2008; Palmer & Strayhorn, 2008; Palmer & Young, 2009). Consequently, Kimbrough and Harper (2006) called for more attention to be paid to Black males at HBCUs. In particular, they noted "with much of the national attention being placed on issues facing Black students at predominantly White institutions. . . the quality of life at HBCUs for African American students—especially African American men—has gone virtually unnoticed" (p. 190). Perhaps if a stronger body of literature focused specifically on the experiences of Black males at HBCUs, institutional leaders and practitioners would not only be more familiar with the contemporary issues of these students but would also have a larger repertoire of resources to help increase persistence.

Data in the current study emerged from a qualitative investigation that focused on factors that promoted academic success for Black males who entered an HBCU academically underprepared and still persisted to graduation. The central question that guided this research was: *What factors do academically underprepared Black males, who entered an HBCU through its remedial program and persisted to graduation, think contributed to their success?* Several themes emerged about factors that influenced the success of the participants in various ways. For example, participants discussed not only their challenges and how they overcame them (Palmer et al., 2009) but also the role the remedial program had on their initial social and academic integration to the university as they transitioned from high school to college (Palmer & Davis, 2012). They also discussed the impact that non-cognitive variables (Palmer & Strayhorn, 2008), social capital (Palmer & Gasman, 2008), student involvement (Palmer & Young, 2009), and family support (Palmer, Davis, & Maramba, 2011) had on their academic success.

In addition to the students, in-depth interviews were conducted with four retention specialists at the university to triangulate the factors that the students described. Specifically, the retention specialists were asked questions that were largely reflective of the questions posed to the Black males about factors promoting their academic success. The interviews with the retention specialists brought up the subject of barriers to the persistence of Black males. These barriers appeared as early as elementary school and continued in high school.

Black Males in the K-12 Educational Pipeline

The social science literature is replete with studies of the bleak conditions and experiences of Black males in education and society in general (Davis, 2003; Jackson & Moore, 2006, 2008; Noguera, 2003; Strayhorn, 2008). Researchers have noted that terms such as *endangered, uneducable, dysfunctional,* and *dangerous* are often used to characterize Black males (Majors & Billson, 1992; Jackson & Moore, 2006, 2008; Strayhorn, 2008).

Research has shown that academic problems hindering the educational progress of Black males begin early, impinging upon their ability to complete high school (Davis, 2003; Epps, 1995;). In elementary and secondary education, teachers and counselors are far more likely to impose negative expectations as they relate to attending college upon Black males than upon their White counterparts (Davis & Jordan, 1994; Epps, 1995; Jones, 2001;). Black males are also disproportionately disciplined, more apt to be expelled, and suspended for longer periods and more frequently than White students (Hale, 2001; Majors & Billson, 1992; Polite & Davis, 1999).

Black males are far more likely to be underrepresented in gifted education programs or advanced placement courses (Jackson & Moore, 2006, 2008) and are overwhelmingly concentrated in special education (Moore, Henfield, & Owens, 2008; Noguera, 2003). Many Black males are disproportionately tracked into low academic ability classrooms (Epps, 1995; Jones, 2001). Many of the aforementioned issues impinge upon Black males' ability to finish school, resulting in high rates of illiteracy and unemployment (Hale, 2001; Majors & Billson, 1992). Black males with lower educational attainment are predisposed to inferior employment prospects, low wages, and poor health and are more likely to be involved with the criminal justice system (Harvey, 2008).

The educational problems that Black males experience in elementary and secondary schools are not restricted to the K-12 setting. Similar trends can be noted in postsecondary education. Although the number of Black males entering higher education increased during the late 1960s and again during the 1980s and 1990s (Noguera, 2003), Black males continue to lag behind their female and White male counterparts with respect to college participation, retention, and degree completion rates (Harper, 2006a; Strayhorn, 2008). The plethora of issues impinging upon college access and success spill over to increased recidivism. According to researchers (Green, 2008; Jackson & Moore, 2006, 2008), the number of Black males in prison exceeds those in postsecondary institutions. A report by the Pew Charitable Trusts (2008) claims one in nine Black males between the ages of 24 and 34 is in jail. Green (2008) also noted that in 2000, there were 188,550 more Black men incarcerated than enrolled in institutions of higher education.

Methodology

I conducted this study at an urban public doctoral research HBCU in a mid-Atlantic state. According to the Office of Institutional Research (OIR) at this university, approximately 6,000 undergraduates were enrolled when our data were collected. Approximately 91% of the students were Black, and their White, Hispanic, Asian, and Native American counterparts comprised 2.5%, 0.9%, 0.7%, and 0.2% of the undergraduate student population, respectively. Consistent with recent research on HBCUs (Kimbrough & Harper, 2006; Palmer et al., 2009; Roach, 2001), the number of Black men graduating in six years has consistently lagged behind Black women at this university where the study took place. On the one hand, data from the OIR indicated that just 46.7% of the Black males admitted in 1998 persisted to their fourth year and only 35.1% graduated in six years. On the other hand, 57.5% of Black females admitted in 1998 persisted to their fourth year and 49.4% graduated in six years, which is more consistent with national retention averages (Harper, 2006a).

Using in-depth interview methods, I sought to explore the academic and social factors promoting the success of Black males situated in a particular context (Lincoln, 2002). Thus, the study's epistemological approach was anchored in the constructivist tradition to construct knowledge, understanding, and meaning through human interactions (Lincoln, 2002). To some extent, grounded theory strategies of continuously asking questions, utilizing research notes, exploring hunches, constant comparative analysis, and memo writing were employed (Charmaz, 2000; Strauss & Corbin, 1998).

Participants

Data for this current study emerged from a project that investigated success factors for 11 Black males who entered an HBCU through its remedial program and persisted to graduation. College remediation is designed to enhance academic deficiencies among underprepared college students through academic support, with program components ranging from a single course offering to more comprehensive academic and social support services, such as tutorial support, counseling, and study skill seminars (Boylan & Bonham, 2007). Students are typically referred to remedial programs when they do not meet traditional academic standards (i.e., GPA, SAT scores, and ACT scores) for admission into the university but demonstrate the potential to succeed in higher education. Participants in this study engaged in a six-week intensive summer remedial program to strengthen their academic skills.

In addition to conducting in-depth interviews with the students, I conducted in-depth interviews with four retention specialists at the institution who were purposefully chosen to triangulate the factors the students described. The interviews with the Black males and retention specialists occurred within the same time frame—that is, these data were not collected weeks or months after the interviews with the Black male students were completed. Consistent with constant comparative analysis, interviews with the students and retention specialists were conducted concurrently to strengthen, add, or refine questions posed to the Black male collegians. Furthermore, the four retention specialists were recruited because of their ongoing work with the director and staffs of the summer remedial program. They were directly responsible for helping students in the program make the initial transition from high school to college. In doing so, they devised and implemented special seminars and workshops for students who participated in the remedial program.

Each of the four retention specialists was Black; three females and one male. The three females worked in the Office of Student Retention and the male worked in the School of Education. One of the female participants was the director of the Office of Student Retention and the remaining two worked in conjunction with her. Three participants had earned various degrees from the university in the study. Specifically, two participants had earned their bachelor's degree, and one participant both her bachelor's and master's degrees. Furthermore, two female participants held PhDs in higher education, one female held a master's in education, and the male participant held a bachelor's degree in social work. The average age of the participants was 51 and they had worked in their capacity for eight or more years. Collectively, they had more than 46 years of experience working in student affairs, with a special interest on student retention and persistence. Table 1 provides details about the participants.

Table 1. The Retention Specialists

Name (pseudonym)	Age	Education	Years in Position	Position
Karen	40	PhD in Higher Education	8	Director of Office of Student Retention, Retention Specialist
Kelly	57	MA in Education	7	Office of Student Retention, Retention Specialist
Lindsay	55	PhD in Higher Education	12	Office of Student Retention, Retention Specialist
Paul	50	Bachelor's in Social Work	19	School of Education, Retention Specialist

Findings

In this section, I present three themes that capture the study's findings: (1) the impact that the lack of motivation and defined goals has on Black male persistence at this institution; (2) that lack of motivation facilitates ineligibility for financial aid, which, in turn, impedes persistence; (3) the hesitancy among Back males to use campus resources to increase their academic potential.

Motivation: A Critical Facilitator of Students' Academic Success

Each retention specialist noted the importance of motivation to academic success of Black males attending this HBCU. They explained that some Black males are not motivated to succeed in college, an attitude that was linked to a lack of firm goals in their pursuit of a college degree. Specifically, Paul, who had earned a bachelor's degree in social work and worked as a retention specialist at the university for approximately 20 years, explained:

> They're [Black males] not focused on the goals, they have no strategy, like when they come to college, they just came to college, they didn't say, 'I want to graduate,' there was no strategy."

Paul reported that when he first came to college, he failed his first semester because he had no specific academic goals. Paul suggested that counselors in middle and high schools need to focus more on helping students identify their passion.

> That is how I came [to college] and I did not do well. I mean, I just want to get there. They [my family] said, "Go to college." And I think what happens is that in middle schools and in high schools, they're not getting out of those students what their passion is. If I were a counselor in those areas. . . if a person ran their mouth a lot—okay that person is in public relations. If a kid wanted to help improve human conditions in life, they'll be good social workers. So I think that we don't really pull out of students what they are really passionate about and therefore when they get to college, they are not as focused and motivated as they should be.

Karen, another retention specialist, who had earned a PhD in higher education and worked at the university for eight years, echoed Paul's sentiment about how not having clear academic goals impedes motivation, which then increases the likelihood of attrition.

> Oh boy! Okay, the key factors that would prevent academic success at the university? First, I think there are motivational factors, that would be number 1, as far as I can see, meaning students coming to college for a number of reasons, and many of those are not connected to motivation to persist from the beginning. you know, coming to college because my parents told me I had to; I don't have anything else better to do, everybody else is going to college, I want to have fun there.

Karen underscored that attending college requires students to take part of the responsibility for their success. To this end, she explained that no one in college is going to act as a parental figure and wake students up for classes. She noted that students, particularly freshmen, have to be motivated to successfully make the adjustment from a highly structured environment—high school—to a relatively low structured environment—college.

> [In college] No one is waking you up every morning. No one is pushing you, you know, when you miss class, no one is calling you and saying, "Hey you missed class.". . . So adjusting to a life of independence that is much less structured than they have been use[d] to is the issue for a lot of Black males. As such, students have to be motivated and take part of the responsibility for their academic success.

Lindsay, another retention specialist, who had earned a PhD in higher education and worked at the university for 12 years, agreed with Paul and Karen. She commented:

> I think that those students who are not focused and directed when they come, who don't have some idea of what they want to do, I think those students are least likely to be successful here.

Lindsay, who also teaches a first-year experience course at the university, later noted that many of these students do not have an understanding of how to successfully adjust from high school to college. She went on to say that many students will eventually become motivated. In fact, she explained that she lacked motivation at first when she entered college and did not become motivated until her junior year.

> Many Black males don't have a real understanding of college compared to high school. They're taken by surprise when they get here. I found that with my students this summer, and I was not as rigorous as some teachers. . . . The students learned a lot. They really did. I would say 90% of my students were serious, but they were just a small group who did not make a good transition from high school to college, and those students tend not to get focused for a long time. I was one of those students. I didn't get focused until my junior year.

Motivation: A Critical Linchpin for Remaining Eligible for Financial Aid

The retention specialists noted the impact that the ability to pay for college has on persistence. They saw a connection between students' motivation and their ability to receive and renew financial aid. Those unmotivated Black males, particularly freshmen, will jeopardize their ability to receive financial aid, thereby hindering their persistence if they heavily depend on it to support their education. In particular, Karen explained:

> Some students become ineligible because of their motivation. . . . They aren't motivated, they're not independent. . . . This has a heavy influence on the financial piece, they all work together. They can't disconnect especially for African American students. . . . "So I'm already am barely paying for college, I'm depending on financial aid, and when I mess up that first time, because of lack of motivation, I'm in jeopardy for losing my financial aid."

Karen continued by noting that students who are not African Americans or those from a higher social class may have more leeway to mess up academically in college because their parents may be able to supplement their financial aid.

> A student who is not African American or from a higher social class can mess up as many times as they want because they are paying cash. So, they are not motivated, their parents can pay for them. . . but for African American students particularly, from lower economic class levels, they may not have family to turn to for financial support.

Kelly, a retention specialist, who had earned a master's degree in education and worked at the university for seven years, echoed Karen's statement about the impact of motivation on students' ability to receive financial aid. She explained that "we lose more students because they are ineligible for financial aid due to poor academic progress."

Similar to Karen and Kelly, Paul underscored the impact that the lack of motivation could have on students' ability to receive financial aid. Specifically, he stated that the majority of students attending this institution receive some form of financial aid. Further, he noted that the continuance of aid is predicated on students' academic progress. If they do not make satisfactory academic progress, Paul explained, their aid will be in jeopardy.

> Because 96% of our students receive some form of financial aid from outside sources that includes: loans, aid, Pell Grant, all different state funding, to them—all of which is determined by satisfactory academic progress. For many Black males at the university, because of motivation, they do not make satisfactory progress, making it difficult to persist.

Lindsay explained that students' guidance counselors may have helped them complete the form to receive financial aid (e.g., FAFSA) the first time, but students may forget to complete the form the next time, which affects their financial aid.

> Students get here as a freshmen, their guidance counselor, maybe somebody helped them, but in order to maintain whatever funding they had that first semester, a lot of students drop the ball. Um, drop the ball not just in not filling out FAFSA, not applying for the monies, which may hurt their chances of funding.

"All by Myself": The Reluctance of Black Males to Use Campus Academic Resources
The retention specialists also believed Black males at this HBCU were less inclined to access support services for academic assistance. They noted that oftentimes when Black males seek support, it is too late in the semester, and very little can be done to improve their chances of passing a specific course. Furthermore, instead of using the campus support services, some males will opt for the "D" or "F." Lindsay, in particular, delineated that Black males tend to isolate themselves and refuse to seek appropriate services.

> I think that men particularly at HBCUs, the men tend to isolate themselves more. They won't yell for help; they won't get the help that they need that is available. They don't use the resources accessibly to help them just pass a class. They'll wait until the last minute; they'll just give up and take the "F" or the "D."

Paul also noted that Black males refuse to use the campus services, talk with the professor, and use peer study groups to help them succeed.

> Black males on this campus won't say, you know, "I need some help. I'm gonna go to the university Center; I'm going to get with a study group, or I'm going to find somebody in my class who's doing well, and ask them for help. Or I'm going to go back to the teacher, and see what I can do, to better understand the information or something like that. They simply refuse to ask for support.

Like the other retention specialists, Kelly explained that Black males at this institution are unlikely to access necessary academic services to increase their likelihood of doing well.

> I think Black males are reluctant to reach out and let people know they are not doing well, or they need help or whatever, you know. I have noticed that quite a bit, and obviously that is going to keep you from succeeding, and that's why we have tutors, the academic development center, Mr. Clark, they have tutors affiliated with them, they're tutors in the residence halls, there are tutors all over the place.. . . But they [Black males] don't use them.

Much like the other retention specialists, Karen explained that Black males were less inclined to use the campus resources to aid in their persistence. Specifically, she noted that "many Black males are so prideful. . . they feel like they could do it [succeed] without anyone's help."

Discussion

Participants in this study described three barriers that impede persistence for Black males at an HBCU: (a) lack of motivation; (b) ineligibility for financial aid because of a dearth of motivation, and (c) reluctance to use campus resources in cases of academic struggles. Research has shown that motivation—a non-cognitive variable—plays a crucial role in the success of Black males attending PWIs (Cokley, 2003; Hrabowski, Maton, & Greif, 1998; Swail, Redd, & Perna, 2003). Further, research has also illustrated the efficacy of non-cognitive variables in the success of Black males at an HBCU (Palmer & Strayhorn, 2008). Some participants noted that Black male freshmen are more likely to experience lack of motivation. The participants' supposition is consistent with research that emphasizes that freshmen are more likely to encounter issues with persistence because they are transitioning from a relatively structured environment— high school—to a relatively structure-free environment—college (Tinto, 1993). Further, some participants explained that the lack of motivation among Black males was inextricably linked to their indecisiveness about a major or career goal. Tinto (1993) argued that prolonged major or career ambiguity could propel students to become less committed to the goal of higher education and increase their likelihood of student departure.

Interestingly, Pace's (1990) Quality of Student Effort supports the relevancy of non-cognitive variables on the impact of students' success in college. To this end, he postulates that the onus is on the institutions to provide resources for students' success. However, the onus is on students to invest energy (e.g., motivation) into the resources to maximize their success. Tinto (1993) supported Pace's Quality of Effort by noting that success in college is determined not by "background factors, which mark students entry into college" (p. 42) but by the extent to which students use the academic resources the college provides to enhance their success.

Participants noted that the lack of effort Black males invest in their academics impacts their eligibility to receive financial aid, which is inextricably tied to their retention and persistence. A number of researchers (e.g., Hu & St. John, 2001; St. John, 2003; St. John, Paulsen, & Carter, 2005; Titus, 2006) have noted a relationship between inadequate financial support and attrition. Although many public HBCUs admit students who rely heavily on financial aid (Allen et al., 2007), public HBCUs generally have lower tuition than private HBCUs or their White counterparts. However, many universities, including the institution in the current study, have increased tuition to compensate for declining state support, thereby making it more difficult for students to finance their education.

Some participants also noted how Black males were less inclined to use the campus academic resources to enhance their academic outcomes. Although one participant noted the impact that pride has on the ability of Black males to seek support, some research has shown that pride may impede Black males from accessing campus resources (e.g., tutorial services, academic advising, talking with professors) to gain assistance with academic problems or concerns. Majors and Billson (1992) characterized pride that Black males display as "*cool pose*"—that is, a façade used to display confidence and masculinity (p. 8). Scholars (e.g., hooks, 2004; Majors & Billson, 1992; Palmer et al., 2009) have noted that Black males' sense of *cool pose* impinges upon their ability to be academically successful. Given the characterization in the literature on the supportive and family like atmosphere of HBCUs one would think that Black males would be more likely to access campus support services (Palmer et al., 2009). Historically, research has shown that Black males at HBCUs are more empowered, assertive, and competitive—outperforming their female counterparts (Fleming, 1984). Certainly additional research is needed to investigate to what extent the institutional environment of an HBCU impacts this notion of *cool pose* for Black males, especially given the widening participation and persistence gaps in higher education between Black men and women compared with students from other racial/ethnic backgrounds.

Recommendations for Institutional Practice

Participants discussed the importance of motivation, a non-cognitive variable, and indicated that Black males, particularly freshmen, were struggling academically because they were not motivated. Given that research has shown that non-cognitive variables are crucial to the academic success of college students, HBCUs should place more emphasis on the cultivation and strengthening of students' non-cognitive skills. Specifically, HBCUs might implement workshops and seminars that focus on the significance of non-cognitive variables to persistence. Institutional activities in freshmen orientations and university 101 courses should also highlight the importance of non-cognitive variables to academic success. Furthermore, HBCUs should encourage better interaction between Black male freshmen and upperclassmen. Upperclassmen should be encouraged to talk to freshmen about those times that they struggled academically and tactics they employed to overcome those struggles. To the extent that HBCUs are able to cultivate and help Black males apply non-cognitive skills to their learning in order maximize their academic success, this will invariably impact their eligibility for financial aid.

Research (e.g., Palmer & Gasman, 2008) has shown that it "takes a village to raise a child." To this end, merely focusing on Black males' non-cognitive skills may not be enough. Thus, HBCUs should emphasize the importance of collaborative efforts between academic affairs and student affairs. For example, one HBCU has promulgated a program called the Male Initiative on Leadership and Excellence (MILE), which involves the efforts of faculty, staff, and administrators. MILE is premised on Kuh's (2009) emphasis on student engagement in educational and purposeful activities. To this end, MILE participants engage in a variety of out-of-the-classroom activities, team building exercises, and service learning projects. According to an evaluation of this program that Chickering, Peters, and Palmer (2006) conducted, MILE has been effective in fostering persistence among Black males, partly because students have formed critical relationships with faculty, administrators, and peers involved in the program, thus providing a stronger network to access.

Furthermore, HBCUs should do more to enhance the supportive campus climate for Black males. This can be done by creating initiatives that weaken the notion that Black males reaching for support runs counter to their masculinity. Again, referring to MILE, not only has this initiative increased Black males' support network among faculty, staff, and administrators but it also has facilitated increased interaction among Black males involved in this program (Chickering et al., 2006). Thus, MILE helped to lessen any form of learned behaviors which made the participants reluctant to actively seek out support. In this regard, MILE participants leaned not just on faculty, staff, and administrators for support but also on each other to help with academic and social concerns.

Conclusion

Research has consistently shown that HBCUs engender a positive and supportive environment for African Americans, thereby fostering retention, persistence, and academic success, but recent research has focused on the low retention and persistence rates among Black males at HBCUs. Using the voices of retention specialists, this chapter has identified barriers to the persistence of Black males attending an HBCU and provided recommendations to enhance persistence. Although this chapter is predicated on only one HBCU, institutional leaders and student affairs practitioners may find the recommendations helpful in increasing Black males' retention and persistence on their campuses.

References

Allen, W. R. (1992). The color of success: African American college students outcomes at predominantly White and historically Black public colleges and universities. *Harvard Educational Review, 62*(1), 26–44.

Allen, W. R., Jewell, J. O., Griffin, K. A., & Wolf, D. S. (2007). Historically Black colleges and universities: Honoring the past, engaging the present, touching the future. *Journal of Negro Education, 76*(3), 263–280.

Bonner, F. A., II, & Bailey, K. W. (2006). Enhancing the academic climate for African American men. In M. J. Cuyjet (Ed.), *African American Men in college* (pp. 24–46). San Francisco: Jossey-Bass.

Boylan, H. R., & Bonham, B. S. (2007). 30 years of developmental education: A retrospective. *Journal of Developmental Education, 30*(3), 2–4.

Brown, C. (2006). The impact of campus activities on African American men. In M. J. Cuyjet (Ed.), *African American Men in College* (pp. 47–67). San Francisco: Jossey-Bass.

Brown, M. C., & Davis, J. E. (2001). The historically Black college as social contract, social capital, and social equalizer. *Peabody Journal of Education, 76*(1), 31–49.

Charmaz, K. (2000). Grounded theory. In N.K. Denzin & Y. S. Lincoln (Eds.), *The handbook of qualitative research* (pp. 509–535). Thousand Oaks, CA: Sage.

Chickering, A. W., Peters, K., & Palmer, R. T. (March, 2006). *Assessing the impact of the Morgan Male Initiative on Leadership and Excellence (MILE)*. Baltimore: Morgan State University.

Cokley, K.O. (2003). What do we know about the motivation of African American students? Challenging the "anti-intellectual" myth. *Harvard Educational Review, 73*(4), 524–558.

Dancy, T. E., & Brown, M. C. (2008). Unintended consequences: African American male educational attainment and collegiate perceptions after *Brown v. Board of Education*. *American Behavioral Scientist, 51*(7), 984–1003.

Davis, J. E. (1994). College in Black and White: Campus environment and academic achievement of African American males. *Journal of Negro Education 63*(4), 620–633.

Davis, J. E. (2003). Early schooling and academic achievement of African American males. *Urban Education, 38*(5), 515–537.

Davis, J. E., & Jordan, W. (1994). The effects of school context, structure, and experiences on African American males and high school. *Journal of Negro Education, 63*(4), 570–587.

Epps, E. G. (1995). Race, class, and educational opportunity: Trends in the sociology of education. *Sociological Forum, 10*(4), 593–608.

Fleming, J. (1984). *Blacks in college: A comparative study of student success in Black and White institutions*. San Francisco: Jossey-Bass.

Freeman, K. (2005). *African Americans and college choice: The influence of family and school*. New York: SUNY Press.

Freeman, K., & Thomas, G. (2002). Black colleges and collegiate choice: Characteristics of students who choose HBCUs. *Review of Higher Education, 25*(3), 349–358.

Fries-Britt, S. L. (1997). Identifying and supporting gifted African American men. In M. J. Cuyjet (Ed.). *Helping African American men succeed in college* (pp. 5–16). San Francisco: Jossey-Bass.

Fries-Britt, S. L. (1998). Moving beyond Black achiever isolation: Experience of gifted Black collegians. *Journal of Higher Education, 69*(5), 556–576.

Fries-Britt, S. L. & Griffin, K. (2007). The Black box: How high-achieving Blacks resist stereotypes about Black Americans. *Journal of College Student Development, 48*(5), 509–524.

Fries-Britt, S. L., & Turner, B, (2001). Facing stereotypes: A case study of Black students on a White campus. *Journal of College Student Development, 42*(5), 420–429.

Fries-Britt, S., & Turner, B. (2002). Uneven stories: Successful Black collegians at a Black and a White campus. *Review of Higher Education, 25*(3), 315–330.

Green, P. C., III. (2008). The impact of laws on African American males. *American Behavioral Scientist, 51*(7), 827–884.

Griffin, K. (2006). Striving for success: A qualitative exploration of competing theories of high-achieving Black college students' academic motivation. *Journal of College Student Development, 47*(4), 384–400.

Guiffrida, D. (2003). African American student organizations as agents of social integration. *Journal of College Student Development, 44*(3), 304–319.

Guiffrida, D. (2004). Friends from home: Asset and liability to African American students attending a predominantly White institution. *NASPA Journal, 41*(3), 693–708.

Guiffrida, D. (2005). Othermothering as framework for understanding African American students' definitions of student-centered faculty. *Journal of Higher Education, 76*(5), 702–723

Hale, J. E. (2001). *Learning while Black: Creating educational excellence for African American children*. Baltimore: The Johns Hopkins University Press.

Harper, S. R. (2005). Leading the way: Inside the experience of high-achieving African American male students. *About Campus, 10*(1), 8–15.

Harper, S. R. (2006a). Reconceptualizing reactive policy responses to Black male college achievement: Implications from a national study. *Focus: Magazine of the Joint Center for Political and Economic Studies, 34*(6), 14–15.

Harper, S. R. (2006b). Peer support for African American male college achievement: Beyond internalized racism and the burden of acting White. *Journal of Men's Studies, 14*(3), 337–358.

Harper, S. R. (2008). Realizing the intended outcomes of *Brown*: High-achieving African American male undergraduates and social capital. *American Behavioral Scientist, 51*(7), 1030–1053.

Harper, S. R. (2009). Niggers no more: A critical race counternarrative on Black male student achievement at predominantly White colleges and universities. *International Journal of Qualitative Studies in Education, 22*(6), 697–712.

Harper, S. R., Carini, R. M, Bridges, B. K., & Hayek, J. (2004). Gender differences in student engagement among African American undergraduates at historically Black colleges and universities. *Journal of College Student Development, 45*(3), 271–284.

Harper, S. R., & Gasman, M. (2008). Consequences of conservatism: Black male undergraduates and the politics of historically Black colleges and universities. *Journal of Negro Education, 77*(4), 336–351.

Harper, S. R., & Nichols, A. H. (2008). Are they not all the same? Racial heterogeneity among Black male undergraduates. *Journal of College Student Development, 49*(3), 1–16.

Harper, S. R., & Quaye, S. J. (2007). Student organizations as venues for Black identity expression and development among African American male student leaders. *Journal of College Student Development, 48*(2), 127–144.

Harvey, W. B. (2008). The weakest link: A commentary on the connections between K-12 and higher education. *American Behavioral Scientist, 51*(7), 972–983.

hooks, b. (2004). *We real cool: Black men and masculinity*. New York: Routledge.

Hrabowski III, F. A., Maton, K. L., & Greif, G. L. (1998). *Beating the odds: Raising academically successful African American males*. New York: Oxford University Press.

Hu, S., & St. John, E. P. (2001). Student persistence in a public higher education system: Understanding racial and ethnic differences. *Journal of Higher Education, 72*(3), 265–286.

Jackson, J. F. L., & Moore, J. L., III. (2006). African American males in education: Endangered or ignored? *Teachers College Record, 108*(2), 201–205.

Jackson, J. F. L., & Moore, J. L., III. (2008). The African American male crisis in education: A popular media infatuation or needed public policy response. *American Behavioral Scientist, 51*(7), 847–853.

Jones, L. (2001). Creating an affirming culture to retain African American students during the post-affirmative action era in higher education. In L. Jones (Ed.), *In retaining African Americans in higher education: Challenging paradigms for retaining students, faculty, and administrators* (pp. 3–20). Sterling, VA: Stylus.

Jones, R. S., Torres, V., & Arminio, J. (2006). *Negotiating the complexities of qualitative research in higher education: Fundamental elements and issues*. New York: Taylor & Francis.

Kim, M. M. (2002). Historically Black vs. White institutions: Academic development among Black students. *Review of Higher Education, 45*(4), 385–407.

Kimbrough, W. M., & Harper, S. R. (2006). African American men at historically Black colleges and universities: Different environments, similar challenges. In M. J. Cuyjet (Ed.), *African American men in college* (pp. 189–209). San Francisco: Jossey-Bass.

Kuh, G .D. (2009). What Student Affairs Professionals Need to Know about Student Engagement. *Journal of College Student Development. 50*(6), 683–706.

Lincoln, Y. S. (2002, November). *On the nature of qualitative evidence*. Paper presented at the Annual Meeting of the Association for the Study of Higher Education, Sacramento, CA.

Lundy-Wagner, V., & Gasman, M. (2011). When gender issues are not just about women: Reconsidering Black men at historically Black colleges and universities. *Teachers College Record, 113*(5), 934–968.

Majors, R., & Billson, J. B. (1992). *Cool pose: The dilemmas of Black manhood in America*. New York: Touchstone.

Moore, J. L., III, Henfield, M. S., & Owens, D. (2008). African American males in special education: Their attitudes and perceptions toward high school counselors and school counseling services. *American Behavioral Scientist, 51*(7), 907–927.

National Center for Education Statistics (2007). *Status and trends in the education of racial and ethnic minorities*. Washington, DC: National Center for Education Statistics.

Noguera, P. A. (2003). The trouble with Black boys: The role and influence of environmental and cultural factors on the academic performance of African American males. *Urban Education, 38,* 431–459.

Pace, R. (1990). *The undergraduates: A report of their activities and progress in college in the 1980s.* Los Angeles: UCLA Center for the Study of Evaluation.

Palmer, R, T., & Davis, R. J. (2012). "Diamond in the Rough": The impact of a remedial program on college access and opportunity for Black males at an historically Black institution. *Journal of College Student Retention, 13*(4), 407–430.

Palmer, R. T., & Davis, R. J., & Hilton, A. A. (2009). Exploring challenges that threaten to impede the academic success of academically Black males at an HBCU. *Journal of College Student Development, 50*(4), 429–445.

Palmer, R. T., Davis, R. J., & Maramba, D. C. (2011). The impact of family support on the success of Black men at an historically Black university: Affirming the revision of Tinto's theory. *Journal of College Student Development, 52*(5), 577–593.

Palmer, R. T., & Gasman, M. (2008). "It takes a village to raise a child": The role of social capital in promoting academic success for African American men at a Black college. *Journal of College Student Development, 49*(1), 52–70.

Palmer, R. T., & Strayhorn, T. L. (2008). Mastering one's own fate: Non-cognitive factors with the success of African American males at an HBCU. *National Association of Student Affairs Professionals Journal, 11*(1), 126–143.

Palmer, R. T., & Young E. M. (2009). Determined to succeed: Salient factors that foster academic success for academically unprepared Black males at a Black college. *Journal of College Student Retention: Research, Theory & Practice, 10*(4), 465–482.

Pascarella, E. T., & Terenzini, P. T. (1991). *How college affects students: Findings and insights from twenty years of research.* San Francisco: Jossey-Bass.

Patton, D. L. (2006). Black culture centers: Still central to student learning. *About Campus, 2*(2), 2–8.

Perna, L. W. (2001). The contribution of historically Black colleges and universities and preparation of African American faculty careers. *Research in Higher Education, 42*(3) 267–292.

Pew Charitable Trusts (2008). One in 100: America behind bars in 2008. Retrieved from the Pew Charitable Trusts Web site: http://www.pewcenteronthestates.org/report_detail.aspx?id=35904

Polite, V. C., & Davis, J. E. (1999). Introduction: Research focused on African American males. In V. C. Polite & J. E. Davis (Eds.), *African American males in school and society: Practices and policies for effective education.* (pp. 1–7). New York: Teachers College Press.

Pope, J. (2009). Men struggling to finish at Black colleges. Retrieved from http://diverseeducation.com/artman/publish/article_12432.shtml

Roach, R. (2001, May). Where are the Black men on campus? *Black Issues in Higher Education, 18*(6), 18–21.

Roebuck, J. B., & Murty, K. S. (1993). Historically Black colleges and universities: Their place in American higher education. Westport, CT: Praeger.

St. John, E. P. (2003). *Refinancing the college dream.* Baltimore, MD: Johns Hopkins University Press.

St. John, E. P., Paulsen, M. B., & Carter, D. F. (2005). Diversity, college, and postsecondary opportunity: An examination of the financial nexus between college choice and persistence for American Americans and Whites. *Journal of Higher Education, 76*(5), 553–569.

Strauss, A., & Corbin, J. (1998). *Basics of qualitative research: Techniques and procedures for developing grounded theory.* Thousand Oaks, CA: Sage.

Strayhorn, T. (2008). The role of supportive relationships in supporting African American males' success in college. *NASPA Journal, 45*(1), 26–48.

Swail, W. S., Redd, K. E., & Perna, L. W. (2003). *Retaining minority students in higher education: A framework for success.* ASHE-ERIC Higher Education Report: *30*(2). San Francisco: Wiley.

Tinto, V. (1993). *Leaving college: Rethinking the causes and curses of student attrition* (2nd ed.). Chicago: University of Chicago Press.

Titus, M. A. (2006). Understanding the influence of the financial context of institutions on student persistence at four-year colleges and universities, *Journal of Higher Education, 77*(2), 353–375.

Wenglinsky, H. H. (1996). The educational justification of historically Black colleges and universities: Policy responses to the U.S. Supreme Court. *Educational Evaluation and Policy Analysis, 18*(1), 91–103.

Chapter Nine

"It's a Manhood Thing"

Pledging, Masculinity, and Identity Development in Black Greek Fraternities

Issam Khoury

Violence in BGFs [Black Greek fraternities] is the product of a particular black male identity resulting from the black man's sojourn in the United States. (Jones, 2004, p. 118)

Society already has this stigma that Black men ain't _____, and so you don't want to be that. You don't want to have had the opportunity to be something and then fall off and become a stereotype. (Student quoted in Watkins et al., 2007, p. 109)

In 1989, Joel Harris, a sophomore at Morehouse College in Atlanta, Georgia, died of a heart attack while participating in a pledge session with members of the Alpha Phi Alpha Fraternity, Inc. (Kimbrough, 1997). Five years later, Michael Davis died after two weeks of intense hazing at the hands of Kappa Alpha Psi Fraternity, Inc. Chapter at Southeast Missouri State University (Chenoweth, 1998). In 1996, Rod Perrymond, a former University of Georgia football player, sued Phi Beta Sigma Fraternity, Inc., for severe bruises to and torn blood vessels in his buttocks after allegedly being paddled (Ruffins, 1997). The following year, an Indiana court awarded Kevin Nash $774,500 in damages for injury to his kidneys, face, neck, and chest, while pledging Omega Psi Phi Fraternity, Inc. (Ruffins, 1997). The new millennium has seen examples as drastic as these. Pledging and hazing, in their worst and most violent form, are still alive and well in the Black fraternal system.

The Black collegiate fraternal movement began in 1906 with the establishment of Alpha Phi Alpha Fraternity. With noble ideals and goals at the heart of this enterprise, the movement quickly spread and has initiated some of the most notable African Americans into its ranks. The initiation process into these ranks remains controversial as members find themselves before courts of law for hazing allegations; chapters get suspended for violating (or more appropriately, getting caught) intake regulations; and national organizations impose moratoria and restrictions out of concern of further lawsuits.

The question arises: "Why did we get to this point in the fraternal intake process where violence is so prevalent?" This chapter will seek to answer that question by placing pledging in the context of the theory of identity development—namely the development of African American men. By centering the theory of multiple identity development, and recognizing the heterogeneity of African American college men, I will posit that pledging and hazing create masculine identities that are both destructive and oppositional. I use the former in the sense of inflicting violence upon other African American men for the supposed goals of uplift, scholarship and manhood, while using the latter to denote that these identities are constructed only in opposition to those identities that are perceived as negative—namely, femininity, weakness, and homosexuality.

Having been initiated into a fraternity more than a decade ago, I have seen firsthand the kinds of activities that permeate throughout the Greek community in the name of "brotherhood." I have seen young men being emotionally and physically abused in the name of gaining strength and "earning your letters." I have heard members talk about "beating the b_____ out of" aspirants because the ultimate goal is manhood. I have seen the paraphernalia proudly displayed with "Bloody" preceding the chapter name as a mark of honor. I have been privy to conversations where some "real" Brothers speak derogatorily about those "paper" Brothers who didn't pledge. And I have personally had more heated discussion than I care to recount with undergraduate fraternity members, trying to find some sort of middle ground as to how we can design and implement a meaningful process that includes the positive aspects of history and tradition while leaving out those parts that have created the kinds of Brothers who bring to their organizations notoriety and disrespect.

However, the importance of this topic is much more than personal. The amount of literature on this topic has slowly increased as the need to understand this phenomenon has become more necessary. Nuwer (1999) attempts to explain the phenomenon through the retelling of the horrific story of Joseph Snell's (failed) attempt to gain entry into Omega Psi Phi Fraternity, Inc. (a process that left him with "flashbacks of the beatings" (quoted in Nuwer, 1999, p. 184). Jones (2004) suggests that pledging is a sacrifice that reaffirms a pledge's sense of manhood and allows him to acquire new status upon initiation. In response to public perceptions of Black Greeks, Hughey (2008) goes even further than that. Recounting a fight between a group of Sigmas and Alphas on the campus of the University of Virginia, he writes a critique of the idea that Black Greeks are "educated gangs."

The tenor of this chapter will offer a critical (and harsh) examination of the role that pledging Black Greek fraternities (BGFs) plays in the identity development of Black men who choose to join these organizations. However, to be so myopic as to suggest that these organizations do not offer much that is positive would be to do them a grave injustice. Harper and Harris (2006), for example, tell of an experience of a young man from Georgia who benefited immensely from the experience of joining a Black fraternity. Seemingly Harper's mini-autobiography, this story is typical of the experience of many young men who choose to undergo the rigors of a pledge process in order to gain affiliation with one of the Divine Nine organizations. Guiffrida (2003) interviews a young African American college student who states, "It seems like being a part of something helps [with networking and creating professional connections]" (p. 308). The literature on the subject also points to numerous benefits in the development of young African American men on college campuses (Harper and Harris, 2006; Harper and Nichols, 2008; McClure, 2006; Moran, Yengo, & Algier, 1994; Murguia, Padilla, & Pavel, 1991; Taylor & Howard-Hamilton, 1995). Most notable among these benefits are brotherhood, creating relationships that are described by members as familial, connecting members to the campus, social integration, networking opportunities, and establishing strong(er) connections to Black history and culture (McClure, 2006). The hundreds of thousands of members of Black Greek Fraternities are clearly a testament to the longevity of the values and ideals of these organizations; the list of notables within each organization is a badge of honor that members publicly display and brag about; and the bonds that are created between brothers testify to the significance of the experience of pledging.

However, to focus on the positive and peripheralize the negatives that are associated with membership would be equivalent to putting blinders on a horse. The whole picture of joining a Black Greek Fraternity needs to be examined, and this chapter will seek to add one more piece to that very complicated puzzle in the hope of expanding our understanding and thus increasing our ability to offer viable solutions to a situation that is clearly a problem.

Black Greek Fraternities

In most articles on this subject, authors offer a short summary of the history of Black Greek Fraternities. That history is well known, and with little debate among scholars, it is accepted that Alpha Phi Alpha Fraternity, Inc., initiated the Black collegiate Greek-Lettered Organization (BGLO) system in 1906. By 1922, three more fraternities and four sororities would be established: Alpha Kappa Alpha

Sorority (1908), Kappa Alpha Psi Fraternity (1911), Omega Psi Phi Fraternity (1911), Delta Sigma Theta Sorority (1913), Phi Beta Sigma Fraternity (1914), Zeta Phi Beta Sorority (1920), and Sigma Gamma Rho (1922). The most recent organization to be founded was Iota Phi Theta in 1963, whose founders were determined to build a legacy and not rest upon one ("About Iota," undated). As early as sixty years after the founding of BGLOs, there already existed a perception that these organizations were elitist, arrogant, and stood as testaments to popularity. Harper and Nichols (2008) confirm this perception in interviews they conducted with thirty-nine Black male undergraduates. There is a sense that members of Black Greek fraternities join organizations in order to perpetuate an elitist attitude that is riddled with arrogance and undergirded by a desire for popularity. At the 2008 Sankofa Conference at Penn State University, a non-affiliated participant offered that the role of Black Greeks is to protect and promote the Black middle class. That statement is a poignant reflection of the fact that Black Greeks are sometimes perceived as disconnected from the larger Black community and that they have become a classist tool. Harper and Nichols (2008) note that not only are members of these organizations perceived as elitist and arrogant, but that among organizations there is an unhealthy and divisive attitude.

In order to counter this divisiveness, the National Panhellenic Council (NPHC) was formed in 1930 to establish "unanimity of thought and action as far as possible in the conduct of Greek letter collegiate fraternities and sororities, and to consider problems of mutual interest to its member organizations" (NPHC, 2007). By 1937, the first eight Black Greek-Lettered Organizations (BGLOs) would combine under the umbrella of the NPHC, and sixty years later, the council would expand to include Iota Phi Theta Fraternity. However, Hughey (2008) claims that the NPHC is the BGLO equivalent of the United Nations, a politically flaccid organization that issues edicts but lacks the requisite power to enforce those edicts. Their 1990, 2000, and 2003 (see appendix) Joint Statements on Hazing stand as proof of this statement.

The Elite Eight (as they were then known, before the induction of Iota Phi Theta into the NPHC) gathered in 1990 to issue their first edict against hazing and pledging. Formally outlawing pledging and hazing, the organizations were committed to reversing the violent trends within the council that left organizations facing courts and lawsuits. The council's 1990 statement abolished pledging completely (including pledge lines, line names, and above-ground processes) in an attempt to eradicate traditions that, as implemented by overzealous members, had sometimes gone awry and ended tragically. In place of pledge traditions, each of the organizations instituted "New Member Intake" programs that were designed to give national and regional fraternity and sorority officials greater control over selection of members (Ruffins, 1997). This statement was reiterated in 2003 (see appendix). The fundamental problem with these statements is that they did not take into account the views and social perspectives of undergraduate members who were actually implementing these processes. Therefore, pledging went "underground," i.e., all the "old" traditions and now-illegal processes that had until then been practiced in the public eye were now made secret and taken out of the sight of officials.

Perhaps the most obvious media critique of public pledging is Spike Lee's 1988 film, *School Daze*. A socially conscious movie dealing with the racial politics of divestment from South Africa, it is a poignant look at how pledging into a BGF was a public spectacle, visible to all members of the campus community. This public spectacle was also portrayed in *The Cosby Show* spin-off, *A Different World*, in which various cast members seek entry into two different organizations, Kappa Lambda Nu Fraternity and Alpha Delta Rho Sorority. As part of their processes, they recite poems, perform "steps," and are pledged in public before the campus community.

The 1990 and 2003 statements did nothing to change these traditions; they only made them private. The NPHC wanted to give national and regional officials more control over the process, but in reality, they ended up with significantly less control. Many members of BGFs saw these statements as efforts to emasculate the process and to undermine the very notions of masculinity that undergird membership in these organizations. The question is "why"?

"Are BGF's Beating Themselves to Death?"

Webster's Dictionary (1984) defines hazing as "1. to harass or persecute with meaningless, difficult, or demeaning tasks; 2. to initiate, as into a college fraternity, by playing rough practical jokes on or exacting demeaning performance from." Hazing is not a new phenomenon. Fisher (2010) examines the history of hazing at Cornell University (also the institution at which Alpha Phi Alpha was founded), which goes back to 1873 when a pledge was blindfolded and was forced to jump to his death off a 37-foot-high cliff. Jones (2004) traces the roots of hazing even farther back to ancient civilizations that practiced rites of passage and to adult lodge groups such as the Knights of Columbus, the Templars, and the Knights of Pythias. Susan Lampkins, founder of the website, Inside Hazing, claims that, since 1970, there has been at least one hazing-related death on college campuses every year (Fisher, 2010).

Where or when did hazing originate in Black fraternities? According to Smoot (n.d.), in the early 1920s, the founders of Alpha Phi Alpha were called to a convention to address the subject of rampant hazing. In BGLOs, hazing has been around for at least eighty years. Furthermore, Kimbrough (1997) confirms that between 1900 and the 1920s, fraternities had incorporated hazing as a part of the pledging experience. However, this does not mean that every member of a fraternity that pledged after 1920 was subject to hazing. On the contrary, there are many accounts of pledging in the 1940s and 1950s with little or no physical hazing at all (Smoot, n.d.). So, what is the difference between pledging and hazing?

According to Smoot, "pledging is a commitment that you are making, not necessarily to the organization, but to yourself. You are committing yourself to a process that is stressful, sometimes dangerous, often times nerve-wracking." Additionally, "[pledging] teaches you accountability, manhood, scholarship, uplift, and to endure throughout all types of situations" (Morgan, 1998). Hazing, on the other hand, was defined at The Broken Pledges videoconference as "'an action' causing danger [or] some sort of discomfort [that is] demeaning [and is] required to get into a group" (Morgan, 1998). Too often these terms are interchangeable, and in the NPHC statements, both processes are made illegal. For the purposes of this chapter, the term "pledging" will be understood as both "pledging" and "hazing."

Dr. Jason DeSousa, Assistant Vice President for Student Affairs at Alabama State University and a member of Kappa Alpha Psi Fraternity, says that "pledging and hazing are an ingrained part of the undergraduate culture" (Ruffins, 1997). For too many, being pledged makes you a "real" member of that fraternity, whereas just going through the officially approved process would only make you a "paper" member of that fraternity. It is here that fraternities face a very obvious dilemma: on the one hand, subscribing to the mandates set by their national headquarters and the NPHC would free local chapters from the possibility of having their charter withdrawn and any potential lawsuits or unnecessary public attention being drawn to their chapter due to the dangers of pledging and hazing; on the other hand, because of the ingrained respect that comes with pledging, members who are not pledged are not respected or seen as legitimate (Anonymous, 1997). This dilemma is best expressed in the words of this anonymous author, who, because he wanted to avoid sanctions for participating in pledging activities, requested his name not be released:

> But although the old men make the fraternity hopefuls sign papers saying they won't pledge and make my brothers and me sign papers saying we won't conduct pledging activities, those old men do not respect anyone who doesn't pledge. So they wink at us as we go underground. If we are caught, all of us—the pledges as well as the brothers—will lose our membership and our charter.

He continues in the article, and as dean of pledges, addresses his pledges while in a car:

> That's why I'm proud of you runts. . . . You didn't have to pledge. You guys could've used the official process, signed your name to a piece of paper and taken a fraternity history test. But then you would have been a brother in name only—

a "paper brother." The documents may make you technically a member, but the brothers won't treat you like a brother. And that's the way it is.

Michael Gordon, the past executive director of the NPHC, Inc., believes that "the desire to be in a brotherhood. . . and involved with something positive is so strong in young people that they are willing to submit to hazing in order to become members" (Morgan, 1998). The fact that young men would be willing to endanger themselves for the sake of belonging is alarming, but what is more scary is the fact that many of them are encouraged to do so by family members who belong to the same fraternity.

[The] same rituals from fifty or sixty years ago that were daunting when carried out by supervised young men carefully picked from America's Black Elite (as African-American seekers of higher education were known at the time), may become deadly when secretly carried out by Black teenagers brought up in a society that equated Black masculinity with violence. (Ruffins, 1997, p. 4)

Defining Masculinity and Constructing Identity

It is the definition and perception of masculinity that seem to undergird the pledge process, and that motivate members of BGFs to engage in such violent processes. There are two dominant paradigms in the literature on masculinity. The first suggests that masculinity is a power relationship that follows Foucault's line of thinking (Lemelle, 2010) that the territory of power is marked by pervasive human interactions whose roles are "outside of the individual" (Lemelle, 2010, p. 15). To elaborate, a number of social forces dictate behavior, and the behavior of individuals is defined by their ever-shifting position of power in society. The social construction of identity dictates behavior, and behavior thus, is only a symptom of an individual's place in the shifting social strata.

Four cultural institutions have constructed Black male identity by imposing Eurocentric values and thus leading to the subjection of Black men: the military, jails, organized athletics, and the entertainment industry. "In each role, expectations for Black males are to produce a particular brand of masculinity" (Lemelle, 2010, p. 53). This leads to the second strand of the literature, which sees masculinity as a performance. Although Lemelle (2010) would suggest that performance of gender would be meaningless had the political, class, and sex roles not been predetermined, the performance of gender is particularly salient in discussions of pledging and masculine identity in BGFs.

Young (2007) offers a poignant dichotomy on this performativity of Black masculinity. He creates two diametrically opposed categories that represent two extremes of masculine identity: niggas and faggots. He compares himself to his fraternity brother whose particular brand of discourse of Black racial authenticity necessitates that "faggots are utterly juxtaposed to niggas" (Young, 2007, p. 60). Although this is an overly essentializing model of Black male identity, this dichotomy is very salient. It offers us one way of understanding how Black male identity in fraternities is constructed.

Stewart (2008) offers an examination of multiple identities among Black college students that complicates Young's portrait. Her male interviewees insisted on not being stereotyped as young Black men but wanted to be seen in their full complexity. Similarly, Harper and Nichols (2008) conducted research that reflects the heterogeneity of Black male identity in college. McClure (2006) further narrows the focus and suggests that no singular Black male identity exists among those who enter fraternities. Each of these perspectives is salient in understanding how identity is formed among men who choose to gain membership in BGFs.

To understand identity theory development, it helps to use the model by Burke and Stets (2009). In this model of identity development, identity has four components: an identity standard, inputs, a comparator and an output. The identity standard is the set of meaning that define the character of the identity. The authors give an example of how the identity standard is set up by examining what "stereotypical" individuals within that group define as the standard, and then establishing a continuum along which other members of that group can be located. The identity standard is thus created from within the cultural group.

The inputs to identity are individual perceptions of their identity. Burke and Stets (2009) differentiate perceptions of identity with the environment—the manipulation of the former is an internal process, and those changing perceptions are meant to match up with the standard. But, what exactly is being perceived? The authors explain:

> It may be perceptions of their own behavior, it may be perceptions of the behavior of others in the form of overt actions or in the form of expressions given off, or it may be combinations of these things and other things as well. (Burke & Stets, 2009, p. 66)

Perceptions are in continuous negotiation with the comparator. The comparator compares the set of meanings that are the identity standard with the perceptions, and produces an error signal. For example, someone might self-correct his actions if he finds himself acting too "feminine." His perceptions (either cues from within or others) of masculinity, based on the identity standard, when negotiated with the comparator let him know that he was too feminine. An error was created. He therefore self-corrects.

In the model, output is behavior that is produced in the environment, and the effect of this behavior is to alter the environment from what it was. Specifically, it alters the symbolic character of the environment. With the symbols changed, everyone in the environment, oneself included, will have changed perceptions, which perceptions feed back up into the identity in a continuing cycle. The meanings are altered. (Burke and Stets, 2009, pp. 66–67). Through this constant cycle, identity is managed, negotiated, and works in consort with and responds to the environment.

Another model of identity development is based on Abès, Jones, and McEwen's Identity Development Model (2007). Although the research that led to the development of this model is based on interviews with three lesbians, it is relevant to our understanding of the meaning-making process among Black men. Lemelle (2010) would posit that the contextual influences are primary in this model as the definition of identity has already been pre-determined. However, the contextual influences in this case are more complex as they include information that is not necessarily determined by hegemonic power structures. These influences then pass through a filter, allowing young Black college men to determine their identity in a new context and forcing them to make sense of the influences and socio-cultural stimuli that have constructed their idea of "self." Through this process, they arrive at a point where their sense of gender and race are incorporated, along with information about what it means to be a Black man in an elite organization that is the fraternity.

Identity, Masculinity and Pledging

These models offer multiple perspectives from which to examine Black male identity development as it relates to pledging BGFs. The accounts that have been provided indicate that a culture of violence is alive and well in the Black fraternal system. This violence is, according to Lemelle (2010), derived from dominant Eurocentric cultural institutions that predetermine the role that Black men play. How Black men then perform their masculinity would seem to be of little consequence, because it could be argued that this performance is merely a representation of a larger, more pervasive, form.

However, I would argue that this interpretation leaves little agency for the players and that the performance is of the utmost importance. The relationship between the structure and the performance is not so one-sided as to suggest that only one imposes upon the other but instead that the performance does and can change the structure. Hence, in the case of pledging, the two form a symbiotic relationship: the structure has been established that paints Black men as violent and ruthless, and it continues and is sustained only by Black men acting according to those predetermined cultural norms. However, not all collegiate members of BGFs are subjected to such extreme brutality and barbarism, and thus, by changing their performance, they complicate the notion that the structure dominates the behavior (performance).

DeSantis and Coleman (2008) interview young Black men who have pledged and who assert that "going through it, hard, is what makes us men. If you don't get the shit beat out of you, you ain't one of us" (p. 295). The performance of male-on-male violence is in itself seen as a masculine act. The performance of physically abusing another man reinforces a brother's sense of masculine identity as strong and physically demanding. Nowhere in the process does the idea of Black-on-Black violence ever surface, for to be a man means to a) be abusive; and b) be strong enough to handle that abuse. This conflicted understanding, I argue, contributes to a thwarted and skewed developmental process for both the fraternity member and the young man being pledged into the fraternity.

The ruthlessness that characterizes many pledge processes and that has led to deaths and too many hospital visits by young men who desire the benefits of membership can also be examined through the lens that Young (2007) offers. In that dichotomy, there are niggas and there are faggots. The diametrically opposed duality necessitates that members of BGFs clearly be niggas, because they certainly cannot be faggots. The performance has to be hypermasculine in order to preserve a sense of identity that is secure. The irony in this is that the idea of "nigga" is, in today's cultural connotation, one that is inherently opposed to that of the fraternal system, which is perceived as elitist, middle class, and bourgeois. Thus, in the performance of this hypermasculinity, Black men reaffirm a sense of being in touch with the identity standard of Blackness while preserving their masculinity.

This sense of masculinity is essentially opposed to homosexuality, and it is this point to which I will now turn my attention. Gay men belong to each of the five fraternities, despite the efforts of some to deny their existence. Thomas (1998) tells of his story of pledging Phi Beta Sigma Fraternity and the internal struggles he faced as a gay man. He says, "I wanted to be a man! I wanted to prove to myself and to others that. . . I could pledge and join a Black fraternity" (p. 13). After he crossed the burning sands, rumors about his sexuality began to surface, one of his fraternity brothers "got all macho and said, 'You better handle your bidiness man; can't have this shit going on!'" (p. 16). That sentiment is typical of attitudes across the five BGFs. DeSantis and Coleman (2008) define masculinity as being "conceptualized, first and foremost, in binary relationship to homosexuality: to be 'manly' is to be virile, attracted to women, and hyper-heterosexual" (p. 294). They interview two young fraternity brothers who both affirm that homosexuality cannot and should not be allowed on a "line"; their understanding of masculinity is one that does not allow for the inclusion of homosexuality in any way. Homosexuality, by definition, is everything that masculinity is not; if masculinity is strong, then homosexuality is weak, if masculinity is the cornerstone of brotherhood, then homosexuality is the antithesis of brotherhood. For members of BGFs, homosexuality is inherently opposed to brotherhood and the process involved in becoming a brother.

To use Abes, Jones and McEwen's model (2007), the equation of homosexuality with weakness comes from the three parts of the model. According to a 2006 General Social Survey cited in Lemelle (2010), 77% of Black men saw homosexuality as always wrong. This astounding figure is part of the contextual influences that Black collegiate men bring with them to college, and they filter this information as being acceptable based on other factors such as Black men's place in society, the hypersexualized entertainment and sports industries, and religious influences. In trying to integrate their identities, Black men center gender and race, and in this centering, an understanding of sexual orientation is important. Blackness and maleness are inextricably intertwined with a heterosexual identity that not only affirms the role of Black men as positive role models in the community but also others gayness as an identity that is simply incompatible with Black masculinity. That 77% of Black men saw homosexuality as wrong is telling in the attitudes of the young men cited by DeSantis and Coleman (2008), and in Thomas' story (1998).

However, the idea that Black male identity is indeed heterogeneous needs to be reaffirmed. In the Thomas (1998) story, he talks of how he reconciled with his chapter brothers who pledged their loyalty to Thomas, regardless of his sexual orientation. Anecdotally, gay men have entered into the ranks of BGFs and have been fully accepted by their brothers without hesitation. As a member of Alpha Phi Alpha, I have had a number of conversations with my own brothers and with members of other fraternities who have told me that their sexual orientation was not an issue when they pledged. The heterogeneity of Black men is a fact, and while masculinity in BGFs is narrowly constructed, to assume that there is only one type of Black man would be to negate the complexity of identity development and the diversity that exists among Black men in varied contexts.

It seems indisputable that the underground pledge is a destructive process that puts masculine identities into oppositional categories that allow for very little flexibility. The brutality of the process indicates that violence is intrinsic in the construction of masculine identity, and that is unhealthy. The exclusive nature of masculinity serves to develop young men who are committed neither to social justice nor to the larger community from which they come. Thomas (1998) says that BGFs who "fiercely resist pressure to openly accept their homosexual members. . . fight a losing battle to hold on to the status quo, which does not even serve their own interests. . . [and] will find themselves outdated and struggling to survive" (p. 19). In order to provide a solution, organizations and institutions have responded to pledging in order to eradicate the dangers associated with that process.

Organizations and Institutions Respond

Because of the NPHC's ban on pledging and hazing, both BGLOs and universities have been forced to effectively deal with infractions of this ban. Following is a list of how different groups have dealt with this:

- The University of Maryland-Eastern Shore has sued both the perpetrators and the victims of hazing in a Kappa Alpha Psi Fraternity chapter. Their rationale is that the only way to end the vicious cycle of hazing is to place some responsibility on those being hazed, in this case, five pledges who were hospitalized following a hazing ritual that involved daily paddling for eight weeks (Ruffins, 1998).

- Omega Psi Phi Fraternity has decided to countersue a former pledge who filed a suit claiming he had been injured by fraternity members during hazing. The fraternity argued that it would not let its good name and reputation be tarnished because of the injury of someone who willingly participated in these activities (hazing) (Ruffins, 1998).

- At Southeast Missouri State University (the site of Michael Davis' horrible death while pledging Kappa), hazing has been classified as a misdemeanor; new pledges sign hazing cards promising to report any hazing activities; leadership retreats are held for the presidents of BGLOs; training is given to university administrators and resident assistants to alert them to signs of hazing; closer links between local affiliates and the national headquarters of each BGLO have been established via the university administration, and the members of the BGLO Chapters have assumed much of the responsibility for ensuring that the Davis incident is never repeated (Chenoweth, 1998).

- Dr. Gloria D. Scott at Bennett College, an HBCU in Greensboro, NC, advises students who arrive on her campus that they should not submit to hazing, and that it is a felony in the state of North Carolina (Morgan, 1998).

Furthermore, suggestions have been offered by many on what might be done as a means of improving the situation of pledging in Black fraternities:

- Educate the undergraduate membership, who seems to be the most resistant to the change toward the membership intake process (Kimbrough, 1997).

- Institute an eight- to ten-week pledging program, consisting of an intensive two-week pre-pledging program, a standard four- to six-week pledge program, whereupon the pledges become members, and then another two-week program which includes the new and existing members of the organization (Smoot, n.d.).

- Sit down with younger members and negotiate a difficult, non-violent (and maybe even silly) pledging process that undergraduates (and their Big Brothers) will accept as legitimate. (Ruffins, Chenoweth, and Evelyn, 1998; Ruffins, 1997).

- Offer a substantial reward or scholarship for anyone who reports hazing, as an incentive for new pledges to uphold the "true ideals" of the organization. (Ruffins, Chenoweth, and Evelyn, 1998).

- Testify against members involved in hazing in criminal courts of law. (Ruffins, Chenoweth, and Evelyn, 1998).

Some of these solutions are drastic and some would arguably engender a level of distrust within chapters and the organization as a whole. In response to the recent moratorium imposed by Alpha Phi Alpha Fraternity, Inc., the national organization has instituted a system that offers undergraduates an opportunity to have input on the design of a new national intake process. This is a critical point in that the voice of the undergraduates was not heard in 1990 when the first ban on pledging was instituted, and thus the process went "underground." By involving undergraduates, organizations have the ability to design processes that are viable and have the buy-in of collegiate members.

In addition to the collegiate voice the ever-increasing body of literature and scholarship on the subject must be utilized. To design processes that are ignorant of the theory of student development without the input of higher education professionals who directly interact with college brothers would be a huge oversight on the part of the national leadership of BGFs.

And finally, each membership intake process needs to include sessions and readings on Black men and identity development, and this needs to be supplemented by a strong grounding in social justice. Today's society is a complex one that does not cater to simple identity constructions. Today's college students are exposed to peers from an array of backgrounds, religious and social systems, and sexualities. Today's job market demands the flexibility and versatility to work with people from all walks of life. To continue with a pledge process that would limit Black masculinity is to do a disservice to prospective members. The viability of BGFs is in jeopardy and it is up to these organizations that were founded on noble principles to respond to changing times, to remain relevant, and to truly rededi-cate themselves to the uplift of all mankind.

Appendix. NPHC Joint Statement Against Hazing (2003)

Joint Position Statement against Hazing

The organizations of the National Pan-Hellenic Council, Inc. (NPHC) are com-mitted to nurturing the ideals of sisterhood and fraternalism in an atmosphere of responsibility and respect. We are also committed to upholding the dignity and self-respect of all persons seeking membership therein. Hazing is antithetical to this commitment and is prohibited by the rules of each NPHC organization. In 1990, the member organizations of the NPHC jointly agreed to disband pledging as a form of admission. At the dawn of a new millennium, we the members of the National Pan-Hellenic Council do hereby reaffirm our unequivocal opposition to hazing and those who seek to perpetuate it.

RESOLUTION

WHEREAS the National Pan-Hellenic Council, Inc. (NPHC) is comprised of local councils drawn from the ranks of 1.5 million college and professional mem-bers of the nine historically African-American fraternities and sororities, namely; Alpha Phi Alpha Fraternity, Inc., Alpha Kappa Alpha Sorority, Inc., Kappa Alpha Psi Fraternity, Inc., Omega Psi Phi Fraternity, Inc., Delta Sigma Theta Sorority, Inc., Phi Beta Sigma Fraternity, Inc., Zeta Phi Beta Sorority, Inc., Sigma Gamma Rho Sorority, Inc., and Iota Phi Theta Fraternity, Inc., and the Council of Presi-dents of these member organizations who come together on issues that promote the common purposes and general good for which these organizations exist; and

WHEREAS these NPHC organizations, operating through chapters located in the United States, the Caribbean, Europe, Africa, and Asia, are proud of their commitment since 1906 to scholarship, community service, leadership and the promotion of sisterhood and brotherhood in an atmosphere of respect and re-sponsibility; and

WHEREAS these NPHC organizations are likewise committed to promoting the self-respect and dignity of all persons seeking membership in the respective orga-nizations; and

WHEREAS hazing is antithetical to this commitment and is strictly prohibited by the constitution, policies and procedures of each NPHC organization; and

WHEREAS "pledging" has been officially abolished as a process for membership and pledge "lines" have similarly been abolished; and all members and prospective members are prohibited from engaging in hazing, pledge or pre-pledge "lines"; and

WHEREAS in 1990, the NPHC organizations issued a joint statement announcing the elimination of pledging and each has instituted within its respective organization, a revised membership development and intake process; and

WHEREAS each NPHC organization has instituted strong policies against hazing and has taken steps to reinforce and strengthen its stand against prohibited conduct: and

WHEREAS as we begin this new century and a renewed commitment to the fundamental principles of brotherhood, sisterhood, human dignity and mutual respect, the NPHC organizations desire to make their commitment against hazing abundantly clear and fully intend for every member, prospective member, parent, university and the general public to be aware of the individual and collective position of the organizations against hazing; and

WHEREAS these NPHC organizations further desire to make known their respective commitment to hold any person who engages in hazing individually and personally liable to the victim and to answer to the law and the organization; and will hold such persons to respond in monetary damages, civil and criminal penalties and severe disciplinary actions by the organization, including expulsion; and

WHEREAS the definition of hazing has been held to include *any action taken or situation created that involves or results in abusive, physical contact or mutual harassment of a prospective Fraternity or Sorority member; and that any such action is considered hazing, whether it occurs on or off the Fraternity or Sorority premises, campus or place where chapters or prospective members meet: and that hazing has also been described to include any action that results in excessive mutual or physical discomfort, embarrassment or harassment; that such activities include, but are not limited to paddling, creation of excessive fatigue, physical or psychological shock, morally degrading or humiliating activities, late work sessions that interfere with scholastic activities and any other activities inconsistent with fraternal law and regulations and policies of the affiliated educational institution and federal, state or local law;* and

WHEREAS such illegal conduct is inimical to the principles for which each organization stands and fails to foster respect for fellow members or preserve human dignity;

BE IT RESOLVED AND RESTATED WITH EMPHASIS ANEW that hazing, pledging, pledge "lines," pre-pledge "lines" or post-intake hazing are strictly prohibited by these NPHC organizations; and

BE IT FURTHER RESOLVED, RESTATED AND MADE KNOWN that these NPHC organizations are committed to eradicate the scourge of hazing and to that end;

That the intake process has been recodified by each organization, which permits the conduct of intake only when specifically authorized by the officer placed in charge of the process and at only such times, places and in the presence of persons specifically authorized and certified to conduct the intake process;

That prospective members and the parents of collegiate applicants are advised that hazing is not a requirement for membership, nor is it tolerated;

That members and prospective members must attest that they are fully aware of the organization's policy against hazing and will not engage in prohibited conduct and that the organization will fully cooperate with law enforcement authorities and with university officials in the investigation and prosecution of hazing or other illegal activity;

That members and applicants for membership are also put on written notice that they will be held responsible to the organization for violation of policies against hazing and the organization will pursue full remedies allowed by the law to obtain indemnification for damages caused by the actions of the members or applicants who participated in illegal, unauthorized or prohibited conduct despite notice to refrain from such conduct;

That each organization shall enforce severe penalties, including expulsion, for proven violations of its policies against and impose sanctions against a chapter involved and cooperate with the university in implementing sanctions by the university;

That members and applicants for membership shall be required to immediately notify the national office of the Fraternity or Sorority, the local chapter advisor, university officials and law enforcement officials of any observed hazing incident or improper activity believed to be in violation of the policy against hazing, without fear of reprisal and their application for membership will not be affected by so doing; and, indeed, failure to report known violations may disqualify a candidate for membership; and, finally,

That these NPHC organizations shall continue to encourage their members to participate in activities which promote high scholastic achievement, sisterhood, brotherhood, loyalty and leadership; and shall continue to affirm sound values and the worth of every member working together to accomplish organizational goals and serve the community.

Harry E. Johnson, Esq. National President Alpha Phi Alpha Fraternity, Inc.

Linda M. White Supreme Basileus Alpha Kappa Alpha Sorority, Inc.
Samuel C. Hamilton Grand Polemarch Kappa Alpha Psi Fraternity, Inc.
George H. Grace Grand Basileus Omega Psi Phi Fraternity, Inc.
Gwendolyn E. Boyd National President Delta Sigma Theta Sorority, Inc.
Arthur R. Thomas, Esq. National President Phi Beta Sigma Fraternity, Inc.
Barbara C. Moore Grand Basileus Zeta Phi Beta Sorority, Inc.
Helen J. Owens Grand Basileus Sigma Gamma Rho Sorority, Inc.
Steven T. Birdine Grand Polaris Iota Phi Theta Fraternity, Inc.

REFERENCES

Abes, E., Jones, S., and McEwen, M. (2007). Reconceptualizing the model of multiple dimensions of identity: The role of meaning-making capacity in the construction of multiple identities. *Journal of College Student Development, 48*(1), 1–22.

"About Iota." (n.d.). Retrieved on February 20, 2010 from http://www.iotaphitheta.org/page2.html.

Anonymous. (1997, June 12). Pledging a brother, not intaking a "paper brother." *Black Issues in Higher Education, 14*(8), 26–27.

Burke, P., and Stets, J. (2009). *Identity theory*. Oxford: Oxford University Press.

Chenoweth, K. (1998, June 25). When Hazing Leads to Death: One Campus' Response. *Black Issues in Higher Education, 15*(9), 20–21.

DeSantis, A., and Coleman, M. (2008). Not on my line: Attitudes about homosexuality in Black fraternities. In G. Parks (Ed.). (2008). *Black Greek-letter organizations in the 21ˢᵗ century: Our fight has just begun*. Lexington: The University Press of Kentucky.

Fisher, J. (2010). The pain of pledging: Hazing at Cornell. *The Cornell Daily Sun* (2010, February 4). Retrieved on February 20, 2010, from http://cornellsun.com/node/40541

Giddings, P. (1988). *In search of sisterhood: Delta Sigma Theta and the challenge of the Black sorority movement*. New York: Morrow.

Guiffrida, D. (2003). African American student organizations as agents of social integration. *Journal of College Student Development*, May/June 2003, *44(3)*, 304–319.

Harper, S., and Harris, F. (2006). The role of Black fraternities in the African American male undergraduate experience. In M. J. Cujet (2006). *African American men in college*. San Francisco: Jossey-Bass.

Harper, S., and Nichols, A. (2008). Are they not all the same? Racial heterogeneity among Black male undergraduates. *Journal of College Student Development, 49*(3), 199–214.

Hughey, M. (2008). "Cuz I'm young and I'm Black and my hat's real low?" A critique of Black Greeks as "educated gangs." In G. Parks (Ed.). (2008). *Black Greek-letter organizations in the 21ˢᵗ century: Our fight has just begun*. Lexington: The University Press of Kentucky.

Jones, R. L. (2004). *Black haze: Violence, sacrifice, and manhood in Black Greek-letter fraternities*. Albany: SUNY Press.

Kimbrough, W. (1997, Spring). The membership intake movement of historically Black Greek-Letter Organizations. *National Association of Student Personnel Administrators Journal, 34*(3), 229–239.

Lemelle, A. (2010). *Black masculinity and sexual politics*. New York: Routledge.

McClure, S. (2006). Voluntary association membership: Black Greek men on a predominantly White campus. *Journal of Higher Education, 77*(6), 1036–1057.

Moran, J. J., Yengo, L., & Algier, A. M. (1994). Participation in minority oriented cocurricular organizations. *Journal of College Student Development*, 35, 143.

Morgan, J. (1998, October 28). The broken pledges of Greek life. *Black Issues in Higher Education, 15*(18), 18–19.

Murguia, E., Padilla, R. V., & Pavel, M. (1991). Ethnicity and the concept of social integration in Tinto's model of institutional departure. *Journal of College Student Development, 32,* 433–439.

National Panhellenic Council. (2007). "About Us." Retrieved on February 26, 2010, from http://www.nphchq.org/

NPHC Joint Statement Against Hazing. (2003). Retrieved on February 26, 2010, from http://www.nphchq.org/docs/NPHCJointPositionStatementAgainstHazing2003.pdf.

Nuwer, H. (1999). *Wrongs of passage: Fraternities, sororities, and binge drinking.* Bloomington, IN: Indiana University Press.

Ruffins, P. (1997, June 12). Fratricide: Are African American fraternities beating themselves to death? *Black Issues in Higher Education, 14*(8), 18–25.

Ruffins, P. (1998, June 25). The persistent madness of Greek hazing. *Black Issues in Higher Education, 15*(9), 14–18.

Ruffins, P., Chenoweth, K., and Evelyn, J. (1998, June 25). Curing the madness. *Black Issues in Higher Education, 15*(9), 16.

Smoot, Chuck. (n.d.). Pledging vs. hazing. Retrieved on November 15, 1998 from: http://www.geocities.com/Athens/5506/essay2.html.

Stewart, D. (2008). Being all of me: Black students negotiating multiple identities. *Journal of Higher Education, 79*(2), 183–207.

Taylor, C. M., & Howard-Hamilton, M. F. (1995). Student involvement and racial identity attitudes among African American males. *Journal of College Student Development, 36,* 330–336.

Thomas, R. (1998). Silent rituals, raging hearts. In S. Windmeyer and P. Freeman. (1998). *Out of Fraternity Row: Personal accounts of being gay in a college fraternity.* Los Angeles and New York: Alyson Books.

Watkins, D., Green, B., Goodson, P., Guidry, J., and Stanley, C. (2007). Using focus groups to explore the stressful life events of Black college men. *Journal of College Development, 48*(1), 105–118.

Young, V. (2007). *Your average nigga: Performing race, literacy and masculinity.* Detroit, MI: Wayne State University Press.

Part Three

Educational Possibilities

Chapter Ten

Slaughtering the Innocents

The (Mis-)Education of African American Males

M. Christopher Brown II

I've taken care of myself. I have.
I've never been in trouble with the law.
I've read hundreds of books, written poems, painted pictures.
I've traveled the world.
I serve my country. I speak 2 languages and I'm working on a third.
I never fathered any children. I've never done drugs or even smoked a cigarette.
   —Antwone Fisher (Washington, 2002)

Jannie Had a Little Lamb

As a child, I was considered a "nice young man" according to most social stan-dards, despite publicly professed pathologies of growing up in a working-class, single parent, female-headed household. Even my familial reality was ma-triarchal—led by my maternal grandmother, the late Deaconess Evelyna Smith Brown. I was a good boy, a church boy, a nerd, a do-gooder, a momma's boy, and indeed my grandmother's child although born of Jannie.

It was my great (mis-)fortune to have been born on the planet earth in the rapidly on-setting final quarter of the twentieth century. I was born after the baby boomers and slightly before generation "x." I was born an only child, who for years was the only grandchild, but I have uncles and aunts barely a decade my senior and a host of cousins more than a decade my junior. I was born after legal desegregation and forced integration but before multiculturalism and multira-cialism. Patricia Williams (1991) in her book-length, autobiographical essay—

The Alchemy of Race and Rights—says that "subject position is everything" (p. 3). Hence, I can assert that I was born in between—not quite, neither, nor.

My communal reality was a formerly all-Black middle class enclave held over from redlining and residential discrimination. We lived on a neighborhood block with three principals, one lawyer, a mortician, and a full complement of working two-parent families although my grandmother worked as a laborer in the laundry of the local medical college. The neighborhood experienced continued decline throughout my youth and is now host to a smorgasbord of criminal activity.

Throughout my K-12 experience, I had many of the same teachers and principals as my uncles and aunts because of the ways in which integrated schools hired away the best African American teachers from the formerly segregated schools (Brown, 2000b; Brown & Bartee, 2007; Brown & Dancy, 2009). The schools located in the community of my youth now struggle to meet Adequate Yearly Progress (AYP) under the national legislation, No Child Left Behind (Lathem, 2011). However, I recall during my matriculation that we had both new and second-hand books. And since I was a "good boy" with good grades I always got issued a new book. I was a student patrol in elementary school—a young gentleman who could always be trusted to carry a note down the hall or take names when the teacher was in absentia.

The disruption to the preceding narrative occurred in fifth grade when my homeroom teacher was imported from the other side of the Cooper River—Mrs. Irby. For whatever reason, Mrs. Irby saw no "good" in me. In a strategem that regularly destroys African American males, I was labeled special education and assigned to ride the short yellow bus and sent to classrooms that specialized in stenographic worksheets as a proxy for academic engagement (Brown & Davis, 2000; Brown & Land, 2005; Kunjufu, 2005). I was caught in a bureaucratic system that had all of the psychometricians and specialists to validate their "label," EMH—Emotionally and Mentally Handicapped. At the tender age of 10, I was emblematic of that biblical scripture from the book of Isaiah chapter 53 and verse 7, "He was oppressed and afflicted, yet he did not open his mouth; he was led like a lamb to the slaughter, and as a sheep before its shearers is silent, so he did not open his mouth."

The Oppressed and Afflicted in American Education

There is a sound body of literature on social differences in academic settings (Brown & Bartee, 2007). In fact, there is even a correlative scholarship base for racial and gender differences in education (Brown & Land, 2005). The raced and gendered constructions of African American males in educational settings are critical reference points for both exploring and understanding the differences in their educational outcomes across the academic spectrum. Arguably, African American males are subject to adverse educational outcomes across the academic pipeline.

In recent years public attention regarding the educational achievement gap, has focused on the scholastic performance and social plight of African American males (Dancy, 2012). On metrics both defining and depicting the context and composition of educational settings, African American males are most often and disproportionately ranked at the worst end of the data spectrum. The fundamental queries must then be, are the vast majority African Americans males inherently unable to engage the educational system, or is the educational system inherently unable to effectively serve African American males? Although there is a complex and complicated host of factors and characteristics embedded in each question, the reality is that many African American males are oppressed and afflicted in educational settings.

There is a nuanced form of "school violence" that remains unexamined in the research literature. Delpit (1995) speaks of a disconnectedness in school settings that can emerge by personnel who teach or supervise "other people's children." Whenever dominant communities operate in nexus with subjugated communities the possibility exists for disparate uses and abuses of power. Freire (1993) suggests "violence is initiated by those who oppress, who exploit, who fail to recognize others as persons" (p. 37). In effect, school violence against African American males has become commonplace and common-stock of the infrastructure of education settings giving rise to higher rates of academic failure and general attrition (Brown, 2012). African American males are perennially penalized via higher rates of suspension, historic levels of expulsion, regularized placement in special education tracks, and wholesale removal from heterogeneous classrooms.

In the Schott Foundation's landmark report *Yes We Can: The 2010 Schott 50 State Report on Black Males in Public Education*, the data revealed an academic crisis of eugenic proportion. The central conclusion was that the American educational system is systemically failing African American males. The report stated that less that 50% of African American males complete high school. African American males attend K-12 schools that are low performing and inadequately funded. African American males are more than double the percentage of White males enrollment in the various special education classifications. And for the scarce cadre of African American males who pursue postsecondary education, less than half graduate. The research findings portray a menacing portrait of a nation of schools that fail African American males on a host of indices with nonchalance and impunity. Although the report goes on to posit ways to improve academic conditions, the damage has already been done to millions of African American males in educational settings.

Polite and Davis (1999) note that "to be an African American male in school and society places one at risk for a variety of negative consequences" (p. 1). They argue that the geographic placement and personnel composition can serve as inhibitors to African American males in their pursuit of academic and social gains. Moreover, Polite and Davis assert that some teachers label African American males as unsalvageable in their early schooling experiences. This notion frames the contextual background of Ferguson's (2000) exploration into the lives of young African American boys attending public school. In *Bad Boys: Public Schools in the Making of Black Masculinity*, Ferguson details ethnographic research she conducted at an urban elementary school over a three-and-a-half-year period. Her study examined the ways in which institutional practices and cultural representations of racial difference are covertly and informally reproduced to support the system of racial inequality in America. Ferguson highlighted two main sources of disparate academic impact on the educational performance of African American males—individual and institutional actions against the subject population and stereotypic racial myths regarding cultural difference.

The elementary and secondary experiences of African American males can also influence their decision to pursue or forgo postsecondary education (Brown & Dancy, 2010). Brown and Hurst (2004) found that although the number of African American males awarded the bachelor's degree increased by 52% since 1977, the number of African American women awarded bachelor's degrees has increased by 112%. What is the nature of this disparity?

Dancy and Brown (2008) published an article in the *American Behavioral Scientist*, "Unintended consequences: African American Male Educational attainment and Collegiate Perceptions after *Brown v. Board of Education*," that examines possible reasons for the disparate educational outcomes for African American males in college and university data. Their study reported descriptions of microaggressions and feelings of victimization on campus from these students. Likewise Dawson-Threat (1997), explored the epistemologies, axiologies, and pedagogies embedded in the student-to-student and faculty-to-student interactions that influence African American males on college campuses.

The social attitudes and internal axiologies of personnel in educational settings have a effect on African American male academic performance. Emotional dissonance and cognitive frustration can interrupt the noble gains of American education, thereby rendering the nation's classrooms hostile environments for African American males. In fact, many African American males are afflicted by subtle incidents and subversive systems of educational incongruence that lead to hegemony and oppression in educational settings. The research reveals a clear narrative regarding the educational experiences of many African American males. It is important therefore to engage academic discourses and educational policies that can speak for the "silent" afflictions and oppressions of African American males across the educational panoply.

A Silence about Race in Educational Settings

There is an ominous quiescence in both the educational discourse and public policy regarding the academic experiences of African American males. Coons and Sugarman (1978) argued that "while our national law forbids and sometimes prevents official segregation, it does not appear likely that affirmative integration will soon become a constitutional norm or habit" (p. 40). In effect there is a widening chasm in the academic worlds of "us" and "them"—African American males and everybody else. There are scores of reports, books, and articles, all examining the educational outcomes of disaggregated student populations.

Like a choral refrain, the data reveal differential outcomes for African American males in academic settings. However, there remains no clear intervention because the subject population is "African American." And in America, "race matters" (West, 1993). Most researchers and policymakers refuse to acknowledge the correlation between race and education (Brown & Land, 2005). Education, like race, is not neutral in conception, application, or implication (Anderson, 1988; Hacker, 1992; Mills, 1997). In fact, education is a raced reality emerging from the patterns of social stratification and pigment prejudice of civic spaces. The existence of performance testing and psychological evaluations serves to both establish and exacerbate educational inequality for African American males. Both Freire (1993) and Macedo (1994) remind us that race is a dominant thread in the tapestry of educational settings. Hence the confluence of race and gender in the academic experiences and performance of African American males is of scholarly concern.

According to Delgado (1990), African Americans and other groups similarly situated engaged their paradigmatic and phenomenological experiences through a powerful racial lens. This is a dominant lens for viewing and interpreting most if not all interactions. Nkomo's (1992) article, "The Emperor Has No Clothes: Rewriting 'Race in Organizations'" explores the responsibility of educational research to account for the allegedly invisible role of race in academic settings. Nkomo (1992) writes,

> The children's fairy tale, "The Emperor's New Clothes," is an excellent allegory for the primary way in which organization scholars have chosen to address race in organizations. For the most part, research has tended to study organization populations as homogeneous entities in which race and ethnicity are either "unstated" or considered irrelevant. A perusal of much of our research would lead one to believe that organizations are race neutral (p. 488).

Likewise, Morrison (1992) posits that

> race has become metaphorical—a way of referring to and disguising forces, events, classes, and expressions. . . . It seems that it has a utility far beyond economy, beyond the sequestering of classes from one another, and has assumed a

metaphorical life so completely embedded in daily discourse that it is perhaps more necessary and more on display than ever before (p. 63).

Arguably then, race is the tone, timbre, and pitch in which they communicate their lived experiences; in other words, they speak race. Hence, to silence the role of race in their academic experiences renders them mute—unable to voice their affliction or oppression. Macedo (1994) termed this the "culture of silence." Thus "silent lambs" are an ideal metaphor for African American males in educational settings. If the lambs could speak, what would they say?

It is imperative to give voice to the educational experiences of African American males. Race gives common voice to the shared experiences of most African Americans and the educational engagements of African American males in particular. We must identify the narratives, ponder the counternarratives, rethink the research, and listen to the silences around this population (Bell, 1989, 1992; Delgado, 1989, 1990; Crenshaw, 1995). Delgado (1989) proffered that marginalized groups have the capacity to use their unsilenced voices to heal the injuries resulting from racial oppression—"testimony." Delgado's scholarship speaks prophetically like the apocalyptic scripture of Judeo-Christianity in the Book of Revelations that asserts "they overcame . . . by the blood of the Lamb, and by the word of their testimony."

A race-conscious discourse must be introduced in academic research and educational policy in order to improve the experiences and outcomes of African American males in educational settings. Macedo and Bartolome (1999) state:

> "[W]e need to give them voice." First of all, we need to become keenly aware that voice is not something to be given by those in power. Voice requires struggle and the understanding of both possibilities and limitations. The most educators can do is to create structures that would enable submerged voices to emerge. It is not a gift. Voice is a human right. (p. 39)

Consequently, researchers of and practitioners in the educational environments in which African American males matriculate must "re-read, re-write, and re-define the place of race in the discourses that surround schooling, learning, and human development" (Brown, 2000a). Education as an industry and educators as a profession must rethink our role in enabling or inhibiting the academic success of African American males.

From Shearer to Shepherd: Rethinking the Role of Educators

Over the years, the education profession has "gotten by" by using intuition, folk wisdom, parenting skills, and some pedagogical craft (Brown & Land, 2005; Brown, Dancy, & Norfles, 2006). Schools and universities have engaged in a series of reform efforts over the past 15 years that have been documented in educational literature (Book, 1996; Goodlad, 1988; Sarason, 1990). The continued emphasis on educational innovation and improved student outcomes has led to a cacophonous engagement of researchers, policymakers, teachers, and the public (Ravitch, 2010). The canyon-like gap between intentions and motivation complicates the best stakeholder efforts toward building equitable educational settings for all students, and most especially African American males. Consequently, the education system has been so involved in navel-gazing that the voice of the African American male experience has been almost silenced (Dancy, 2012).

Many of the difficult realities grown in educational settings emerge from a deep, dark soil—mixed and mired with social problems, economic influences, and community realities. The students who arrive at classroom doors across our nation have complex and complicated lives, capabilities, needs, and aspirations. The confluence of familial, social, and educational realities has profound implications for African American male academic performance. Too many African American males are relegated to classrooms that fail to facilitate their intellectual growth, emotional development, and civic engagement. In many educational settings, African American males are regularly "devalued, ignored, and displaced" (Brown & Davis, 2000). This tragic reality has the potential to lead these students toward psychological dependency and disruptive social behavior (Comer & Poussaint, 1992).

According to Brown & Bartee (2000), in their article, "African American Students in the Desegregated P–16 Pipeline: Opportunities, Outcomes, and Value-Based Ideologies," educators play in critical role in the "stoppage," "leaks," and "flow" of the educational pipeline. They say that educational settings, like shears, can cut short the academic attainment and aspirations of African American students. Hence, school contexts and personnel dispositions serve as hidden hands in the shearing of African American male educational attainment. Wade Boykin (Quoted in Neisser, 1986) states:

> What a child does or does not do is essentially the question of academic performance. It is what Black children do not do in school that create the need for the present volume. The issue of what a child can do, in contrast, is one of cognitive competence. In its strong form, it implies maturational constraints or structural limitations on ability; in a weaker form it refers to what a child cannot do at present but could in the future if conditions were favorable. (p. 7)

Rather than shearing the educational opportunities and outcomes of African American males, educators must shepherd this population's academic ambitions and attainment.

Freire (1998) in *Teachers as Cultural Workers: Letters to Those Who Dare to Teach*, Brown and Davis (2000) in *Black Sons to Mothers: Compliments, Critiques, and Challenges for Cultural Workers in Education,* and Dancy (2012) in *The Brother Code: Manhood and Masculinity among African American Men in College,* all do two important things. First, all three books provide important insights into the problems embedded in the educational settings that serve African American males. Second, each book provides useful guidance on how schools, colleges, teachers, faculty, principals, presidents, deans, and support staff influence the possibilities of the African American male students they serve. For many African American males in educational settings access to educational opportunity has not yet been translated into attainment of equitable outcomes.

Educational settings must engage in mutually transformative relationships with African American males. Educational settings must provide a quality education for all students and conceptualize modes of delivery that effectively serve all students. George Counts (1932) argues that:

> Education as a force. . . must bridge the gap between school and society and play some part in the fashioning of those great common purposes which should bind the two together. . . . If the schools are to be really effective, they must become centers for the building, and not merely for the contemplation of our civilization (pp. 28, 34).

Educational settings must assume responsibility for this critical role within society. The adoption of an ethos of serving all students can positively impact the experiences of African American males across the academic continuum.

In order for the educational data trends for African American males to improve, researchers and personnel in educational settings must address what forms of knowledge and learning are given preference as well as the modes of interaction that maximize educational attainment for all populations. The rising tide of effective engagement in educational settings will raise the boat of positive and productive African American male educational experiences. Reformation, revitalization, and reconstitution of the educational spaces that African American males occupy portend a rethinking of the role of educators in various classroom situations, interactive scenarios, and academic settings. The ability of African American males to maximize their performance and potential on academic metrics and social indices will depend upon the willingness of educational settings to respond to their needs and interests.

Classrooms and Coffins: Concluding Thoughts

Despite the faults and failings of the public educational system that serves most African American males, I managed to survive. As a result of good teachers (Ladson-Billings, 1994), a village of mothers (Brown & Davis, 2000), and mentoring (Brown & Dancy, 2011) combined with internal locus of control (Brown, 2011), resilience (Brown & Bartee, 2007), and the sheer will to prevail, I successfully navigated the academic pipeline. I graduated in the college preparatory track from high school. I completed the bachelor's degree in four years *cum laude*. I earned a master's degree in one year and a Ph.D. in three years. I served on several university faculties and have been tenured and promoted from the rank of assistant professor past professor to the rank of university professor. I directed a national research center, have been a dean at a research university, served as a provost of a highly selective liberal arts college, and now serve as president of the nation's oldest historically Black land-grant university.

My ability or providence in successfully matriculating through various educational spaces and social frames does not negate the power and damage of the coordinated system of educational settings that "mis-educate" African American males (Woodson, 1933). Moreover, as a silent lamb in the fifth grade banished to the educational slaughtering house, it was the voices of resistance from my mother, a teachers' aide, and the school guidance counselor that yelled out before the shearers "Please do not cut this one." My mother was persistent in the face of the bureaucracy of shearers that her only begotten son was not just a lamb, but a man-child destined for the promised land (Brown, 1965). The all-Black teacher's aide staff in the special education contingent of my middle school viewed their role as one of shepherd and not shearer. Those teacher's aides, especially Mrs. Brown (no kin), protected me from bullies and led me through my individualized education plan. They made certain that I did more than work sheets and forced the principal to mainstream me into gifted and talented courses. Although afflicted and oppressed, I had shepherds who spoke for me during my "dumb silence."

In the divinity of time, my guidance counselor and I were members of the same church. Mrs. Brown (again no kin) was my Sunday School teacher and church youth director. Her parents and my grandmother were friends and lived just one block apart. She and my mother, as well as my older uncles and aunts, grew up and attended school together. Without fail, she would interrupt the stratagem to lead me into the slaughterhouse. She was the guidance counselor in my elementary school, and by the time I emerged from the special education experience in middle school she had been promoted to guidance counselor in my high school. Time and time again, she would be my "ram in the bush."

As an African American male, I was oppressed and afflicted in an educational setting but I had no voice with which to speak. In fifth grade, I was led like a lamb to the slaughter when labeled emotionally and mentally handicapped. There was nothing I could say to disprove the diagnosis of the school psychologist or the pronouncements of Mrs. Irby. Like so many African American males, based on my new label, I was marked for potential social services and the likelihood of imprisonment. I escaped the academic slaughterhouse. Fortunately, I had my mother, my teacher's aide, and my guidance counselor—all three of whom were named Mrs. Brown. But, what about the other little lambs in educational settings across the nation? Who will speak out in the racial silence about the conditions of their academic experiences?

The time has come for concerned citizens and contentious educators to work toward transforming the educational settings in which African American males seek academic knowledge, pursue career skills, and develop social dispositions. The current outcomes for African American males are insufficient to advance their or our collective aims. There is trouble in the nation's schoolhouses. There is a crisis on college campuses. Similarly, the complex nexus of other educational contexts continues to yield woeful academic outcomes for African American males. It behooves me to declare we have too many funerals for American American males and an insufficient number of graduations for them across all levels of the educational spectrum.

Finally, "Coffin for Head of State" is one of my favorite songs by the late Nigerian musical prophet and civil dissident Fela Anikulapo Kuti. His mother—the reknowned feminist and anti-colonial activist, Funmilayo Ransome Kuti—was thrown out of a second-story window by the Nigerian military during a raid and died after months in a coma (Veal, 2000). Fela (as he was affectionately called) took the coffin containing her corpse to "supreme presidential residence"—the equivalent of our White House. The president did not open the door of the residence for days until the coffin was removed. Fela's song asserts "Dem no wan take am. / Who go wan take coffin? / Dem must take am, / For the bad bad bad things, / Wey dem don do."

Who will carry the coffins of the African American males slaughtered by inadequate personnel, insufficient engagement, and ineffective educational spaces?

In his book *The Fire Next Time,* James Baldwin (1962) writes, "This is the crime of which I accuse my country and my countrymen, and for which neither I nor time nor history will ever forgive them, that they have destroyed and are destroying hundreds of thousands of lives and do not know it and do not want to know it. . . . It is their innocence which constitutes the crime" (p. 3). *The time has come to stop slaughtering the innocent.*

References

Anderson, J. (1988). *The education of Blacks in the south, 1860–1935.* Chapel Hill: The University of North Carolina.

Baldwin, J. (1962). *The fire next time.* New York: Vintage.

Bell, D. (1989). The final report: Harvard's affirmative action allegory. *Michigan Law Review, 87,* 2382–2410.

Bell, D. (1992). *Faces at the bottom of the well: The permanence of racism.* New York: Basic Books.

Book, C. (1996). Professional development schools. In J. Shulman (Ed.), *Handbook for research on teacher education* (2nd ed., pp. 194–210). New York: Macmillan.

Brown, C. (1965). *Manchild in the promised land.* New York: Signet.

Brown, M. C. (2000a). Involvement with students: How much can I give? In M. Garcia (Ed.), *Succeeding in an academic career: A guide for faculty of color* (pp. 71–88). Westport, CT: Greenwood.

Brown, M. C. (2000b). Seeing the invisible color Black: Race-ing the collegiate desegregation discourse. *Race, Ethnicity and Education, 3,* 259–270.

Brown, M. C. (2011). Making it on the broken pieces of capital and context. In R. D. Bartee (Ed.), *Contemporary perspectives on capital in educational contexts* (pp. ix–xiii). Charlotte, NC: Information Age.

Brown, M. C. (2012). Black boys and blackboards: Examining African American males and masculinity in collegiate spaces. In T. E. Dancy, & M. C. Brown, *African American males and education: Researching the convergence of race and identity.* Charlotte, NC: Information Age.

Brown, M. C., & Bartee, R. D. (2000). African American students in the desegregated P–16 pipeline: Opportunities, outcomes, and value-based ideologies. *National Alliance of Black School Educators Journal, 4,* 15–25.

Brown, M. C., & Bartee, R. D. (2007). *School matters: Why African American students need multiple forms of capital.* New York: Peter Lang.

Brown, M. C., & Dancy, T. E. (2009). An unsteady march toward equity: The social and political contexts of African American educational attainment. In M. C. Brown & R. D. Bartee, *The broken cisterns of African American education: Academic performance and achievement in the post-Brown era* (pp. 17–42). Greenwich, CT: Information Age.

Brown, M. C., & Dancy, T. E. (2010). African American male collegians and the sword of Damocles: Understanding the postsecondary pendulum of progress and peril. In V. C. Polite & E. M. Zamani-Gallaher (Eds.), *The state of the African American male* (pp. 249-263). East Lansing: Michigan State University Press.

Brown, M. C., & Dancy, T. E. (2011). Mentorship, induction, and the professional development of educators of color: Practicing theory, theorizing practice. *Journal of School Leadership, 21,* 607–634.

Brown, M. C., & Davis, J. E. (Eds.). (2000). *Black sons to mothers: Compliments, critiques, and challenges for cultural workers in education.* New York: Peter Lang.

Brown, M. C., & Hurst, T. (2004). *Educational attainment of African American males post-Brown v. Board of Education.* Fairfax, VA: The Frederick D. Patterson Institute of the United Negro College Fund.

Brown, M. C., & Land, R. R. (2005). *The politics of curricular change: Race, hegemony and power in education.* New York: Peter Lang.

Brown, M. C., Dancy, T. E., & Norfles, N. S. (2006). A nation still at risk: No Child Left Behind and the salvation of disadvantaged students. In F. Brown & R. Hunter (Eds.), *No Child Left Behind and Disadvantaged Students in Urban Schools* (pp. 341–364). Greenwich, CT: Information Age Publishing.

Comer, J. P., and Poussaint, A. F. (1992). *Raising Black children: Two leading psychiatrists confront the educational, social, and emotional problems facing Black children.* New York: Plume/Penguin.

Coons, J. E., & S. D. Sugarman. *(1978). Education by choice: The case for family control.* Berkeley: University of California Press.

Counts, G. S. (1932). *Dare the school build a new social order?* New York: John Day.

Crenshaw, K. (Ed.). (1995). *Critical race theory: The key writings that formed the movement.* New York: The New Press.

Dancy, T. E. (2012). *The brother code: Manhood and masculinity among African American men in college.* Charlotte, NC: Information Age.

Dancy, T. E., & Brown, M. C. (2008). Unintended consequences: African American male educational attainment and collegiate perceptions after *Brown v. Board of Education. American Behavioral Scientist, 51,* 984–1003.

Dawson-Threat, J. (1997). Enhancing in-class academic experiences for African American men. In M. J. Cuyjet (Ed.), *Helping African American men succeed in college,* 31–42. San Francisco: Jossey-Bass.

Delgado, R. (1989). Storytelling for oppositionists and others: A plea for narrative. *Michigan Law Review, 87*, 2411–2441.

Delgado, R. (1990). When a story is just a story: Does voice really matter? *Virginia Law Review, 76*, 95–111.

Delpit, L. (1995). *Other people's children: Cultural conflict in the classroom.* New York: The New Press.

Ferguson, A. A. (2000). *Bad boys: Public schools in the making of Black masculinity.* Ann Arbor: University of Michigan Press.

Freire, P. (1993). *Pedagogy of the oppressed.* New York: Continuum.

Freire, P. (1998). *Teachers as cultural workers: Letters to those who dare to teach.* Boulder, CO: Westview.

Goodlad, J. (1988). School-university partnerships for educational renewal: Rationale and concepts. In K. Sirotnik & J. Goodlad (Eds.), *School-university partnerships in action: Concepts, cases, and concerns* (pp. 3–31). New York: Teachers College Press.

Hacker, A. (1992). *Two nations: Black and White, separate, hostile, unequal.* New York: Macmillan.

Kunjufu, J. (2005). Keeping Black boys out of special education. Chicago: African American Images.

Ladson-Billings, G. (1994). *The dreamkeepers: Successful teachers of African American children.* San Francisco: Jossey-Bass.

Lathem, J. (2011, July 29). Only 27% of elementary, middle schools make AYP. *Live 5 WCSC.* Retrieved from http://www.live5news.com/story/15172525/only–27-of-elementary-middle-schools-make-ayp

Macedo, D. (1994). *Literacies of power.* Boulder, CO: Westview.

Macedo, D., & Bartolome, L. (1999). *Dancing with bigotry: Beyond the politics of tolerance.* New York: St. Martin's.

Mills, C. W. (1997). *The racial contract.* Ithaca, NY: Cornell University Press.

Morrison, T. (1992). *Playing in the dark: Whiteness and the literary imagination.* Cambridge: Harvard University Press.

Neisser, U. (Ed). (1986). *The school achievement of minority children: New perspectives.* Hillsdale, NJ: Lawrence Erlbaum Associates.

Nkomo, S. M. (1992). The emperor has no clothes: Rewriting "race in organizations." *Academy of Management Review, 17*(3), 487–513.

Polite, V. C., & Davis, J. E. (1999). *African American males in school and society: Practices and policies for effective education.* New York: Teachers College Press.

Ravitch, D. (2010). *The death and life of the great American school system: How testing and choice are undermining education.* New York: Basic.

Sarason, S. (1990). *The predictable failure of educational reform*: Can we change course before it's too late? San Francisco, CA: Jossey-Bass.

Schott Foundation, The. (2010). *Yes, we can: The 2010 Schott 50 State Report on Black Males in Public Education.* New York: Author.

Veal, M. (2000). *Fela: The life and time of an African musical icon.* Philadelphia: Temple University Press.

Washington, D. (Director). (2002). *Antwone Fisher* [Film]. San Diego: Fox Searchlight.

West, C. (1993). *Race matters.* Boston: Beacon.

Williams, P. J. (1991). *The alchemy of race and rights.* Cambridge, MA: Harvard University Press.

Woodson, C. G. (1933). *The mis-education of the Negro.* Washington, DC: Associated Publishers.

Thematic Bibliography on Black Males in Education

Timothy K. Eatman

The original volume, *Black Sons to Mothers: Compliments, Critiques, and Challenges for Cultural Workers in Education,* which the current volume reflects and extends, did not include a stand-alone bibliography. Notwithstanding, the chapters in both books present a wealth of scholarship and useful information about the phenomenological lives of African American males granting special emphasis on educational dimensions. This bibliography provides a focused sampling of the best research on the subject generated over the past decade.

Organized into three sections: I. Parenting, Mentoring, and General Educational Issues, II. Primary and Secondary Education, and III. Higher Education, this bibliography has been constructed to pivot among both traditional and evolving genres of knowledge creation and dissemination. Sections may contain books, articles and reports, theses and web resources. The final category, web resources is drawn broadly to include salient knowledge in and/or presented through non-traditional scholarly formats including websites, audiovisual artifacts (i.e., speeches, interviews, developed as podcasts, webinars and other presentations), web-based studies as well as databases or annotated bibliographies. One will also find information on high-profile organizations and programs that serve this crucial area. It is important to note that the sections of this bibliography are not intended to be mutually exclusive. Therefore some items could easily have been placed in several sections.

This bibliography represents some of the most compelling current scholarship and general information about the education of Black males available today. Taken together, references in the chapters and this bibliography (which may represent a fair amount of overlap) will lead those interested in the educational experiences of Black males to substantive and useful resources.

The African American Male: An Annotated Bibliography (1999) compiled by Jacob U. Gordon is probably the most recent comprehensive annotated resource specifically focused on Black males. The structure of my current bibliography benefits from that work. With the exception of a few classic and overlooked pieces, this work includes items published within the ten-year period 1999–2009. Finally, it should be noted that although the focus here is on the education of Black males, several items address quality education in its broadest sense.

I. Parenting, Mentoring, and General Educational Issues

Articles and Reports

Grantham, T. (2004). Multicultural mentoring to increase Black male representation in gifted programs. *Gifted Child Quarterly, 48*(3), 232–245.

Hébert, T. (2001). "If I had a new notebook, I know things would change": Bright underachieving young men in urban classrooms. *Gifted Child Quarterly. 45*(3), 174–194.

Lee, C. (2000). *The state of knowledge about the education of African Americans.* Washington, DC: Commission on Black Education, American Educational Research Association.

Lee, C. D. (2008). 2008 Wallace Foundation Distinguished Lecture—The centrality of culture to the scientific study of learning and development: How an ecological framework in education research facilitates civic responsibility. *Educational Researcher, 37*(5), 267–279.

Maryland, Brooks, D., & Johnson, O. M. (2006). [Report]. [Maryland]: *Task Force on the Education of Maryland's African-American Males.* Maryland State Department of Education. 200 West Baltimore Street. Baltimore MD 21201

Nebbitt, V. (2009). Self-efficacy in African American adolescent males living in Urban Public Housing. *Journal of Black Psychology, 35*(3), 295.

Stoops, N. Educational attainment in the United States: 2003. *Current Population Reports.* June 2004

The Schott Foundation for Public Education. (2008). *50 State Report on Public Education and Black Males.* Retrieved October 15, 2009, from http://www.blackboysreport.org/.

Eooks

Du Bois, W. E. B. (1966). *The souls of Black folk* (Modern Library Edition). New York: Blue Heron.

Gordon, J. U. (1999). *The African-American male: An annotated bibliography.* Westport, CT: Greenwood Press.

Hewlett, S. A., Rankin, N., et al. (2002). *Taking parenting public: The case for a new social movement.* Lanham, MD: Rowman & Littlefield.

Hrabowski, F. A., Maton, K. I., & Greif, G. L. (1998). *Beating the odds: Raising academically successful African American males.* New York: Oxford University Press.

Kafele, B. K. (2009). *Motivating Black males to achieve in school and in life.* Alexandria, VA: ASCD.

Thompson, G. L. (2007). *Up where we belong: Helping African American and Latino students rise in school and in life.* San Francisco: Jossey-Bass.

West, C. (1993). *Race matters.* Boston: Beacon Press.

West, C., & Ritz, D. (2009). *Brother West: Living and loving out loud: A memoir.* New York: Smiley Books.

Woodson, C. G. (2000). *The mis-education of the Negro.* Chicago: African American Images.

Theses

Derrick, L. (2009). Exploring mentoring relationships between African American high school males and African American male principals. Unpublished Ed.D., Bowling Green State University, United States—Ohio.

Gilliam, A. (2009). The effect of communalism and verve on the academic performance of African-American elementary school students. Unpublished M.S., Howard University, United States—District of Columbia.

Howell, A. (2009). Cultural self-efficacy and leadership: Adolescent African-American male perspectives through digital diaries. Unpublished Ed.D., Cambridge College, United States—Massachusetts.

Williams, P. (2009). Exploring teachers' and Black male students' perceptions of intelligence. Unpublished Ph.D., University of Miami, United States—Florida.

Web Resources

Kunjufu, J., (2009) Black Boys and Special Education—Change Is Needed! Teachers of Color: The Unique Resource Guide for World-Class Teachers Retrieved October 22, 2009, from http://www.teachersofcolor.com/2009/04/black-boys-and-special-education-change-is- needed/

Michigan Reach-out: A Center Linking College and Community Mentors with Children and Teens (2009) Retrieved August 12, 2009 from http://www.reachoutmichigan.org/index.htm

National CARES Mentoring Movement (2009) Retrieved August 12, 2009 from http://caresmentoring.com/

National Public Radio (Producer). (2006, Feb. 20) African American Boys in Crisis [Podcast]. Retrieved October 22, 2009 from http://www.npr.org/templates/story/story.php?storyId=5225088

II. Primary and Secondary Education

Articles and Reports

Berry III, Robert Q. (2005). Voices of success: Descriptive portraits of two successful African American male middle school mathematics students. *Journal of African American Studies* (formerly *Journal of African American Men*), 8(4), 46–62.

Bonner, F., II, Jennings, M., Marbley, A., & Brown, L. (2008). Capitalizing on leadership capacity: Gifted African American males in high school. *Roeper Review, 30*(2), 93.

Braddock, J. H., Royster, D. A., Winfield, L. F., & Hawkins, R. (1991). Bouncing back: Sports and academic resilience among African-American males. *Education and Urban Society, 24*(1), 113–131.

Fultz, M., & Brown, A. (2008). Historical perspectives on African American males as subjects of education policy. *The American Behavioral Scientist, 51*(7), 854.

Ladson-Billings, G. (2006). From the achievement gap to the education debt: Understanding achievement in U.S. schools. *Educational Researcher, 35*(1), 3–12.

Milner, H. Richard, IV. (2007). African American males in urban schools: No excuses—teach and empower. *Theory into Practice, 46*(3), 239.

Monroe, C. (2005). Why are "bad boys" always black? Causes of disproportionality in school discipline and recommendations for change. *The Clearing House, 79*(1), 45–50.

Moore, J., III, Henfield, M., & Owens, D. (2008). African American males in Special Education. *The American Behavioral Scientist, 51*(7), 907.

Noguera, P. (2003). The trouble with Black Boys: The role and influence of environmental and cultural factors on the academic performance of African American males. *Urban Education, 38* (4): 431–459.

Skiba, R. J., Michael, R. S., Nardo, A. C., & Peterson, R. (2000). The color of discipline: Sources of racial and gender disproportionality in school punishment (Policy Research Report SRS1).

Bloomington, IN: Indiana Education Policy Center. Retrieved May 29, 2007, from http://www.indiana.edu/~safeschl/cod.pdf

Task Force on the Education of Maryland's African-American Males. (2006). Baltimore: Maryland State Department of Education. http://www.marylandpublicschools.org/MSDE.

Tate, W. I. (2008). The political economy of teacher quality in school mathematics. *The American Behavioral Scientist, 51*(7), 953.

Thompson, L. R., & Lewis, B. F. (2005). Shooting for the stars: A case study of the mathematics achievement and career attainment of an African American male high school student. *The High School Journal, 88*(4), 6.

Books

Brown, M. C., and Davis, J. E. (2000). *Black sons to mothers: Compliments, critiques, and challenges for cultural workers in education.* New York: Peter Lang.

Butler-Derge, S. R. (2009). *Rites of passage: A program for high school African American males.* Lanham, MD: University Press of America.

Ferguson, A. A. (2000). *Bad boys: Public schools in the making of Black masculinity.* Ann Arbor: University of Michigan Press.

Kunjufu, J. (2005). *Keeping Black boys out of special education.* Chicago: African American Images.

Kunjufu, J. (2001). *State of emergency: We must save African American males.* Chicago: African American Images.

Kunjufu, J. (1995). *Countering the conspiracy to destroy Black boys.* Chicago: African American Images.

Ladson-Billings, G. (2005). *Beyond the big house: African American educators on teacher education.* New York: Teachers College Press.

Ladson-Billings, G. (1994). *The dreamkeepers: Successful teachers of African American children.* San Francisco: Jossey-Bass.

Landsman, J., & Lewis, C. W. (2006). *White teachers, diverse classrooms: A guide to building inclusive schools, promoting high expectations, and eliminating racism.* Sterling, VA: Stylus.

Lewis, C. W., & Erskine, K. F. (2008). *The dilemmas of being an African American male in the new millennium: Solutions for life transformation.* West Conshohocken, PA: Infinity.

Orfield, G. (Ed.). (2004). *Dropouts in America: Confronting the graduation rate crisis.* Cambridge: Harvard Education Press.

Polite, V. C., & Davis, J. E. (1999). *African American males in school and society: Practices and policies for effective education.* New York: Teachers College Press.

Sandler, S. (2000). *Turning to each other, not on each other: How school communities prevent racial bias in school discipline.* San Francisco, CA: Justice Matters.

Tatum, B. D. (2003). *"Why are all the Black kids sitting together in the cafeteria?" And other conversations about race.* New York: Basic Books.

Thompson, G. L. (2004). *Through ebony eyes: What teachers need to know but are afraid to ask about African-American students.* San Francisco: Jossey-Bass.

Toldson, I. A. (2008). *Breaking barriers: Plotting the path to academic success for school-age African-American males.* Washington, DC: Congressional Black Caucus Foundation, Inc.

Theses

Mahany, K. (2009). A study of the impact of single sex classes on the self-efficacy of urban African American adolescent males. Unpublished Ph.D., Capella University, United States—Minnesota.

Pitts, R. (2009). The relationship of ethnic identity and bicultural competence to academic achievement among urban African-American adolescents. Unpublished Ph.D., Temple University, United States—Pennsylvania.

Prier, D. (2009). Understanding hip-hop as a counter-public space of resistance for Black male youth in urban education. Unpublished Ph.D., Miami University, United States—Ohio.

Stanford, M. (2009). How black and white urban school teachers view African American males. Unpublished Ph.D., State University of New York at Buffalo, United States—New York.

Williams, P. (2009). Exploring teachers' and Black male students' perceptions of intelligence. Unpublished Ph.D., University of Miami, United States—Florida.

Web Resources

Jordan Coleman (2007) *Say It Loud* Film. Retrieved October 1, 2008 from http://www.sayitloud-film.com/

Open Society Institute & Soros Foundation Network (2009). U.S. Programs Black Male Achievement. Retrieved October 22, 2009, from http://www.soros.org/initiatives/usprograms/focus/cbma.

Open Society Institute (Producer). (2009, Nov. 2) Can We Talk about How Race Affects Our Classrooms? [Podcast]. Retrieved October 22, 2009 from http://www.soros.org/initiatives/baltimore/events/classrooms_20091102

Washington Keon Media (Producer). *Beyond the Bricks* Documentary (2009). Retrieved October 30, 2009 from http://www.beyondthebricksproject.com/

III. Higher Education

Articles and Reports

Beamon, K., & Bell, P. A. (2006). Academics versus athletics: An examination of the effects of background and socialization on African American male student athletes. *The Social Science Journal, 43*(3), 393–403.

Cross, T., & Slater, R. B. (2000). The alarming decline in the academic performance of African American men. *The Journal of Blacks in Higher Education, 27,* 82–87.

Dancy, T. E., & Brown, M. C. (2008). Unintended consequences. *The American Behavioral Scientist, 51*(7), 984–1003.

Flowers, L. A. (2006). Effects of attending a 2-year institution on African American males' academic and social integration in the first year of college. *Teachers College Record, 108*(2), 267–286.

Hall, R. E., & Rowan, G. T. (2000). African American males in higher education: A descriptive/qualitative analysis. *Journal of African American men, 5*(3), 3–14.

Hall R. E. (2001). The ball curve: Calculated racism and the stereotype of African American men. *Journal of Black Studies, 32*(1), 104–119.

Harper, S. (2008). Realizing the intended outcomes of *Brown. The American Behavioral Scientist, 51*(7), 1030.

Jackson, J. (2008). Race segregation across the academic workforce. *The American Behavioral Scientist, 51*(7), 1004.

Roach, R. (2001). Where are the Black men on campus? *Black issues in Higher Education, 18*(6).

Wilson-Sadberry, K. R., Winfield, L. F., & Royster, D. A. (1991). Resilience and persistence of African-American males in post-secondary enrollment. *Education and Urban Society, 24*(1), 87–102.

Books

Allen, W. R., Epps, E. G., & Haniff, N. Z. (1991). *College in black and white: African American students in predominantly white and in historically Black public universities.* Albany: SUNY Press.

Cuyjet, M. J. (2006). *African American men in college.* San Francisco: Jossey-Bass.

Fleming, J. (1984). *Blacks in college: A comparative study of students' success in Black and White institutions.* San Francisco: Jossey-Bass.

Gordon, J. U. (2002). *The black male in white America.* Hauppauge, NY: Nova Science.

Jones, L. (2002). *Making it on broken promises: Leading Black male scholars confront the culture of higher education.* Sterling, VA: Stylus.

Smith, W. A., Altbach, P. G., & Lomotey, K. (2002). *The racial crisis in American higher education: Continuing challenges for the twenty-first century.* Albany: SUNY Press.

Theses

Martin, G. (2009). A comparison of African-American athletes' nurturing experiences at historically black and historically white colleges/universities. Unpublished Ed.D., The University of North Carolina at Greensboro, United States—North Carolina.

Noble, R., III. (2009). The impact of self-efficacy on the mathematics achievement of African American males in postsecondary education. Unpublished Ph.D., The University of North Carolina at Chapel Hill, United States—North Carolina.

Pouncil, M. (2009). Acting Black: Black men and doctoral dissertation completion. Unpublished Ed.D., University of California, Irvine and California State University, Long Beach, United States—California.

Roberts, A. (2009). Institutional factors supporting the enrollment and persistence of African-American males in Virginia community colleges. Unpublished Ph.D., Old Dominion University, United States—Virginia.

Web Resources

National Public Radio (Producer). (2006, June. 14). Racial Balancing in Higher Education [Podcast]. Retrieved May 20, 2007 from http://www.npr.org/templates/story/story.php?storyId=5484494

National Public Radio (Producer). (2006, Feb. 20). Program Addresses Gender, Racial Disparities in Higher Ed [Podcast]. Retrieved January 8, 2007 from http://www.npr.org/templates/story/story.php?storyId=5225085

The Todd A. Bell National Resource Center on the African American Male. (2009). The Ohio State University. Retrieved October 22, 2009, from http://oma.osu.edu/currentstudents/bell-resource-center/

Washington Post/Kaiser Family Foundation/Harvard University African American Men Survey. (2006). Survey Snapshot: Views and Experiences of Young Black Males. Retrieved January 8, 2007 from http://www.kff.org/minorityhealth/upload/7535.pdf

About the Editors and Contributors

About the Editors

M. Christopher Brown II, Ph.D. is the 18th president of the nation's first historically Black land-grant institution, Alcorn State University in Lorman, Mississippi. Dr. Brown has earned a national reputation for his research on education policy, governance/administration, and institutional contexts. He is especially well known for his studies of historically black colleges, educational equity, educational contexts, and professorial responsibilities. Dr. Brown has lectured and/or presented research in various countries on six continents.

In addition to authoring or co-authoring more than 100 journal articles, book chapters, and publications related to education and society, Dr. Brown is the author/editor of fifteen books and monographs—*The Quest to Define Collegiate Desegregation* (1999), *Organization and Governance in Higher Education* (2000), *Black Sons to Mothers* (2000), *Equity and Access in Higher Education* (2002), *Studying Diverse Institutions* (2003), *Black Colleges* (2004), *Unique Campus Settings* (2004), *Achieving Equitable Educational Outcomes with All Students* (2005), *The Politics of Curricular Change* (2005), *The Children Hurricane Katrina Left Behind* (2007), *School Matters* (2007), *Still Not Equal* (2007), *Ebony Towers in Higher Education* (2008), *The Broken Cisterns of African American Education* (2009), and *The Case for Affirmative Action on Campus* (2009).

Dr. Brown received a Bachelor of Science degree in elementary education from South Carolina State University, a Master of Science degree in educational policy and evaluation from the University of Kentucky, and a Doctor of Philosophy degree in higher education from The Pennsylvania State University with a cognate in public administration and political science. Dr. Brown was initiated into the Mu Lambda chapter of Alpha Phi Alpha Fraternity, Inc. in March 2004.

T. Elon Dancy II, Ph.D. is a professor of higher education at the University of Oklahoma in Norman. He received a Ph.D. from Louisiana State University with an emphasis in Higher Education. His research agenda investigates the intersection of race, gender, and culture in colleges and universities as well as other educational settings. More specifically, his scholarship addresses boys and men in schools and colleges and the ways in which gendered constructions intersect with race, class, sexual orientation, and other social categories. His work also considers how identity constructions, pipeline issues, and environmental norms influence, improve, and contest Black males' retention, persistence, experiences, and socio-cognitive outcomes.

Dr. Dancy has written scholarly publications that engage the sociology, history, and politics of schooling/postsecondary education. He was named Emerging Scholar by the Association for the Study of Higher Education Council on Ethnic Participation (2006). He was the AERA-J 2008 Outstanding Dissertation Award Runner-Up and the LSU College of Education Dissertation of the Year Award Honoree (2007–2008).

Dr. Dancy is the author of *The Brother Code: Manhood and Masculinity among African American Men in College* and editor of *Managing Diversity: (Re)Visioning Equity on College Campuses*. He has been presenter and/or lecturer of more than 50 peer-reviewed papers and topics related to education and society. He is senior editor of the *College Student Affairs Journal*, and an Emerging Education Policy Scholar of both the Thomas B. Fordham and American Enterprise Institutes. Dr. Dancy was initiated into the Gamma Delta chapter of Alpha Phi Alpha Fraternity, Inc. in March 2000.

James Earl Davis, Ph.D. is Interim Dean of the College of Education, and Professor of Educational Leadership and Policy Studies. His work has appeared in numerous academic journals, including *Gender & Society, Urban Education, Youth & Society, American Journal of Evaluation, Review of Research in Education,* and *Educational Researcher.* He is co-author of *African American Males in School and Society: Policies and Practices for Effective Education* and *Black Sons to Mothers: Compliments, Critiques, and Challenges for Cultural Workers in Education.*

A former National Academy of Education/Spencer Foundation Postdoctoral Fellow, Dr. Davis has been on the faculty at the University of Delaware and Cornell University. He has also served as a Visiting Scholar in the Institute for Research of Women and Gender at the University of Michigan and in the Center for Education Research at the University of Wisconsin-Madison. His work has been funded by the Spencer Foundation, National Science Foundation, Marcus Foundation, and the U.S. Department of Education. In the local community, Dr. Davis is a board member of the YouthBuild Charter School, Public Citizens for Children and Youth, and the Germantown Friends School.

Dr. Davis earned a B.A. in Sociology from Morehouse College, a Ph.D. from Cornell University, and completed a postdoctoral fellowship in the Division of Education Policy at the Educational Testing Service, Princeton, NJ. His research focuses on gender-based educational policy, issues of equity and access in higher education, urban school reform, and gender and cultural studies. Specifically, Dr. Davis has investigated social contexts of learning, including various school settings with a concern for how gender and race are related to students' achievement and engagement, particularly Black boys and young men. Dr. Davis was initiated into the Rho chapter of Alpha Phi Alpha Fraternity, Inc. in March 1995.

The Contributors

TIMOTHY K. EATMAN, PH.D. is an educational sociologist in the Higher Education department at Syracuse University and Co-Director for the national consortium, Imagining America: Artists and Scholars in Public Life, headquartered there. He joined the Syracuse University community in the fall of 2007 after a postdoctoral fellowship at the University of Michigan in the Center for the Study of Higher and Postsecondary Education. Dr. Eatman has also worked as Associate Director for Research and Policy for the Academic Investment in Math and Science (AIMS) program at Bowling Green State University. This work emanates from his research interests in students from traditionally underrepresented groups in higher education. Dr. Eatman is co-author of Scholarship in Public: Knowledge Creation and Tenure Policy in the Engaged University, a widely cited IA report on faculty rewards for publicly engaged scholarship that also discusses the aspirations and decisions of graduate students and early-career publicly engaged scholars. Most recently, he has been working with the University of the Free State in Bloemfontein, South Africa, to review its service learning and community-engagement enterprise. Dr. Eatman was initiated into the Eta chapter of Alpha Phi Alpha Fraternity, Inc. in April 1988.

MARK A. GOODEN, PH.D. serves as an Associate Professor in the Educational Administration Department. He is also Director of The University of Texas at Austin Principalship Program (UTAPP). His research interests include the principalship, anti-racist leadership, urban educational leadership and legal issues in education. His research has appeared in *Brigham Young University Education and Law Journal, Education and Urban Society, The Journal of Negro Education, Educational Ad-*

ministration Quarterly, The Sage Handbook of African-American Education and *The Principal's Legal Handbook.* He currently serves on the Executive Committee for the University Council of Educational Administration (UCEA), Chair of the Barbara Jackson Scholars Advisory Board, and he has served on various committees for the American Educational Research Association. He is also Chair of The University of Texas Elementary School Management Board. Dr. Gooden was initiated into the Delta Delta chapter of Alpha Phi Alpha Fraternity, Inc. in March 1991.

ISSAM KHOURY IS A DUAL-TITLE PH.D. candidate in Higher Education and Comparative and International Education at the Pennsylvania State University. He earned a Bachelors degree in Political Science from Virginia Tech, a Masters degree in Arabic Literature from Ohio State University, and a second Masters degree in International Affairs from Penn State. He has worked in the U.S., Qatar, Oman, and the UAE. Mr. Khoury was initiated into the Alpha Rho Lambda chapter of Alpha Phi Alpha Fraternity, Inc. in March 2000.

H. RICHARD MILNER IV, PH.D. is Associate Professor of Education in the Department of Teaching and Learning and the Department of Leadership, Policy and Organizations (secondary) at Peabody College of Vanderbilt University. Professor Milner's research, teaching and policy interests are urban education, teacher education, African American literature, and the sociology of education. In 2007, Dr. Milner was promoted to associate professor and granted tenure at Vanderbilt University, becoming the first African American in Peabody College's 225-year history to earn tenure and promotion. Dr. Milner has published more than sixty (60) journal articles and book chapters, and he has published five books. His most recent book, published in 2010 by Harvard Education Press, is: *Start Where You Are but Don't Stay There: Understanding Diversity, Opportunity Gaps, and Teaching in Today's Classrooms.* It has been honored with two major awards: (1) the 2012 American Association of Colleges for Teacher Education Outstanding Book Award, and (2) a 2011 American Educational Studies Association Critics' Choice Book Award. Dr. Milner was initiated into the Beta Delta chapter of Alpha Phi Alpha Fraternity, Inc. in February 1994.

ROLAND W. MITCHELL, PH.D. is an Associate Professor in the Department of Educational Theory Policy and Practice at Louisiana State University. He currently serves as the Assistant Director of the School of Education in the College of Human Sciences. In addition, he is Program Leader for Higher Education Administration and Co-Director of the Curriculum Theory Project. He has a B.A. in History from Fisk University a M.Ed. in Higher Education from Vanderbilt University and a Ph.D. in Educational Research from The University of Alabama. He teaches courses that focus on the history of higher education and college teaching and his articles have appeared in leading education journals such as *Urban Education, International Journal of Qualitative Studies in Education* and *The Journal of Negro Education*. Roland is the Co-Editor of the *College Student Affairs Journal*, Higher Education Section Editor of the *Journal of Curriculum Theorizing*, and director of the Louisiana State University Writing Project's Teaching African American Boy's Summer Institute. His cu°rrent research interests include theorizing the impact of historical and communal knowledge on pedagogy. Dr. Mitchell was initiated into the Delta Phi Lambda chapter of Alpha Phi Alpha Fraternity, Inc. in November 1999.

ROBERT T. PALMER, PH.D. is Assistant Professor of Student Affairs Administration at Binghamton University. Dr. Palmer has authored well over 65 refereed journal articles, book chapters, and other academic publications and has produced six books: *Black Men in College: Implications for HBCUs and Beyond, Black Graduate Education at HBCUs: Trends, Experiences, and Outcomes, Fostering Success of Ethnic and Racial Minorities in STEM: The Role of Minority Serving Institutions, Racial and Ethnic Minority Students' Success in STEM Education, STEM Models of Success: Programs, Policies, and Practices*, and *Community Colleges* and *STEM: Examining Underrepresented Racial and Ethnic Minorities*. Dr. Palmer earned his Ph.D. in Higher Education Administration from Morgan State University in 2007, M.S. in Counseling with an emphasis on Higher Education at West Chester University of Pennsylvania in 2003, and the B.S. in History at Shippensburg University of Pennsylvania in 2001. Dr. Palmer was initiated into the Delta Lambda chapter of Alpha Phi Alpha Fraternity, Inc. in March 2007.

TERRELL L. STRAYHORN. PH.D. is Associate Professor of Higher Education at The Ohio State University, where he also serves as Director of the Center for Higher Education Research and Policy (CHERP), Senior Research Associate in the Kirwan Institute for the Study of Race & Ethnicity, and Faculty Associate in the Todd Bell National Resource Center for Black Males. He holds joint appointments in the Department of African American & African Studies, Sociology, and Engineering Education. Author of five books, over 80 refereed journal articles and chapters, more than 130 conference papers and reports, Professor Strayhorn maintains an active and highly visible research agenda focusing on major policy issues in education such as equity/diversity, access/retention, and student development, learning, and success. In 2011, *Diverse Issues in Higher Education* named him one of the nation's Top Emerging Scholars. Strayhorn is co-editor of *Spectrum: A Journal on Black Men*, published by Indiana University Press; associate editor of the *NASAP Journal*, and serves on several editorial boards. He received a BA degree from the University of Virginia (UVA), a MEd degree in educational policy studies from UVA's Curry School of Education, and a PhD in higher education from

Virginia Tech. Dr. Strayhorn was initiated into the Alpha Mu Lambda chapter of Alpha Phi Alpha Fraternity, Inc. in Spring 2007.

GEORGE L. WIMBERLY, PH.D. is the Director of Social Justice and Professional Development at the American Educational Research Association (AERA). He manages the AERA dissertation and postdoctoral fellowship programs and develops and implements professional development activities that build research capacity among graduate students and early career scholars. He is the Co-principal investigator on the National Science Foundation funded project, Advancing Knowledge and Building the Research Infrastructure in Education and STEM Learning. Much of his research focuses on educational transitions and educational attainment among African American students. He has previously worked in policy research at ACT, Inc., where he developed policy reports on college planning. He earned his bachelor's degree from the College of the Holy Cross and master's and doctoral degrees in sociology from the University of Chicago. Dr. Wimberly was initiated into the Omicron Eta Lambda chapter of Alpha Phi Alpha Fraternity, Inc. in March 2008.

Studies in the Postmodern Theory of Education

General Editor
Shirley R. Steinberg

Counterpoints publishes the most compelling and imaginative books being written in education today. Grounded on the theoretical advances in criticalism, feminism, and postmodernism in the last two decades of the twentieth century, Counterpoints engages the meaning of these innovations in various forms of educational expression. Committed to the proposition that theoretical literature should be accessible to a variety of audiences, the series insists that its authors avoid esoteric and jargonistic languages that transform educational scholarship into an elite discourse for the initiated. Scholarly work matters only to the degree it affects consciousness and practice at multiple sites. Counterpoints' editorial policy is based on these principles and the ability of scholars to break new ground, to open new conversations, to go where educators have never gone before.

For additional information about this series or for the submission of manuscripts, please contact:

> Shirley R. Steinberg
> c/o Peter Lang Publishing, Inc.
> 29 Broadway, 18th floor
> New York, New York 10006

To order other books in this series, please contact our Customer Service Department:

> (800) 770-LANG (within the U.S.)
> (212) 647-7706 (outside the U.S.)
> (212) 647-7707 FAX

Or browse online by series:

> www.peterlang.com